World Trade Poli

MW01156853

World Trade Politics is the most detailed overview available of the development of the global trading system since World War II. An ideal text for advanced undergraduates and graduates in courses on trade politics, international political economy, international organizations, US or EU foreign policy and global governance, the book:

- explains the prominent leadership role of the United States and European Union negotiators in shaping global economic policy;
- explores the challenges before developing state officials in trying to achieve fuller participation and benefits from international trade;
- draws on extensive interviews with leading politicians and negotiators to give the inside track on why international bargaining succeeds or fails;
- analyzes the international trade regime within a wider discussion of why international institutions succeed and fail;
- develops and tests theory of international political leadership that can be applied more generally in international relations research.

By tracing the evolution of the international trade regime through an extensive wealth of primary sources and theoretical discourses on international relations and foreign policy, David A. Deese makes an important contribution to our empirical understanding of the evolution of the multilateral trading system.

David A. Deese of the Department of Political Science at Boston College is editor of *The New Politics of American Foreign Policy* and the book series *The Library of Essays in International Relations*. His research focuses on international organizations, political economy, and foreign policy.

World Trade Politics

Power, principles, and leadership

David A. Deese

Routledge
Taylor & Francis Group

LONDON AND NEW YORK

First published 2008
by Routledge
2 Park Square, Milton Park, Abingdon, Oxon, OX14 4RN

Simultaneously published in the USA and Canada
by Routledge
711 Third Avenue, New York, NY 10017

Routledge is an imprint of the Taylor & Francis Group, an informa business

© 2008 David A. Deese

Typeset in Times New Roman
by Keystroke, 28 High Street, Tettenhall, Wolverhampton

British Library Cataloguing in Publication Data
A catalogue record for this book is available from the British Library

Library of Congress Cataloging in Publication Data
A catalog record for this book has been requested

ISBN 13: 978–0–415–77404–8 (hbk)
ISBN 13: 978–0–415–77405–5 (pbk)
ISBN 13: 978–0–203–94603–9 (ebk)

To Pattie

Contents

viii *Contents*

Preface

The modest claim of this book is to contribute an unusually comprehensive narrative of the international trade regime, in terms of its long evolution over time, which is framed by a theoretically informed set of arguments. If it is "original" in any sense it would be first in the integration of: a) many high quality existing cases and empirical studies from different time periods; b) interviews with many senior officials and negotiators; and c) the politics of foreign policy with trade politics at both domestic and international levels. Second, the book aims to also modestly advance the development and testing of international political leadership theory, in part to stimulate its application to the analysis of other international regimes. Future scholarship will hopefully also more fully develop and specify leadership theory in international contexts

It is essential to recognize the critical contribution of many leaders in trade policy, past and present, who were gracious in their willingness to grant the author one or more research interviews. This includes each of the former US cabinet heads for international trade (US Trade Representatives, or USTRs) from Robert Strauss (for Jimmy Carter), Senator William Brock and Clayton Yeuter (Ronald Reagan), Carla Hills (George H. Bush), and Mickey Kantor and Charlene Barchefsky (William Clinton), as well as Gene Sperling, former Head of the National Economic Council, Dan Glickman, former Secretary of Agriculture, Commissioners Jennifer Hillman and Marcia Miller (International Trade Commission), and Senator Robert Packwood. In addition, Peter Allgeier, Deputy USTR to Robert Zoellick (USTR for George W. Bush) for international negotiations and the WTO, Dorothy Dwoskin, David Walters, Bruce Hirsh, Christina Sevilla, Steve Jacobs, and Thelma Askey were also generous with their insights and explanations of key decisions, meetings, and negotiations. Similarly, I truly appreciate the opportunity to interview in detail former senior US officials Warren Lavorel, Ambassador John Veroneau, Jeff Lang, Alan Wolff, Clyde Prestowitz, Gary Horlick, Brad Figel, Claude Barfield, and Edward Gresser

At the World Trade Organization in Geneva (WTO) invaluable interviews were provided by senior officials Stuart Harbinson, Rufus Yerxa, Patrick Low,

Keith Rockwell, Alain Frank, Roderick Abbott, Valerie Hughes, Evan Rogerson, Nacer Benjelloun-Touimi, Clem Boonekamp, Jean-Maurice Leger, Carmen Pont-Vieira, Carmen Luz-Guarda, Hiromi Yano, Gretchen Stanton, and Edwini Kessie. My meetings with former WTO and senior national trade negotiators Julio Lacarte, David Hartridge, Andy Stoler, and Ake Linden were crucial to this project. I am also grateful to Julio Lacarte for his visit to Boston College, and to Enrique Iglesias, President of the Inter American Development Bank, who took the time to meet with me in Washington, D.C. in order to discuss the Uruguay Round negotiations.

I had the important opportunity to interview senior government trade officials from countries worldwide in Geneva; Cancun, Mexico; or their capital cities. These include Ambassadors Alejandro Jara (currently a WTO Deputy Director General) and Eduardo Perez Motta, Bruce Gosper, Abdel-Haimd Mamdouh (currently a senior WTO official), Peter Thompson, David Shark, Jesus Zorilla Torra, Haran Virupakshan, Didier Chambovey, Detlev Brauns, Wolfgang Hantke, Nelson Drangu, Maigari Buba, Cristian Espinosa, and Simon Farbenbloom. Former senior officials Paulo Batto, John Weekes, Paul Tran, Anthony Hill, Frieder Roessler (at the Advisory Centre for WTO Law), and Shishir Priyadarshi (at the South Centre) were most gracious in providing vital insights and corrections.

I could not have conducted several research visits to Geneva from 2002–2005 without the vital support and assistance of Janet Spettel, Jany Barthel-Rosa and the library staff at the WTO in Geneva, as well as the special consideration of Patrick Low, Keith Rockwell, and Bruce Wilson. Former GATT-WTO official Richard Blackhurst also offered important suggestions and ideas.

In terms of the extensive existing scholarship on the politics of trade, foreign policy and international institutions completed over past decades, this author is deeply indebted to key theorists, authors of narratives and case studies, government officials, and private individuals from numerous organizations and countries. This book's arguments are built directly from the work of James McGregor Burns, Erwin Hargrove, Jean Blondel, and Jameson Doig on political leadership, and of Oran Young, Duncan Snidal, David Lake, and Robert Keohane, on international political leadership. The book formulates propositions concerning trade politics and foreign policy based on scholarship by Judith Goldstein, Mac Deslter, Susan Aaronson, Helen Milner, Lisa Martin, Steve Dryden and Christina Davis, among others. The main argument about international political leadership also draws heavily on the bargaining and negotiation literature of scholars such as Mark Lax, James Sebenius, John Odell, Daniel Druckman, and James Fearon, and the insights about international trade policy and law of Gilbert Winham, Patrick Low, John Jackson, Frank Garcia, Alan Oxley, Ernest Preeg, Rorden Wilkinson, and Richard Steinberg. In addition, it relies on careful empirical studies of the GATT-WTO and international trade regime in key periods of time by scholars such as John

Croome, Hugo Paeman, Jarrod Wiener and many others. The online information resources of the International Centre for Trade and Sustainable Development (ICTSD) are extremely useful. Finally, this project would not be possible without the research on international organizations and multilateralism of scholars such as Miles Kahler, Kenneth Abbott, John Ikenberry, Joseph Nye, John Ruggie, Andrew Moravcsik, and Martha Finnemore.

I recognize with gratitude the recommendations and points offered by several anonymous reviewers. Their contribution is considerable. The text also benefited from important insights offered by Timothy Crawford, my colleague at Boston College, and more generally from the wisdom of Gilbert Winham. The difficulty with such specific acknowledgments, of course, is that this five plus year research project and the resulting book depend on many other authors and sources that are simply too numerous to mention here. Suffice it to say that I have tried to recognize all these other important sources and individuals throughout the book.

Truly invaluable research support for this project was provided by Boston College in the form of a sabbatical year Research Incentive Grant, as well as several research expense grants and numerous graduate and undergraduate research assistants. I cannot include here the name each of the many PhD, MA, and undergraduate students at Boston College who made key contributions to this project, but their efforts were absolutely essential to this book. I am grateful to each for a range of vital accomplishments. Finally, I am most grateful to my wife Pattie for her support as I conducted many research trips for this project, but even more for her love and patience.

Abbreviations

ACP	African, Caribbean, Pacific
ACWL	Advisory Centre on WTO Law
AGOA	African Growth and Opportunity Act (United States)
APEC	Asia Pacific Economic Cooperation
ASP	American Selling Price
CAFTA	Central American Free Trade Agreement
CAP	Common Agricultural Policy (of the European Community/European Union)
CED	Community of Economic Development
CXT	common external tariff
EC	European Communities/European Community
EEC	European Economic Community
EFTA	European Free Trade Area
EU	European Union
FIPs	Five Important Persons
FOGS	Negotiating Group on the Functioning of the GATT System
FTA	free trade agreement
FTAA	Free Trade Area of the Americas
GATT	General Agreement on Tariffs and Trade
GSP	generalized system of preferences
HST	hegemonic stability theory
IMF	International Monetary Fund
INGO	international non-governmental organization
ITO	International Trade Organization (planned)
KTR	Kennedy Trade Round
LDC	least developed country
MAI	Multilateral Agreement on Investment
MFN	most favored nation
MTN	multilateral trade negotiation
NAFTA	North American Free Trade Association
NAMA	non-agricultural market access

NGO	non-governmental organization
NTB	non-tariff barrier
NTM	non-tariff measure
OECD	Organisation for Economic Co-operation and Development
PNTR	permanent normal trade relations
RTAA	Reciprocal Trade Agreements Act (United States)
STR	Special Trade Representative
TEA	Trade Expansion Act (United States)
TNC	Trade Negotiating Committee (GATT)
TRIMS	trade-related investment measures
TRIPS	trade-related aspects of intellectual property rights
UNCTAD	United Nations Conference on Trade and Development
UNDP	United Nations Development Programme
UR	Uruguay Round
USDA	United States Department of Agriculture
USTR	United States Trade Representative
VER	voluntary export restraint
WTO	World Trade Organization

Part I

Coverage, concepts, and theories

1 Why study international political leadership and the global trade regime?

Despite its modest beginning in 1947–1948, the GATT-WTO has evolved into what is arguably the most effective and authoritative of all the global inter-governmental organizations.[1] Even with its still modest staff and operating budget,[2] the WTO and its associated global trade regime maintain unprecedented influence in comparison to other international regimes.[3] Its members have gradually and incrementally built very substantial functions and authority into this relatively small organization. It facilitates the resolution of a wide range of trade disputes through either pre-judicial settlements or obligatory, enforceable rulings, guides ever more ambitious and encompassing rounds of global trade negotiations, offers training and special support for new and least developed states, binds a steady flow of new members to its procedures and specific policies, and reviews and shapes the trade policies of each of its 150 members. Its membership could well expand to as many as 170 or more states over the next decade. Despite its "weakness" in terms of the lack of an executive board and the relatively small staff and budget, the WTO serves as no less than the multilateral organizational mechanism underlying a truly global trade regime.[4]

This study is modest in its focus on the GATT-WTO-based negotiations that have gradually led to an ever-expanding set of law, rules, procedures, and norms governing trade worldwide. This work is necessarily narrow in this way because of the difficulty of tracking the many connections and implications of the overall global trade regime. It cannot hope to identify and explain the extent to which this regime connects with national and regional trade institutions worldwide. For example, even the substantial number of small states which are not yet WTO members are certainly affected by the trade regime. The 150 member states are involved either directly or indirectly in almost all trade worldwide, including even the areas such as oil and certain agricultural sectors not covered by WTO agreements. The small states outside the WTO are connected through not only trade exchanges with large trading entities such as the USA and EU but also bilateral or regional arrangements with WTO member states. More generally, although trade relations have distinctive regional characteristics, and trade is heavily affected by national security concerns, the influence of global trade norms and practices is pervasive.

For this reason, it is reasonable to focus on the GATT-WTO-based negotiations as a surrogate or focal point for the global trade regime. Indeed, trade policy activists, journalists, experts, and officials have tended through history to look to the GATT-WTO as both the key indicator of health of the global regime and the antidote to perceived sickness in the regime. In other words, when GATT-WTO negotiations and agreements have been perceived as healthy, the global regime is generally assumed to be strong, When trade rules seem to be ignored and national protectionist measures and high-visibility disputes between major trading states seem to be on the rise, the GATT-WTO process is seen as the first antidote. In fact, weak economic performance in key states, regionally, or globally has also triggered US presidents, EU leaders, GATT-WTO director generals and other political leaders worldwide to call for renewed effort and emphasis on GATT-WTO negotiations as an essential response. The fact generally seems to be lost that any direct effects on economic growth from ongoing or emerging trade rounds will not occur until years later.

It must be noted that this book is not mainly about the most institutionalized or formalized roles, functions, and capabilities of the WTO. The basic idea of a new international organization for trade, the WTO, was in part to make available a more predictable and substantial organizational framework which could carry out more effectively not only authoritative dispute settlement but also the day-to-day roles of information collection, policy and regulatory reviews, working-group-level negotiations on new agreements, training, and technical support. Many members sought to escape the boom–bust environment wherein the capacity of the organization seemed to be dominated by, or at least closely tied to, the up and downs of the current round of global negotiations, or the lack of one. In this sense, this work focuses on negotiating rounds, or what was intended to become relatively less important over time owing to the more centralized and independent (especially in legalized dispute settlement) nature of the WTO as an international organization.[5] In fact, the perceived influence and importance of the WTO and global trade regime are still closely associated by media and even some expert opinion with the ongoing negotiating round. When the round seems to be in trouble, prevailing opinion, at least as expressed in the media, seems to be that the WTO is less important, if not threatened with irrelevance!

At the same time, the book is quite relevant to these formalized roles of the WTO. First, in dispute settlement the decisions of panels and the Appellate Body for appeals affect the environment, and even the likely outcomes, of negotiations. Longer term, over the first decade of operations these dispute settlement bodies have established a substantial body of international trade law that resolves many uncertainties and sets the parameters for negotiations. Furthermore, this existing law combines with the most recently completed agreements to set the entrance requirements for new members such as China, which in turn shape their negotiating behavior for years after their entry as a new member. Second, the need for negotiations over new agreements arises in part from perceived problems with the operation in practice of existing ones. Thus, the direction of negotiations, particularly in later drafting stages, affects member states' behavior with regard to existing rules and procedures. Finally, the importance and reputation of the GATT-WTO and the broader trade regime depend on their ability to keep up with technology, basic economic trends, and the needs of members. This, in turn, has required continual broadening of the trade sectors and issue areas covered by GATT-WTO agreements. Thus, for example, the WTO's ability to extend its coverage to all agricultural trade is crucial in the current Doha Round because of agriculture's fundamental economic importance to many least developed and developing country members, its economic and political role for many larger developing and most developed states, and its symbolic role in demonstrating whether the global trade regime can become a central factor in economic development through agricultural trade.

Aside from the worldwide visibility and controversy associated with the WTO and global trade regime, and the current Doha Round of negotiations in particular, why dedicate an entire book to the relatively narrow economic domain of international trade negotiations? To the extent that the reader is intrigued by international relations, foreign policy, international law, international economics and business, or international leadership, there are several important answers. First, political leadership in international contexts is not only, or even mainly, about power, dominance, coercion, or states as unitary actors. Many books published in international relations and foreign policy during the first decade of the twenty-first century focus on questions of "empire," "unipolarity," and "hegemony," and most often with emphasis on the policies and actions of the United States. Indeed, at this time in international political history, prevailing modes of thinking would not suggest an investigation of leadership at all. And it is certainly nor popular in the United States, other countries or internationally to speak of American leadership in light of the failed intervention in Iraq. One prominent commentator argues that "[o]ne reads about America's desire for leadership only in the United States . . . everywhere else one reads about American arrogance and unilateralism."[6] Furthermore, the widespread public opposition to US policies in Iraq and the Middle East more generally only reinforces deeply held skepticism among publics worldwide about the negative aspects of economic globalization, and US and WTO roles therein.

For these exact reasons, however, it is urgent to reexamine international political leadership, and to separate this inquiry from the different domain of theories focused on hegemony and unipolarity. What is the constructive potential for international political leadership in the first quarter of the twenty-first century? To what extent must this leadership be joint in order to be effective? How have large, medium, and small powers worked out their leader and participant roles in a core issue area (international trade) of international political economy, international organizations, international economic law, foreign policy, and international business? What role can officials of a public international organization play in facilitating leadership, and joint leadership in particular? How do US, European, and other leaders understand and determine trade-offs between national security and foreign economic goals? Even for scholars in the field, all are familiar with theories related to "hegemony" whereas many are not even aware that there is a distinct body of theory about international political leadership.

A second reason to investigate trade negotiations is that their long and rich experience offers key insights for officials and states involved with many other important global, multilateral, and regional treaties and regimes across a wide range of issue areas in various stages of development. Whether operating with only the modest supporting structure of an arrangement such as the North American Free Trade Association (NAFTA), or with the more elaborate organizational basis of the International Monetary Fund (IMF), many treaty systems and broader international regimes will benefit from studying the failures in trade leadership at the global level so as to avoid or mitigate such failures in the future and the successes in order to emulate them. While the GATT-WTO experience is less applicable to the process of creating new agreements or regimes in the twenty-first century, it is centrally relevant to the development and enhancement of existing treaty systems and regimes. In this way, the study aims to help address a relative dearth of work on the long-term evolution of international regimes.

Third, the international trade system offers an experience that is quite distinct from those of the Bretton Woods international monetary system and the international development loan institutions (originally the World Bank and later the IMF as well). Instead of the comprehensive International Trade Organization (ITO), which was stillborn, the GATT began with a very narrow mandate and an extremely informal institutional structure. From these tentative beginnings, the story of international trade is one of long-term, episodic development built upon a long series of successes and failures at key turning points in ever more ambitious rounds of negotiations. After fifty years of GATT-based negotiations, the Uruguay Round culminated with the new WTO and a much more broadly based global regime. In sharp contrast, the monetary and development regimes began as relatively elaborate organizations, involving the IMF and World Bank respectively, but then gradually experienced collapse or basic failures in accomplishing their core mission, as well as shifts in the fundamental focus of their operations.

In sum, the long experience of leadership of GATT-WTO-based international trade negotiations may suggest a solution to the single most fundamental problem confronting international organizations in the twenty-first century: How is it possible to simultaneously keep engaged and committed both the most powerful member states, which rightfully expect a disproportionate role in decision making, and the least powerful states, which rightfully expect to participate in meaningful ways? Students of political science or international relations are often perplexed, if not offended, by the relative inequality of influence among the member states in public international organizations in terms of influence over decision making, despite the one state–one vote principle. Furthermore, critics who would either abolish or reform the WTO and its trade regime, and even leading European trade negotiators, have all complained about the lack of formality and organization in decision making. At the same time, serious thought should be given to how many different negotiators and state officials, on behalf of many different states, have provided leadership in the context of GATT-WTO-based negotiations. There can be no doubt that, historically, US and European heads of state and negotiators have been the main leaders, yet a wide array of other states have consistently produced leaders of substantial importance to the negotiations. Most important, a very substantial number of states gradually have built a political culture around the training and advancing of highly effective trade negotiators. This book argues that a very few of these have joined US and EU officials in providing vital joint leadership, and that this trend will surely continue into the future.

Approach and methodology

The approach in researching this book was to seek out the primary and most relevant secondary, scholarly sources available and then conduct elite interviews to cover gaps in the primary sources or resolve inconsistencies in the secondary materials. Wherever possible, the research cross-checked primary and scholarly secondary sources not only against each other but also with elite interviews. This involved considerable archival research at the WTO in Geneva, numerous government missions in Geneva, national government offices in key trading states, and major university libraries. For the empirical analysis of key decisions, meetings, and other events, this included interviewing the person deciding, someone else present at the time, or the most reputable chronicle of the event, preferably one written by someone who was present. Normally an interview of at least one additional participant or observer was conducted. Elite interviews were conducted in parallel with archival research at the WTO, government missions in Geneva, government offices in several key states, and non-governmental organizations in Geneva and other capital cities. Of course scholarly research provided an invaluable and reliable record when it was based heavily on an appropriate combination of documents, other primary sources, and interviews. In the case of most of the processes traced and mapped for this book, the secondary literatures are invaluable. They generally provide solid and comprehensive coverage of the events, particularly micro-level analysis of the eight complete GATT trade rounds. Several sources should be listed, but key examples include Gilbert Winham's classic work on the Tokyo Round (1986) and John Croome's comprehensive history of the Uruguay Round (1995). Indeed, in some cases a leading participant has written an account of key events, for example EC trade negotiator Hugo Paemen's coauthored book on the Uruguay Round (Paemen and Bensch 1995). That coverage extends through completion of the Uruguay Round in 1993–1994, but is not available for the final case studies: the WTO ministerial meetings in Seattle of 1999, Doha of 2001, Cancún of 2003, and the Doha Round preliminary agreement of summer 2004, which were based heavily on interviews and primary materials. Insights from the Cancún, Mexico, ministerial meeting of 2003 are based on the author's coverage of the meeting, participation in press and NGO briefings, and numerous interviews on-site. The rich description provided by past researchers on negotiations through the Uruguay Round allowed this book to focus on empirical questions where the literature is either in disagreement or insufficient in coverage.

However, work that tends to sacrifice historical accuracy on the altar of advancing theory was not weighted equally with theoretical explanation that was careful to get the history right. In other words, some scholars are clearly more committed to their theory than to the empirical cases or data. This book takes the other path, in part because there is considerable divergence between the scholars working in the different traditions outlined above. Equally important to the theoretical context is an accurate map of the causes of macro-level decisions taken with respect to regime development. At the same time, as explained above, the research questions are drawn from the most pertinent theoretical literatures and integrated into a political leadership of international regime negotiations approach. In this way, the cases are designed to contribute to our understanding of state sovereignty, international bargaining and cooperation, and the role of institutions in each of these areas.

The book's methodology represents a blend of archival research, interviews of political elites, and process tracing in the tradition of historical institutionalism.[7] It maps out the background conditions, the crises, coalitions, and cleavages, and the barriers to change involved with the key events that were intended to develop the international trade regime through GATT-WTO-based negotiations.[8] Each time that member states attempted to make major changes in the organization or regime is considered to be a defining period. Equally important, the book relies on analysis of the turning or focal points in negotiating, as related to bargaining stages or phases, as is explained in Chapter 2. Thus, the study aims to include all of the major turning points in the evolution of the trade regime.

It is important to explain how the cases will address the challenges of avoiding circular reasoning and causal relations, and distinguishing normal bargaining behavior from international political leadership, including how to understand when successful bargaining outcomes are due to leadership rather than power. For these purposes, three key methodological steps are taken. First, political and international political leadership are defined in detail, and divided into two main types, structural and entrepreneurial, which can be traced and analyzed in interaction and contrasted with each other. Leadership as defined in this study emphasizes the clarity and precision of leaders' ideas and policies (including the pursuit of collective international in addition to national interests), the degree of committed and persistent goal seeking, and the continual building and maintenance of coalitions or consensus groups (at both domestic and international levels).

Second, particularly for structural leadership, the bargaining proposals and subsequent compromises offered before and during negotiations are compared to known national positions in order to identify any elements that represent broader, or collective, interests. In this way, initial proposals and positions can also be contrasted with subsequent ones to identify shifts toward collective interests. In addition, leadership in this sense is also distinguished from integrative bargaining, which takes some account of others' positions. Leadership reaches a higher threshold than simply taking other parties' positions into consideration when forging a bargaining strategy. In the trade context, political leadership aims to advance the development of the global trade regime, but it does so by offering new ideas or approaches, and often by offering to move earlier and further than other parties. Finally, as explained below, cases are contrasted in sets of failed and successful attempts in order to help differentiate causal mechanisms and pathways.

Thus, a history of more than fifty years can be summarized as a series of attempts at international political leadership to advance the regime through negotiations. In each case, the initial conditions are compared to the outcomes, both positive and negative, with respect to the dimensions of the dependent variable or factor, as explained further in Chapter 2. The key stages and turning points are identified and traced to determine the precipitating actions and events.

An important aspect of trade regime development is the extent to which its defining periods are rounds or negotiations. Still, it is clearly acknowledged that the work and development of the organization also occur gradually during the periods between major negotiations. Indeed, the individual missions and ambassadors in Geneva that are so actively and consistently engaged in the business of the GATT-WTO help to establish its member-driven nature. Still, this study is based on the assumption that the fundamental causal factors underlying the organization's evolution can be understood by explaining the attempts to advance it. Because failed attempts are assumed to be at least as important in this regard as successful ones, they are closely scrutinized and subjected to critical analysis. Indeed, the overall history of the trade regime appears as a cycle of failure and crisis building to an agreement, which in turn creates conditions leading to the next failure.

In order to establish causality accurately, the empirical research design focuses heavily on these critical events. They were defined as "failures" and "successes" in the narrow sense that political actors, mainly states but also the EC, either agreed or did not agree to advance their level of coordination and collaboration within the GATT-WTO framework. These labels are not intended to carry a normative message or judgment, because GATT-WTO member states sometimes differ sharply as to whether a given agreement was preferable to no agreement. For example, certain Caribbean member states that sought to block the initiation of a new round of negotiations would consider the Seattle Ministerial of 1999 to be a "success" and the Doha meeting of 2001 to be a "failure." Furthermore, decisions made by officials on behalf of states cannot be considered to be morally or socially optimal.[9]

Central to the research design is conducting a detailed contrast of failure and success at turning points to develop the global trade regime in this sense of whether member states reached agreement or not. Contrasting cases are used to highlight those factors most present when agreement was and was not reached. The approach is designed to sharpen and enhance the analysis through precise comparison of the decision processes traced. In this way, the research aims to isolate more reliably and accurately the causal factors driving regime development. Furthermore, this approach lends itself to testing and confirmation by other scholars. It also allows future research to build on the foundation provided herein by substituting different cases or inserting additional ones.

Within this framework, the eight cases of failure can be subdivided into six significantly different types of attempts at international cooperation: (1) Beginning a new round of multilateral negotiations (1982 and 1999); (2) completing a round (1990 and 1991–1992); (3) ratifying and implementing a major agreement (ITO of 1948); (4) completing a round that failed to meet most of its initial goals and purposes (the Dillon Round, 1960–1962); (5) agreeing on the mid-term framework for a round; and (6) coping with widespread divergence of member state behavior from trade rules and procedures (1970s–1985). The book emphasizes the more recent five cases in this group. The author determined on the basis of both research and past scholarship that the more revealing cases would be those occurring after an important transition in the mid-1970s, as explained in subsequent chapters.

The eight cases of success include reaching agreements to launch a new round or complete a round or mid-term framework. The three agreements to begin a round include the Tokyo Round in 1973, the Uruguay Round in 1986, and the Doha Round in 2001. The four successful completions are: (1) the early GATT rounds of 1947 to 1956; (2) the Kennedy Round in 1967; (3) the Tokyo Round in 1979; and (4) the Uruguay Round in 1993–1994. This research approach specifically does not assume that each of these cases is equally important. Certainly, reaching a mid-term agreement is not in general as important as finalizing or even opening an entire round. Therefore, for both sets of cases, failures and successes, those of clearly greater importance, such as the closing of the Uruguay and Tokyo Rounds, are assessed in greater length and emphasized in the conclusion.

For organizational and analytical purposes, the total of sixteen cases studies is divided into three time periods. First is the background period of 1947 through 1973. Relatively brief treatment of the earlier five cases is offered in order to provide background and historical perspective. Next is the crucial period from the mid-1970s through the mid-1990s, with seven case studies that are rich in implications for both policy and theory, concluding with the agreement to create the WTO. The third and final focus period is 1999 through 2004, which grounds the analysis in the current period to ensure relevance and accuracy for the present and future.[10] Finally, despite the emphasis of the cases on key events and specifically defined time periods, the empirical work also took account of key events and decisions during the intervening periods.

The analysis of what caused the success and failure of major initiatives from 1947 through most of the Uruguay Round incorporated and synthesized a large set of literatures. The book is truly indebted to key scholars and researchers who have carefully documented particular rounds of GATT negotiations, issue areas, and countries. At times, however, on the core questions of this project the literature was either inconsistent or incomplete. In other cases, the picture could be completed relatively consistently, but only by carefully piecing together the most relevant past work from different disciplines and perspectives. For example, the failure of the ITO in the late 1940s is well documented but not as well understood or agreed in terms of key causes. Finally, for the earlier cases through much of the 1970s it is difficult to rely on interviews as an important part of the research design because most of the key officials are no longer available.

Still, beginning with the period of the Carter administration in 1977, and corresponding with Prime Minister Callaghan in Britain, President Giscard in France, Chancellor Schmidt in Germany, and Roy Jenkins as president of the EC, interviews play an increasing central role in the book. Entering the 1980s and the attempt to launch the Uruguay Round in 1982, even more of the key government and GATT officials are still available, and recollections can be checked against each other, other primary sources, and key books, articles, and reports. For the most recent contrasting cases of 1999–2001 and 2003–2004, interviews with officials from a wide range of different countries play a central role in the research, but they are both cross-checked against all the other available sources and interpreted in light of the natural human inclination to view favorably one's own historical record and to avoid criticizing the president, prime minister, or cabinet head served recently.[11]

In sum, the purpose of this study is to determine how and why international negotiations fail or succeed. It asks how bargaining is catalyzed by ideas and proposals, how it is guided by committed officials with a range of positive and negative levers, and how it is facilitated, punctuated, and revived by highly experienced entrepreneurs. It emphasizes the role of coordinated leadership by groups of two to four officials, as well as the strategic construction of consensus groups.

The book proceeds next in Chapter 2 with a synthesis and argument about theoretical expectations in approaching the case studies. It offers several specific propositions or hypotheses about regime development. Chapters 3 through 5 are organized historically. Chapter 3 contrasts the successful early negotiations with the collapse of the planned ITO, and the very limited outcomes of the Dillon Round with the successes of the Kennedy Round and the launch of the Tokyo Round. Chapter 4 presents the completion of the Tokyo Round and the multiple failures and successes of the Uruguay Round, as well as the non-GATT-governed trade behavior that parallels negotiating rounds in the 1970s and 1980s. The final sets of contrasting cases in Chapter 5 are, first, the failed Seattle ministerial of 1999 and the success in Doha, Qatar, two years later in 2001 in launching the Doha Round, and second, the collapsed Cancún, Mexico, ministerial of 2003, and the July Package agreement of August 1, 2004. The concluding chapter, Chapter 6, analyzes the theoretical expectations in light of the case studies. It also assesses the implications of these findings for the reform of the WTO-based international trade system. Finally, it draws out the most relevant insights for international bargaining, international institutions, and cooperation in economic, security, environmental, and other domains.

2 Political leadership in international institutionalized bargaining

Introduction

How, in fact, did the so-called Bretton Woods non-institution become the basis for what is perhaps the most important and authoritative of all the current international organizations and regimes? This book investigates the hypothesis that the pace and character of development in the global trade regime were largely determined until the early to mid-1970s by the international political leadership of key US officials, who were assisted or supported in the consensus-building process by officials representing Britain and the other largest European states. From the mid-1970s until the late 1990s, this study expects that it was driven by the leadership of officials representing the core US–EU "duopoly," who were in turn supported in the pyramiding process by a small group of other influential officials which gradually increased in size over time. Finally, beginning in the late 1990s the large and increasingly diverse WTO membership, along with an ever more complex and broad set of negotiating issue areas, is expected to required further expansion of even the core leadership group.

At the same time, it is hypothesized that national policy makers must constantly balance their incentives to lead in trade policy against their domestic political constraints and competing foreign policy priorities. On average, it is expected that domestic political and political economic constraints will prevail or converge with politicians' episodic use of trade protectionism for electoral or other short-term political purposes. In other words, the preferences of political leaders and trade policy makers will be determined endogenously, or by domestic political pressures or goals most of the time. Still, the balance can and does shift under certain circumstances in favor of the incentives to provide leadership in foreign economic policy.

This chapter proceeds as follows. First, it outlines the hypothesis that US, US–EC/EU and small-group leadership have been the crucial pivots in determining the pace and character of institutional trade expansion. Second, it explains the critical role of pyramiding, or gradually expanding the circle of consensus, in the GATT-WTO negotiating process. Thus, it expects both structural and entrepreneurial leadership to be crucial. Although more difficult to document, the role of ideas and intellectual leadership is also important. Additionally, the interactions of structural, entrepreneurial, and intellectual leadership help to predict not only the outcomes of key bargaining events but also change in the nature of the core leadership group. Finally, the conclusion synthesizes from the chapter the analytical approach that will focus and structure the case studies.

How are we to understand and explain the evolution of the global trade regime? Many scholars in international relations seem to believe that there is a well-established prevailing understanding about why and how the GATT-WTO and its global regime have evolved. This work challenges that basic notion. It turns out that there are, in fact, various prevailing "wisdoms." Each of the "standard" accounts is significantly different from the others in important ways. Several make important contributions, but none of them alone is adequately comprehensive, precise, and accurate to explain regime development.

Most prominent among the prevailing understandings is the idea of hegemony and the associated theory of hegemonic stability. Most analysts would agree that "hegemony" is the ability of a single state to dictate (or at least dominate) in establishing and enforcing the primary rules and arrangements of international relations. Some scholars emphasize US hegemony in money and trade after World War II, "[b]ut there has been no global, system-wide hegemon during the past two centuries. Contrary to myths about Pax Britannica and Pax Americana, British and American hegemonies have been regional and issue-specific rather than general."[1] Thus, for the purposes of analyzing power internationally, it is essential to specify whether the focus is global or regional, and general or issue-specific. To whatever extent the United States is claimed to have been hegemonic after World War II, its hegemony certainly did not extend to the Soviet bloc, China, and a substantial number of countries outside Western Europe and the Western Hemisphere. US leaders were in general most concerned about avoiding another world war and winning the political and economic competition with the Soviet bloc, and this often required making major political and economic trade-offs within the Western alliance. At key points from the 1940s into the 1960s, US leaders ceded major economic benefits and advantages to Japan and European states, and traded away global economic priorities for the perceived demands of unity and integration in Europe.

In sum, it can be argued that the United States generally "centered" the Western economy around itself for the first two decades after the war, but it is difficult, if not impossible, to show that it was able to dominate the rules and arrangements for trade. Important compromises and trade-offs were made in negotiating the fundamental international trade principles and institutions, particularly with the emergence of the Cold War in 1947.[2]

Proponents of hegemonic stability theory (HST) and its variations contend that institutionalized cooperation is most likely when power is concentrated in a single state, since only a hegemon can subsidize the material requirements of its less able partners.[3] This overlaps with the theoretical approach herein, but while HST concentrates on relative wealth, structural leadership begins with political ideas, will, and initiative, also emphasizes skillful negotiation and demonstrations of commitment to reluctant partners, and combines non-material factors. While HST emphasizes the objective distribution of resources, it neglects the question of how material wealth affects policy and ultimately determines institutional outcomes. Moreover, HST posits a direct relationship between relative power and regime maintenance. When a hegemonic state begins to fall, so too should the institution it supports.[4] The notion of leadership, integrating elements of hegemonic leadership scholarship, suggests a more dynamic relationship between key states and regimes: long-term returns balance the magnanimity offered by a leading state to persuade its partners to adhere to institutional principles. In Keohane's terms, hegemonic leadership is about persuading other states that their interests are served by deferring and following the leader, that at a minimum they are better off inside rather than outside the international institutions built by the hegemon. Indeed, since leadership implies a willingness to suffer short-term political costs for long-term benefits, the inevitability of hegemonic decline is mitigated by membership in healthy regimes.[5]

Empirically, HST is difficult to justify. When the United States was at the peak of its dominance in the immediate post-war period, it declined to ratify the International Trade Organization.[6] The president and Congress chose to opt out of the deal. A half-century later, a relatively less powerful United States signed and ratified the agreement to create the World Trade Organization. Dependence on the US market had declined with the progression of European integration and Asian development, and regional trade agreements had begun to balance US preeminence and capture part of US trade. Hence, key partners improved their alternatives to further expansion of the US-driven international trade regime. "The hegemony theory taken alone," observe John Odell and Barry Eichengreen, "would surely imply that the United States would have been more likely to ratify the ITO Charter than the WTO."[7]

If hegemony and its related theories are not adequate to explain the international trade issue area, then what else might be? A second account is offered by the rational choice or economic school: States pursue their interests in part through international organizations because they are welfare-enhancing. States design and rely on them to reduce transaction costs and enhance information flows. This line of analysis has led in part to a rich body of work in the tradition of not only neorealism but also neoliberalism, which accepts the basic assumptions of realism.[8] The important "rational design" project seeks to map out how and why states structure international organizations in order to solve cooperation problems. In particular, it has advanced thinking about a common set of key variables and characteristics such as centralization, control, and flexibility of institutions.

In this tradition, game-theoretic analyses of cooperation, which assume strategic rationality of actions and reactions, have provided key insights and considerations. This study shares in part this approach's emphasis on the preferences of leaders. Part of the richness of trade bargaining involves shifts over time in leaders' preferences over outcomes, processes, and negotiating fora. Preferences are important to the concept of leadership developed below in that they have varied across different heads of state and their senior officials involved in formulating and executing trade or foreign economic policies. More important, however, is that these preferences tend to vary considerably less than the nature or degree of leadership by key officials. Preferences are only one dimension of leadership in trade negotiations.

Game theory also contributes key insights through the "battle of the sexes" game, which advances understanding of the basic nature of joint leadership – the subtle blend of competition and cooperation inherent in the small leadership group. Individuals can co-lead when they share a common and underlying purpose even when they differ about the exact nature of the ends to be pursued and the means to be applied. In other words, even among officials cooperating closely to provide joint leadership at key periods, their relationship is shaped substantially by competition between the states' interests they represent and their own preferences about optimal outcomes. Despite their core common purpose of guiding the negotiations to success, they compete actively as they forge joint bargaining positions and papers, and as they engage in subsequent compromises and efforts to broaden the group of states joining in their consensus group at key points in the negotiating process. At the same time, game theory fails to account for much of the richness involved in complex international negotiations, including differences in the level of information held by negotiators, decisions not based on fully rational behavior, and the substantial range of possible solutions and equilibria in each bargaining round.

Even more useful is the earlier analysis of two-level games and more recent modifications that highlight how governments must simultaneously manage the domestic and bureaucratic politics of formulating and adjusting their negotiating proposals, and the international process of negotiating, reaching agreement, and winning the legislature's approval of such deals. Trade liberalization is certainly a critical case of such dual domestic and international complexity and challenges. Trade policy involves the ability to make credible threats and commitments, to balance vital interests across different foreign policy issue areas, to coordinate bargaining strategies among actors, and to assert leverage based on global, regional, and bilateral agreements. The multiple-level and issue bargaining game is especially important for the EU, where negotiators at the global level must simultaneously maneuver among the member states, the Commission, and the Council. At the same time, European (or EU) negotiators may be able to block or soften a US proposal for global trade liberalization by convincing US officials that it poses a credible threat to European unity or institutions.

Indeed, foreign policy makers and international negotiators must not only balance domestic and foreign policy interests but also adjudicate between competing foreign policy goals. The latter is explained, in part, by Destler's concept of the "economic complex" in competition with the "security complex" in US foreign policy decision making.[9] In this context, trade liberalization is managed and advocated by the economic complex, which must usually give way to higher-priority security policies whenever the two domains of policy are in conflict. Most often, European unity and institutional development is expected to be the US security or diplomatic goal that trumps trade policy. At the same time, the policies advocated by the two complexes are not always in conflict. US officials' leadership of GATT-WTO bargaining can be constructed on the argument or strategy that a deepened global trade regime advances US security and diplomatic leverage. Specifically, when increased European integration is perceived to be a threat to US global leadership, US officials may well commit to a stronger trade regime specifically as a means to advance vital international political interests.

Still, states or officials do not negotiate or "lead" as unified actors. Individuals lead and negotiate. Leadership is about individuals who are committed to making positive changes in their environments for collective purposes. For this reason, it is necessary to integrate theories and cases of leadership from domestic and cross-cultural contexts as well as international systems and institutions. Even in the relatively institutionalized international contexts examined in this book, leadership is not basically different from that in other domains of politics. Power and influence are certainly central, but so are fundamental principles and beliefs concerning what is right for constituents at home, and even in other countries. Furthermore, the range of issue areas where institutionalized bargaining occurs is ever-expanding, for example into "core national interests" such as security and economic as well as human and transnational ones.[10] Regardless of the issue area, leadership of negotiations means managing multi-level processes, and especially addressing concerns and opposition that rise and wane among constituents and groups in the leader's domestic political environment.

Also in this rationalist tradition, it is often emphasized that a secretive club drove the GATT-WTO process. Judith Goldstein and Lisa Martin, for example, explain that "[e]arly rounds were akin to clubs" in that "[d]eals were struck among a small group of like-minded representatives, behind closed doors. Later rounds eschewed this general negotiating form."[11] This account must be elaborated and integrated into a more systematic framework that also takes account of domestic political forces and competing foreign policy goals, particularly in the leading member states, and bargaining theory.

Therefore, another approach, that of international bargaining or negotiating theory, is most useful for this study. Scholars such as Willliam Zartman, James Sebenius, David Lax, Gilbert Winham, and John Odell, to mention a few, have made fundamental contributions by assessing the dynamics and strategies of bargaining. In general these scholars assume intelligent, strategic behavior – that is, the pursuit of a set of goals – but with the understanding that bargaining interactions often take place over time in sets of rounds, which can increase the perceived opportunities to reach an acceptable deal. One important focus is "pyramiding," or the process of gradually adding parties to build an ever-larger "consensus" group for negotiated agreements. Pyramiding in this sense can substantially restructure the perceived future, as compared to the status quo. If most of the major trading states reach agreement, most others must consider a new and different reality as the alternative to signing up.[12] In other words, it is necessary to consider how parties perceive the alternatives to an emerging agreement, and how these perceptions in turn affect their negotiating behavior. Also fundamental is the work of John Odell, emphasizing, for example, the importance of whether states' bargaining strategies take account of other parties' interests and positions, or whether they seek only to maximize their own relative gains.

Liberal institutionalists take a further important step by asking not only how and why institutions endure but how they develop autonomous functions over time. Recent scholarship on "legalization" extends this approach, building significantly in fact on trade and the WTO among other issue areas, and examines the implications of organizations with substantial autonomy or independence. Even more recent work focuses specifically on the relative independence of international organizations in terms of decision-making procedures, a supranational bureaucracy, and dispute settlement mechanisms, and finds that independence is enhanced by the passage of time and economic interdependence.[13] Of course, although this work naturally finds that among regional organizations the EU has the ideal type of relatively independent and authoritative bureaucracy – the Commission – Moravcsik finds that even Commission bureaucrats have less important entrepreneurial roles than those of member state officials.[14] Insights from this work are integrated directly into this study to help define and delineate the dimensions of the GATT-WTO and trade regime which have developed over time, as well as to help explain how certain entrepreneurial director generals have facilitated decision making.

The next – sociological or constructivist – approach focuses squarely on the organizations as independent, bureaucratic actors with their own agendas, and directly probes the nature and sources of their influence. It provides a fuller argument about them as autonomous actors and then investigates the implications.[15] This way of viewing public international organizations is also helping to generate a rich body of conceptual and empirical analysis, for example on the vital relationships between non-governmental organizations and international organizations, which is important background to this study. Indeed, it is certainly fruitful to study the WTO dispute settlement function from this perspective. For this study, the constructivist emphasis on ideas is fundamental to intellectual leadership, as explained later in this chapter. Leaders are motivated to act on their preferences in part as a result of their underlying ideas and belief systems. Still, in this book the rationalist assumptions prove more central because of the very limited nature of the GATT as a sparse negotiating forum for many years, its very gradual and long-term development as an organization, and the fundamentally decentralized or dependent nature of even the WTO in most of its basic norms and operational roles. In other words, the main emphasis of this work is not on how the organization has shaped its members but rather on how officials, states, and coalition building have developed the international organization and regime.

A final important approach, which closely parallels the rationalist or economic one outlined above, emphasizes domestic political economic factors in the United States and its major allies as the principal driving force of the international trade regime. Some leading trade scholars, such as Judith Goldstein, trace the roots to early US protectionism and exclusions, especially for agriculture, while others, such as Patrick Low, would point more to the EEC-EC-EU's Common Agricultural Policy (CAP) and regionalism.[16] Others highlight the complexities and limitations of reaching decisions on common negotiating policies among EU members. Another scholar, Robert Paarlberg, drawing on international food and agricultural issue areas in particular, emphasizes the need for a sequential process of "leadership" which must begin at home and only thereafter execute foreign policy initiatives.

Just like the concept of a "club," the notion that domestic politics, including the balancing coalitions, play a major role is crucial to understanding GATT-WTO and regime evolution. Important work in political economy on domestic trade policy coalitions, for example, establishes the central role of factor mobility, the level of collective action costs, and the type of political institutions. In this tradition, Mansfield and Busch argue that states are likely to enact protectionist measures against trading partners when the incentives of pressure groups and policy makers converge. More specifically, their results confirm the need to integrate societal models (highlighting that deteriorating macro-economic conditions can create widespread demands for protection) and statist models focusing on the insulation or autonomy of policy makers from groups pressing for liberalization.

They also find that large states with market power are inclined to exploit their position by means of predatory policies, especially against small states. In fact, "[t]he incentives for larger countries to be open are simply considerably weaker than those facing smaller countries."[17] The gains from open trade through scale economies, specialization, and price reductions to consumers are relatively less important for states with larger domestic markets. In sum, economic and political economic approaches emphasize that leaders' preferences are often endogenous. They are the agents, rather than principals, reacting to domestic political forces and interests, which are also inclined toward predatory policies by the market power of large trading states.

When combined, these important political economic approaches suggest a fundamental intellectual puzzle addressed by this book. Given these considerable societal and institutional pressures, along with the protectionist privileges of the most powerful states, how do US or EU foreign policy goals prevail over domestic constraints, thus enabling cooperation? The situation is further complicated by the need for domestic constraints to be overcome in the United States and the largest European states (and in intra-EC or EU decision making) at approximately the same time. It would not be surprising, then, if domestic constraints dominated most of the time, and political leaders were unwilling or unable to exert their preferences for trade policy liberalization.

At the same time, committed political leaders who believe strongly in liberalization might be able to capitalize on periods of deteriorating domestic macroeconomic and international economic conditions. They might mobilize domestic political support by arguing that it is especially urgent in these circumstances to reduce trade barriers to catalyze growth and forestall protectionist impulses, which are likely to trigger counterproductive international retaliation. Furthermore, particularly in states where electoral rules and districts are less favorable to narrow economic interests, leaders can be expected to mobilize domestic groups favoring liberalization in order to balance protectionists. Finally, the predatory commercial inclinations of large states may be overcome when their leaders seek trade policy liberalization as a means to accomplish broader foreign economic, diplomatic, or security goals.

Thus, domestic approaches alone cannot explain the episodic occurrence of foreign economic policy thrusts to liberalize policies and advance the trade regime. Is there an alternative theory or conceptual approach that might more fully illuminate this crucial area of international political economy?

Defining political leadership

In his important work *Leadership*, James Burns emphasizes that leaders seek recognition and status as well as power in order to advance collective purposes. At the same time, they must be able to separate their personal motivations from reasons of state. Contemporary definitions of political leadership almost always emphasize the accomplishments of leaders based on some blend of personal characteristics and interpersonal capabilities. Burns argues that leaders "appeal to and respond to the needs and other motives of would-be followers with acts for reciprocal betterment or, in the case of transforming leaders, the achievement of real change in the direction of 'higher' values."[18] Drawing on classical political philosophy beginning with Thucydides, a leader is wise and open-minded in sizing up situations, as well as advisers and other officials, and thinking through appropriate measures and policies. In contemporary terms, the leader blends a grasp of historical context with the ability to make decisions with complexity and incomplete information.

Furthermore, leaders are often driven by a focused and sustained dedication, a deep sense of purpose toward accomplishing their program or policies. Clearly, political leadership is about motivation and goal seeking. In addition, however, it can be argued that the most effective political leaders "transcended their environments and transformed their circumstances as only great men can do, and thereby bent history to their will."[19] Leadership at its best helps guide us toward future agreements, practices, and institutions that advance higher political and human values.

Even as a baseline, however, leadership from the earliest political writings is recognized as requiring restraint and moderation, or prudence, both personally and in policies and actions. Both Thucydides and Clausewitz emphasize that a leader can discern the appropriate relationship between policies and public support. Specifically, a leader is sufficiently modest and pragmatic to recognize when a policy is not working, and flexible enough to change course. Leadership could be argued to be the ability to discern among three different situations with regard to following or educating and trying to change the views of citizens: first, when it is appropriate to avoid, abandon, or modify a policy lacking public support; second, when it makes sense to conduct a campaign to educate and persuade publics to accept an unpopular measure; and third, when on occasion it is important to persist with a policy or position despite public opposition. In any case, leaders in international politics must remain credible to citizens at home, and even abroad, and moral in their policies, both domestic and foreign. As one of the most astute American strategists has demonstrated,

> especially in this world of abundant and rapid communications, any of our policies abroad that are either conspicuously immoral to begin with or likely to lapse into behavior that can easily be so labeled, whether justly or not so justly, is likely to prove quite inexpedient and ultimately self-defeating.[20]

Thus, it is logical that "[t]he ultimate test of practical leadership is the realization of intended, real change that meets people's enduring needs."[21] At the same time, a leader seeks to achieve a common or collective purpose in addition to his or her own policy agenda. Thus, self-interest must be moderated with a sense of fairness and flexibility in recognizing differences among followers or constituents and the need to make compromises and adjustments in the process of goal seeking.

Mobilizing followers is a subtle task. In a political context, "leaders have a special role as activators, initiators, mobilizers."[22] Indeed, the roles of leaders and followers are interchangeable. Effective political mobilization requires that leaders understand their followers' needs and transform them into hopes and aspirations.

In their study emphasizing individual leadership by highly effective American executives in public agencies and organizations, Doig and Hargrove identify two key variables: coalition-building skills and skillful use of rhetoric and symbols. Creating followers, or coalition building, is a strength of almost all successful leaders, while "rhetorical leadership" is not as common. It involves the creation of myths through symbols and language that connect institutional innovation with deeper principles. In addition, "[s]kill and politics can be reinforcing; both are important in explaining achievement." Successful leaders almost always "had the personal support of elected executives as patrons."[23] Finally, success requires not only a mutually beneficial relationship between leader and head of state but also favorable or at least neutral trends in broader political opinion.

Just as Doig and Hargrove favor leadership by individuals over interest groups or organizations, this study emphasizes international leadership by individuals rather than by "states" or "hegemons." Even in international relations, states do not innovate in foreign policy and negotiations. Individuals do. At the same time, some forms of leadership in international relations may require support from both the elected "patron" at home and in terms of "domestic attitudes, political structures, and decision making processes."[24] In his explanation of whether the hegemonic state is willing or not to "lead," Keohane builds from Kindleberger's earlier arguments about British decline, the United States, and lack of leadership in the interwar period. Keohane emphasizes conditions under which a state can and cannot lead as a result of domestic political constraints. Instead, this study asks how senior appointed leaders and, often, their elected "patrons" build and maintain political support at home and manage the constraints of public opinion, interagency committees, and legislative oversight.

Thus, most definitions and applications of political leadership emphasize the ability to influence people in their beliefs and actions, and the capability to enact change in political institutions or practices. Definitions almost always highlight the accomplishments of leaders based on some blend of personal characteristics and interpersonal capabilities. Leadership surely includes the ability to use symbols and rhetoric to educate and persuade people to tolerate, or acquiesce, if not agree fully, with a policy or course of action. Leaders are "effective" because they create some lasting legacy by getting things done, particularly by recognizing the constraints in their political environments and working to mitigate or overcome them.[25] They have the ability to capitalize on the constraints or difficulties in their political environments by using them to mobilize people and institutions to action, and to build and shape coalitions. In sum, political leaders integrate ideas and rhetorical skills with commitment and persistent coalition building. In addition, at the international level leaders may also have important levers of influence available when they represent powerful or particularly engaged states.

Political leadership of institutionalized international negotiations

International political leadership in this study includes the contributions of individual officials acting on behalf of their government, officials representing public international organizations, and nongovernmental experts and analysts from a wide range of organizations. The nature and extent of their leadership will be assessed in the terms discussed above. In addition, for analytical clarity and simplicity, political leadership at the international level is assessed primarily in terms of two separable, although reinforcing, forms. First, "structural leadership" represents efforts of officials on behalf of states, most often those states with the greatest commitment to the issues under negotiation and/or the power resources that can be applied to the bargaining. Second, "entrepreneurial leadership" is the building and shaping of coalitions, and the persistent pursuit of the ways and means of forging agreements. A third type of leadership, "intellectual," is also important but significantly more difficult to track in practice. It is the promotion of the ideas and language that prove central to how the negotiators define the issues and possible solutions or ways to map out agreements.

Building upon the general international leadership approach of Charles Kindleberger, Young emphasizes these three different types of leadership of negotiations within international regimes: "Much of the real work of regime formation in international society occurs in the interplay of bargaining leverage, negotiating skill, and intellectual innovation."[26] The process of identifying and contrasting these distinct three forms aims specifically to establish the existence and absence of leadership independent of the outcomes it is associated with. It directly integrates the role of power or structural leverage, and thus elements of hegemonic leadership, material factors, and the domestic political economy of the largest trading states; the role of agency or political will and initiative, and thus elements of rationalist and bargaining perspectives; and the role of ideas, and thus elements of the sociological, institutionalist, and even constructivist perspectives. This book integrates key elements of Young's conceptual framework into the political leadership approach explained above, and applies it across the entire period of the international trade regime in all stages from the founding, but with special attention to its maintenance and development since the late 1970s.

Intellectual leadership

Political leaders draw heavily on their belief systems and those of senior advisers to produce broad directions and goals. In any one issue area, beliefs are transformed into more specific policies and initiatives to be pursued in order to effect lasting change in the political environment. At the same time, ideas from a wide range of experts, academics, and non-governmental and public institutions make their way into international negotiations. However, the exact sources and pathways of these ideas and even proposals can be very difficult to track with precision.

The intellectual leader "relies on the power of ideas to shape the thinking of the principals in processes of institutional bargaining."[27] Once key ideas have taken hold among parties, structural and entrepreneurial leaders may deploy or advocate them as an ideology to justify policy change. "Embedded liberalism" in particular "provided a coherent argument in support of free trade," and the rationale not only for creating the GATT in the 1940s but also for deepening and broadening its authority through the 1960s.[28] Thus, intellectual leadership has been central to both US and small-group consensus building to develop the authority of the global trade regime since the 1940s.

Even as the effective balancing of domestic needs and international arrangements enshrined in embedded liberalism was undermined by structural changes in domestic and international political economy evident by the 1970s, liberalism and liberalization in both political and economic terms assumed a new visibility and role in intellectual discourse and state practice. The "Washington consensus" was influential most fundamentally in the third wave of democratization that began in the mid-1970s, accelerated with the converging ideas of Reagan, Thatcher, and Kohl in the early and mid-1980s, and was catalyzed again by the collapse of the Cold War in the late 1980s and the Soviet Union in 1991. Economic globalization, enabled in part by the global GATT-based trade regime, was both driven by, and central to the further spreading of certain ideas of neoclassical liberalism.

On the other hand, ideas about the costs and disadvantages of economic globalization in general and the WTO in particular have come increasingly into play. Non-governmental organizations (NGOs), international non-governmental organizations (INGOs), and related transnational networks based mainly in the OECD states which oppose, or seek to revise, the WTO or global trade rules have pressed important arguments about increasing accountability in the negotiating process and integrating economic development as a central consideration in trade policy. In certain cases their ideas have been influential on the negotiating positions and initiatives of least developed and developing states. Thus, the persuasiveness of the ideas brought to bear in the negotiating process is one important part of both structural and entrepreneurial leadership in advancing the global trade regime.

Therefore, where possible this study attempts to identify the source of key ideas and proposals, but for the most part this is extremely difficult to establish reliably. For this reason, this work generally maps out how structural and entrepreneurial leaders employed ideas and rhetoric in their attempts to forge agreements that would advance trade liberalization. The degree of leadership is assessed in part by analyzing the emphasis and priority attached to the main policies announced for international trade liberalization and the WTO negotiations in particular.

Structural leadership

Structural leaders possess and clearly signal a serous commitment to actively, consistently pursue specific policies and initiatives. The degree of leadership can be assessed quite directly by the level of activity and consistency of action by senior policy makers.

International structural leadership includes the frank presentation, explanation, and advocacy of these policies and initiatives to domestic political constituents as necessary to gain authority to negotiate and approve international trade agreements. It is "rhetorical" in the sense of applying language and various channels of communication to win the support or acquiescence of interest groups, legislative leaders, and the legislature as an institution in the pursuit of policies and initiatives. In the foreign policy domain, this means establishing negotiating authority, involving legislators and other key individuals from business and NGOs, and gaining support for negotiated international agreements. These actors will closely track and cue on the level of perceived commitment by the head of state or prime minister to the policy, and his or her degree of support for the most involved minister or cabinet head.

Influencing people and accomplishing political change is inherently about education and public relations. For a head of state, prime minister, or cabinet head, this means communicating with people directly and through the media. Equally important is a degree of frankness and honesty in explanation and justification. Even the clearest and most strongly held idea or policy will not make a leader if the politician concerned lacks a reputation for sincerity and integrity. Lyndon Johnson was both genuine and credible in his leadership of policies and measures involved in the Great Society but much less so in his pursuit of the war in Vietnam. Leaders can change their emphasis or even their themes in explaining and justifying a policy, but integrity and credibility become ever more important as the justifications for policies change over time. Leadership of domestic political interests is assessed by tracing the degree of support established among the most interested and active groups.

International political leadership means proposing policies, carefully applying a wide range of levers of influence, and creatively guiding parties to compromises and deals. It requires flexibility and compromise in interactions with foreign governments, public international organizations, and INGOs. Just as in the domestic political environment, here leadership is about judging the timing and nature of key compromises required to win the agreement of key actors. It also involves mobilizing and carefully applying a wide range of levers of influence. Influence must be applied not only in the specific issue area at hand but also through arrangements and compromises linked from one issue area to another, including those in different trade agreements and between trade and other economic and even security deals.

Leaders in the context of international economic policy and extended bargaining certainly must be both patient and effective in working with people who disagree or who are reluctant, forging compromises, and applying a wide range of resources and levers of influence. Recognizing how and when to offer compromises is crucial to international trade policy leadership for two reasons. First, leaders must signal that they are taking careful account of other parties' positions, interests, and even their constituents. In the language of bargaining theory, they indicate that they are pursuing an "integrative" strategy, or one allowing for gains by others as well as oneself. A narrow "distributive" strategy excludes significant gains for other parties, and therein makes agreement unlikely if not impossible.

Second, however, a leader in international economic policy making must do more than this. He or she must guide the process of consensus-based decision making, and even incorporate other key leaders into the leadership circle or small group. Educating, mobilizing, building support at home, and developing an integrative bargaining strategy are all essential. Yet it is equally important to work effectively across sharply different political economic cultures and decision-making styles or approaches. Even in international institutional contexts, where many of the embedded procedures are adapted from US practices and legislation, leadership is inherently about recognizing and incorporating different institutional cultures or traditions.[29] Leaders must respect and apply not only the evolved procedures of the international institutional environment but also those of other actively involved states. Importantly, bargains in international issue areas generally require more patience and consensus building than in the United States, where majority rule decision-making processes are more widely practiced and accepted.

A structural leader has specialized skills in converting power based on material resources into bargaining leverage for the advancement of agreements on the negotiating issues. He or she is usually the trade minister or lead negotiator of a state with a major stake in a specific trade issue area. This study investigates what will be called two dimensions of structural leadership, as drawn from the work of Young, Lax and Sebenius, Winham, and others: (1) the implications of asymmetries in the distribution of power among parties; and (2) pyramiding, or winning over new parties and managing negotiating coalitions. At the same time, this approach assumes that in order to provide structural leadership, policy makers must be willing and able to overcome protectionist domestic interests and coalitions, while simultaneously adjudicating between competing foreign policy goals. Most of the time, leaders' trade policy preferences are endogenous. They are agents, rather than principals, who react to domestic political economic pressures and the predatory inclinations of the largest trading states with market power. However, this is not always the case, and this chapter also explains the exceptional cases of when and how structural leaders are successful in overcoming domestic constraints and other foreign policy purposes.

First, in assessing structural leadership in terms of both the overall negotiation and each negotiating issue, there are major asymmetries in the distribution of power and influence among the major bargaining parties. In addition, related to this more "positive" and resource-based form of power is "negative" or blocking leverage. Thus, for example, a state or coalition with relatively little to lose from a failure to reach, or a delay in reaching, agreement can exert considerable pressure by stalling, blocking, and making public commitments to persist. Indian officials have often applied this form of leverage in GATT-WTO negotiations. Conversely, the party with relatively more to gain from an agreement can be expected to consider the use of bribes in the form of side payments or rewards to induce parties to join its consensus group. US officials seeking agreement to launch the Uruguay Round, and particularly to include services in the GATT, provide an illustration of this situation.[30]

Structural leaders, who stand to gain the most when agreement is reached, should also be expected to take the initiative in making substantive proposals for liberalizing trade which go first or farthest on the policy area at hand. They aim to keep foreign trade policy in pace with international economic and technological change. No matter what stage from pre-negotiation to issues about implementation, monitoring and enforcement, the structural leader attempts to catalyze the negotiating process by moving first or exceeding (or at least meeting) the best offer on the table.

GATT-WTO initiatives usually begin with structural leaders from the state or states with by far the most material resources – that is, control of access to very large markets. Still, early on they seek to induce substantial deals and agreements among increasingly larger sets of member states, and ultimately to shape the agenda and advance the multilateral trade regime. This marks a crucial difference between hegemony or dominance and international political leadership. These can be differentiated in part by evaluating the degree of domestic or broader interests being pursued by a state in what John Odell terms a continuum of negotiating strategies from "pure distributive" to "pure integrative." Distributive, "value-claiming" strategies are narrow attempts to garner the best deal possible from international negotiation, whereas "value-creating" integrative strategies are designed to generate visible mutual benefits.[31] Because integrative strategies highlight the shared gains from cooperation, Odell expects that these tactics facilitate institutional expansion. Distributive strategies may help individual states achieve optimal gains, but make agreement difficult and decrease the chances for long-term cooperation. Pure distributive and integrative strategies are ideal types; in reality, states employ mixed approaches in different times and settings.[32] In this study, these terms are applied to the strategies and proposals of leaders, and structural leaders in particular.

Thus, a structural leader signals a clear, costly commitment to the negotiation process during key periods of time, which requires showing his or her willingness to make substantial compromises if others will do the same in finalizing the negotiating agenda.[33] This may also include explicit signals of willingness to negotiate compromises in particular elements of these early initiatives. The only major exception to this expectation is when this leader perceives a clear positional disadvantage to being out-front on a controversial issue when his or her state or organization is identified as having a strong self-interest therein. For this reason, when a structural leader expects that his or her proposal will be opposed precisely because it is so closely identified with self-interests, that leader can be expected to ask or suggest that another leader, most likely an entrepreneurial one, take the initiative, which in turn effectively becomes leadership on the original leader's behalf.

As suggested by several scholars in international relations, comparative politics, and American politics over past decades, political leadership is "collective" not only in the sense of the intimate connections between leaders and followers but also in its potentially joint nature. This study goes farther than most in the past in arguing that international political leadership is in fact most often inherently joint in nature. First, even the heads of states or cabinet heads most accomplished as leaders still rely on leadership by subordinate officials, and particularly so in international contexts. Second, structural leadership internationally often involves a small number of individuals working jointly. Not entirely unlike the process of leadership in the US Senate or Congress, it is often the case that no one leader can get it done. One leader may well be the first mover, the most influential, or the most visible, but accomplishing significant and enduring change may often require joint leadership. Even in the most often cited case of US (usually "hegemonic") leadership in creating the post-World War II, or Bretton Woods, international economic institutions, this study argues that the intellectual leadership was provided jointly by US and British officials. The structural leadership of US officials succeeded only by integrating British ideas, proposals, officials, and negotiating experience and insights fully into the negotiation process. Especially where the issues are complex, there are many players, and the stakes are high, we should expect joint leadership. Two individuals or even small groups of leaders are required in order to master technical complexity adequately, manage multiple issue areas, represent widely diverse geographic constituencies, and build communities of support among the many players with an important stake.

In this context, leadership includes the ability to share responsibility and blend ideas, policies, and levers and resources of influence. Small groups of two to four officials of leading states, sometimes closely supported by a senior official of the international organization, provide "collective leadership." Importantly, they lead together because their ideas, commitments, rhetoric, and influence among other members and coalitions are individually and jointly required for successful consensus-based decision making. The emphasis, even more than on resources and tangible levers of influence, is on their ability to mobilize support from groups of other actively involved states with clear stakes in the process. Leaders in the small group each add a comparative advantage in their ability to guide or convince key individuals, usually negotiators or ministers, from a range of states, regions, and issue areas. Co-leadership substantially improves the diplomatic and economic connections available for effective pyramiding. Thus, this approach directly incorporates the situation "where two or more countries take on the task of providing leadership together, thus adding to the legitimacy, sharing the burdens, and reducing the danger that leadership is regarded cynically as a cloak for domination and exploitation."[34]

This study sets out to examine closely individuals co-leading mainly in their structural, but potentially also in their entrepreneurial, roles. Co-leadership or collective leadership in the structural form is expected to be produced by small sets of officials representing two, three, or even four of the largest, most engaged trading states. Entrepreneurial leadership may also flow from multiple individuals both in concert and on their own. Young expects the efforts of multiple entrepreneurial leaders to be especially constructive for popularizing issues and brokering interests.[35] The next logical step is to scrutinize the possible role of certain coalitions of parties as entrepreneurial leaders, such as the Cairns Group in the agriculture area during and after the Uruguay Round.[36]

On more purely theoretical grounds, collective leadership is analyzed by scholars such as David Lake, Duncan Snidal, and Robert Pahre. In particular, Lake emphasizes the important difference between theories of hegemony and those of leadership. In his plea for separating these two different approaches, he argues that leadership theory has made more progress than theory about hegemony. At the same time, Snidal establishes that there is no reason that leadership cannot be provided by more than one state at the same time.[37] Lake argues that small groups of more than one country are increasingly likely to provide joint leadership in part as its costs and difficulties increase. Pahre applies game theory to ask how multiple leadership affects both the incentives to lead and the overall supply of public goods. He finds some positive effects on leaders, for example less buck passing, when a second or third leader is added. Furthermore, he finds that effects of multiple leadership are at least not necessarily negative for the supply of public goods. Despite the limitations of formal theory of public goods, Lake also advances thinking by showing that the question of the benevolent, as opposed to exploitative or coercive, nature of leadership is of only secondary importance. In sum, together these and other scholars have effectively established the fundamental potential and promise of joint or collective leadership theory, while also calling for the much fuller articulation and testing of leadership theory.

The second dimension of structural leadership is pyramiding, or winning over additional parties, through the judicious use of party arithmetic, process opportunism, and strategic sequencing, as explained below. Pyramiding refers to the process of gradually attaining consensus by reaching agreement among a small group of negotiators and working outward. This means, in the first instance, working to win the agreement of the next state judged to be the most important or influential with other states on the negotiating issue at hand. Once the first two states are in agreement, then it involves turning to the next most influential state, and therein constructing the inner, or core, consensus group one step at a time. The concept of pyramiding is central to an institution-alized, yet still informal, process in the GATT-WTO so-called Green Room bargaining. Typically, ten to twenty trade ministers are invited by the GATT-WTO director general to join an intensive small-group bargaining session in an attempt to break an impasse during a ministerial meeting. In general, ministers are selected first because they represent essential states, the largest traders, or states particularly engaged and committed on the issue at hand. A closely related and crucial criterion for selection is the minister's ability to represent, and subsequently win the agreement of, several or even many other member states.

Lax and Sebenius argue that subgroup agreements are difficult to overturn.[38] First, once states commit to positions, they are unlikely to back down in the force of external pressures. Domestic audience costs prevent easy reversals, and prospect theory demonstrates that negotiators are less willing to give up on existing agreements than they are to seek new ones.[39] Second, agreements become focal points for further negotiations. The codified terms of coopera-tion are psychologically attractive and difficult to discard.[40] Participation in the GATT has been defined by its serial approach to liberalization. Each ministerial meeting and overall round has significantly built on the last one and anticipated the next. In fact, by the Uruguay Round the final agreement contained specific schedules for continued negotiations on two key areas. In this way, members intended to avoid, or at least mitigate, the problem of getting a new round under way by establishing very precise requirements for further talks. Third, renegotiations are costly and uncertain because negotiating faith deteriorates as agreements fail.

Finally, opponents to expanded cooperation may be thwarted, divided, or co-opted. As more parties accede to the agreement, opportunity costs for remaining neutral increase. Agreements reached among a core group of key players are thus hard to resist, even if third parties feel left out of the process, or upset at being presented with a fait accompli. As one veteran diplomat observes, "what becomes apparent at the [multilateral] negotiation session is often less a product of that meeting than a result of the painstaking groundwork that has occurred, on a bilateral basis, in the weeks or months preceding."[41]

But pyramiding is not inevitable. Agreements, even among influential and wealthy states, do not automatically catalyze path-dependent expansion. Even though core group agreements tend to spread, the process must be carefully managed. The principles binding together members of the core group do not naturally spread to the periphery. Efforts to pursue expanded membership too quickly may fail, because the process depends on the gradual socialization of new members. This takes time. The main structural and entrepreneurial leaders must not only convince other states of the logic of institutionalized cooperation but also demonstrate their success within a common framework.

Lax and Sebenius outline three methods by which bilateral or small group bargaining may expand. The party arithmetic governing negotiations describes how adding or subtracting parties affects the prospects for cooperation. Tacit coalition building increases the bargaining range "by adding parties to the interaction that desirably affect no-agreement alternatives."[42] For example, bringing in a second competitive bidder in a trade deal may raise the acceptable price the original buyer was willing to spend. Adding parties gives more players a stake in negotiated outcomes, and the potential for linkage and greater mutual benefit increases. This may break an impasse between two or three states that can only offer each other so much. Conversely, subtracting parties from unwieldy bargaining fora may increase bargaining range by limiting the number of necessary side payments needed to appease all parties at the table. Explicitly or implicitly subtracting dissenting coalition partners from a single negotiating side makes agreement more likely.

One way of cooperating is to ignore voices of dissent and work with those with a greater shared interest. In time, the recalcitrant party may be persuaded to reconsider his or her opposition and brought into an agreement concluded without him or her. Maintaining the proper balance between adding and subtracting parties is tricky; it must be carefully managed by structural and entrepreneurial leaders. Aggressive expansion may only be pursued after the principles embedded in subgroup agreements visibly guide the policy of key states over an extended period. In general, voices of dissent are not ignored in international bargaining, because most cultures and international organizations aim for broad-based consensus decisions.

Process opportunism describes efforts to garner influential allies and prevent the emergence of opposing coalitions. Structural leaders in particular increase the chances for agreement by quietly gaining support for cooperation before formal talks commence. They exhibit skill in forging powerful coalitions and deterring states from joining opposing and blocking coalitions. They employ secrecy, partial communication, and imperfect information to harden alliances before proposals are made public.

The logic of process opportunism for individual agreements is essentially the logic of the key states approach, writ small. The probability for bilateral or subgroup cooperation increases once tacit agreement is reached among key players, domestic or international. During pre-Uruguay Round meetings, for instance, structural leaders from the Quad states were able to diffuse growing unrest in developing states. Brazil and India expressed particular dissatisfaction with the US desire to expand the GATT into new areas including services and investment without first addressing existing controversies. The Uruguay Round proceeded only after entrepreneurial leaders of smaller and medium-sized states and GATT mediators persuaded key developing members to relax their demands.[43] Thus, process opportunism has been important to the ability of structural leaders from the largest states to restrain the blocking power that newer players and their coalitions have acquired over time.

Implicit in this process is the concept of strategic sequencing, or the decisions about the order in which allies are sought. Because the process involves purposeful incremental expansion, the "pyramiding phenomenon necessarily implies some order of actions that can be chosen with the goal of affecting perceptions of the target zone of possible agreements."[44] To achieve effective multilateral cooperation, domestic opposition must be controlled before taking on large international commitments. Sequencing internal and external commitments thus has the effect of first mitigating internal dissent before limiting external opposition.

Domestic constraints and competing foreign policy goals

US and European domestic political constraints from national elections to opposition by key legislative committee chairs or specific interest groups regularly affect the GATT-WTO negotiating process.[45] Political economy models and theories help to explain the fact that states are likely to confront the strongest protectionist pressures when the incentives of pressure groups and policy makers converge. Mansfield and Busch, for example, find most persuasive an integration of societal, statist, and market power models of trade policy making. Societal models explain how widespread nationalist pressures can be generated by deteriorating macroeconomic conditions. Statist approaches focus on the degree of insulation or autonomy of policy makers from groups pressing for liberalization. The greater their insulation, the stronger the incentive under certain conditions to impose tariffs or other barriers to win votes in swing states or provinces or favor among important constituencies. Finally, they also find that large states with market power are inclined to exploit their position with predatory policies, especially against small states.

For these reasons, the most fundamental challenge to structural leadership is mobilizing and sustaining domestic political support for trade policy liberalization during key points in the bargaining process. Leaders' preferences do not have to be exogenous throughout the bargaining. Instead, leaders must be willing and able to make trade policy a higher priority when required for international cooperation. In general, this means at the points when the domestic political mandate or authority is established for the negotiations to begin and when the content of specific agreements is reviewed for approval.

Essentially, the outcome for policy makers can be assessed with respect to three required steps or stages. First, they must decide whether to pursue trade liberalization or to seek political gains by the use of protectionist measures. Second, when they pursue liberalization, their leadership of trade policy must prevail over domestic constraints. Often, protectionist interests in the domestic setting are offset, at least in part, by countervailing pressure from supporting interests. Finally, unless trade policy liberalization converges with other important foreign policy goals, policy makers must determine that trade policy takes priority.

Particularly important to structural leadership by US negotiators is the "veto point" protectionist threat from Congress, which must grant trade negotiating authority to the president or approve a final trade agreement. US structural leaders wield less negotiating credibility among the GATT-WTO membership if they do not have a specific grant of negotiating authority from the Congress. Furthermore, lowering the barriers to trade almost certainly raises the ire of import-competing industries, agriculture (especially in the EU, Japan, South Korea, and Switzerland, but also in the United States), and organized labor. The most vocal protectionist interest groups constitute substantial voting constituencies and important campaign contributors. US structural leadership requires that politicians make trade-offs and explain the benefits expected to offset losses. To be credible, a structural leader must demonstrate the ability to cope with protectionist pressures, and, ultimately, to ratify bargained agreements and integrate them into domestic legislation and regulations. This requires the commitment of substantial effort toward constructing and maintaining a minimum winning coalition of domestic interests. Thus, the audience costs incurred in the support of expanded institutional trade are significant. Therefore, when structural leaders overcome serious challenges at home, they signal their own commitment to wary institutional partners.[46]

There are three basic ways to accomplish this. The first is to balance such protectionist pressures with support from exporters, producers who import components of their products, and groups or associations focused on global markets. Structural leaders must mobilize positive pressure for progress on a negotiating round from their supportive and potentially supportive business communities. A well-known phenomenon in GATT-WTO rounds is that difficult issues or focal points are unlikely to be resolved without a substantial level of interest in the overall round from business and industry groups.

One important tool for this purpose is cross-issue linkage to broaden the stakes of negotiation, thereby mobilizing domestic pro-trade interests.[47] While threats often lead to backlash, and the resort to legalism may arouse suspicions of lost autonomy, linkage strategies give incentive to those domestic groups that support liberalization. Focusing on the difficult area of agricultural subsidies and tariffs, Davis finds that linkage serves to reduce the influence of protectionist agriculture ministers, thus reducing the domestic opposition to agreement.[48] During the Uruguay Round, the use of linkage mobilized European and Japanese industrial exporters to lobby for agricultural liberalization. Because they came to believe that the United States would not support further cooperation without action on an agreement on agriculture, they pressured their respective governments to work towards compromise. In Japan, the leading business association endorsed GATT director general Arthur Dunkel's "single package," and the government made important concessions on rice barriers. In Europe, linkage reduced the perception of CAP inviolability in Europe, thus facilitating the Blair House agreement in 1990 and breaking the EU–US impasse.

A second way to overcome domestic opposition is to lead a campaign to educate and persuade opponents and citizens more generally of the urgent necessity to achieve a foreign diplomatic or security goal through liberalization. For example, in 1993–1994 the Clinton administration argued that NAFTA was expected to help lock in Mexico's recent economic and political reforms. In the aftermath of the September 11, 2001 attacks on the United States, US Trade Representative (USTR) Zoellick argued before congressional committees that trade liberalization was one important tool for fighting the underlying causes of terrorism. The third approach is for leaders to forcefully emphasize the economic necessity or advantages of opening trade markets overseas and at home. For this purpose, they might take the case to the media, legislative leaders, and even citizens at large that liberalization is urgent during difficult economic conditions, both as a positive catalyst for economic growth and as an offset against the destructive, retaliatory impulses of fearful populist pressures.

In sum, the main challenge to structural leadership is domestic constraints, and the steady state may well be that leaders' preferences are endogenous. Indeed, it is likely that success is rare precisely because of the difficulty of overcoming domestic pressures, as well as variation among leaders in the strength of their beliefs in liberalization. Additionally, protectionist pressures in one key state can trigger reactionary impulses in other states, making it even more difficult for leaders to overcome domestic opposition. At the same time, there are important examples of where clear opposition to agreements has been shifted to neutral or positive. The puzzle of this book is to explain how and why this occurs.

Entrepreneurial leadership

The third type of leader, entrepreneurial, is "an individual who relies on negotiating skill to frame issues in ways that foster integrative bargaining and to put together deals that would otherwise elude participants."[49] Specifically, this involves careful and strategic shaping of the agenda to increase the chances of agreement, innovative introduction of policy options to resolve breakdowns, and brokering deals. It has traditionally been central to GATT-WTO negotiations. In part because of the lack of a formal executive board for regular decision making, the trade regime has been advanced with the entrepreneurial leadership of individuals from a surprisingly large number of member states. They are typically officials acting on behalf of a state, the GATT-WTO, or a negotiating group or committee empowered by the member states. GATT-WTO negotiating committees are often headed by an official from a smaller or middle-sized state who is chosen first for his or her entrepreneurial and management capabilities, but also because his state has little or no direct stake in the specific negotiating area.

The entrepreneurial leader offers skillful, creative guidance and brokering of international trade bargaining, or the "ability to seize upon a particular issue in which others have an interest and to coax them to cooperate towards its ultimate resolution."[50] Leadership is not simply the product of resources and power; that is, a leader cannot influence behavior simply because he or she is wealthier or has a more formidable army.[51] Rather, it involves the ability to emphasize and structure key incentives and convince potential allies that long-term cooperation is in their interest even if it implies some loss of domestic policy autonomy. A leader provides not only resources but also "time and skills in structuring a multilateral incentive matrix."[52]

It often involves "persuasion," in the sense of "changing people's choices of alternatives independently of their calculations about the strategies of other players."[53] An entrepreneurial minister or ambassador, state, or group adeptly demonstrates and draws attention to the benefits of membership, highlighting not only likely gains but also the avoidance of possible losses, and adherence to institutional norms and principles, to skeptical states.[54] This leader frequently shapes and sometimes sets the agenda to enhance the prospects for agreement. Because accession to international regimes threatens state sovereignty, this is no easy task. Even very visible, shared interests, including areas of substantial overlap, may not be enough.

Entrepreneurial leadership also requires the leader to make use of careful initiatives and manipulation in forging constructive linkages across issues, particularly within the domain of international trade, but helpful linkages can be forged between trade and other issue areas and international regimes. Cross-issue linkages can be crucial in international trade because when formulated systematically they offer the possibility of increasing trade-offs and balancing perceived gains and losses.[55] Furthermore, as is noted above, these linkages serve as an important means for mobilizing domestic interests favoring liberalization. In the end, in order to conclude an agreement, entrepreneurial leaders may work closely with structural leaders to apply several different tools of diplomacy to persuade leaders of other key states and build coalitions of support, but they do not cross over the sometimes subtle line between a spirited effort at persuasion, and coercion or domination.[56] Finally, entrepreneurship also involves the skillful integration and blending of ideas about the negotiating process and content. Ideas generated from outside as well as inside the formal trade policy community can be important, but most often ideas are shaped and introduced by inside participants.

Finally, the construction and manipulation of turning points and reversals in the GATT-WTO negotiation process is extremely important. Entrepreneurial leaders in particular appear to rely substantially and consistently on the use of focal or turning points. Relatively sudden events or decisions that originate outside the negotiating process sometimes can be managed or shaped to create intense political pressures on parties outside the consensus group. The strategic construction of more minor, but still significant, focal points in the form of new ideas, procedures, proposals, or coalitions internal to the negotiating process is also important to trade bargaining.[57] The shaping or management of reversals in response to failed meetings may contribute to a cyclical pattern of sequential failures and successes. Explaining how the actions of entrepreneurial, and at times structural, leaders help to create this failure–success pattern of GATT-WTO negotiations is an important goal of this book.

Entrepreneurial leaders, working closely with structural leaders, usually responding to a failure or deadlock in the bargaining, formulate special procedures to redirect the process. They may seek to appoint a new committee or committee chair, propose a new formula or draft text, declare a crisis in the trade regime, or establish a heightened sense of time urgency for compromising and reaching agreement. External events such as US or European national elections, or domestic and international economic crises, can be manipulated and applied to forge a turning or critical point in the process.

More often, however, entrepreneurial activity in the trade regime is built upon events internal to the process.[58] Leaders use "mini-lateral" or mini-ministerial, "Green Room," and ministerial meetings in an effort to break a deadlock and reach an interim or framework agreement. It is generally understood that as a draft agreement appears to key structural and entrepreneurial leaders to be approaching the required degree of consensus, a ministerial meeting will be scheduled. This allows the GATT-WTO director general and the minister acting as chair of the General Conference to apply greater pressure on all members to make final compromises and reduce disagreements to the level where a ministerial meeting is likely to induce the final bargaining required to reach agreement.

Conclusion

Trade policy makers are substantially constrained most of the time by domestic politics and national political economic interests. Indeed, at certain times these interests converge with those of policy makers who use protectionist trade measures to achieve short-term electoral or other political gains. Thus, policy makers' interests by trade sector or trade issue area do not always mesh with the GATT-WTO regime or the main interests of other key GATT-WTO member states. More often than not, these specific and shorter-term interests dominate.

Furthermore, even when domestic politics are not dominant, trade policy and other foreign policy goals do not always converge. When they diverge, trade policy must compete for priority, and there is substantial experience indicating that the policies of the US security complex can trump those of the economic complex when they are in competition. Particularly during the Cold War era, US national security or Department of State officials favored European unity over development of the international trade regime, at least when they believed the latter undermined the former. In sum, for both domestic and foreign policy reasons, in general we must "expect global political leadership from domestic politicians to be rare, and the governance of globalization to remain disarticulated and disjointed."[59]

Still, during key decision processes and periods, leaders' broader, longer-term interests and commitments to the trade regime are expected to prevail. In fact, in trade policy in particular it can be argued that certain structural leaders, including heads of state and cabinet officers, as well as entrepreneurial and intellectual leaders, pursue coherent strategies of international leadership. Thus, the central argument is that during focal points or decisive junctures in the evolution of the GATT-WTO process, if leadership is provided, then the process is much more likely to be successful in reaching agreement, and if it is not provided, then it will not end with an agreement.

This analysis takes as its starting point the assumption that leadership "is a critical determinant of success or failure in the processes of institutional bargaining that dominate efforts to form,"[60] develop, and sustain international regimes. Leadership of the bargaining process is considered fundamental and central to the negotiating process within the GATT and certainly other organizations, regimes, and negotiations. Two crucial components of structural leadership are pyramiding and managing supporting and opposing coalitions. Therefore, wherever the empirical evidence makes it possible, this work focuses especially on leadership aimed at expanding the consensus group. Why do states decide to join, or not join, the consensus group? What are the perceived benefits of joining and how central are relative gains? Given the central role of domestic political economic factors in international trade, how can they be adequately accounted for in a leadership approach? Specifically, how do trade and other foreign policy officials balance protectionist pressures and trade policy liberalization goals, as well as liberalization against other foreign policy goals?

The puzzle: assessing development and enhancement of the trade regime

In this investigation, the survival and growth in influence of the international trade regime will serve as the dependent variable, or the factor to be explained. The GATT-WTO-based regime provides a rich subject for investigation because of its changing status through time. The contrast is sharp between the original form of the GATT and its modest rules, as opposed to the current global trade regime and the WTO structure and authority. For clarity and precision, this work focuses more specifically on the expansion of the regime primarily in terms of how changes in its role and functions have been proposed at key junctures, and ultimately how they have been rejected or accepted by the negotiating members in the failure or success of the final proposed agreement.

Naturally, elements of subjectivity must influence any judgment of the degree of enhancement of the trade rules and institutions, but past analyses, particularly those such as the "rational design" and "legalization" approaches, have provided effective measures.[61] The case studies take into account the following dimensions of the trade regime at each of the key periods from 1947 to 2001:

- the durability of fundamental operating principles;
- the level of precision in defining the rules and procedures for conduct of members;
- the extent of independence and authority vested in GATT-WTO implementation and interpretation of rules, including dispute settlement;
- the effectiveness of monitoring, reporting and enforcement of the agreed rules and procedures, while acknowledging that a degree of flexibility is sometimes required in their application;
- its accountability to member states and legitimacy of decision-making, including particularly the participation and representation of members;
- the breadth of regime membership (overall numbers but also major trading states); and
- the scope of trade and related issue area coverage.

Part II
The practice of political leadership in international trade negotiations

3   The founding

World War II to the turbulent 1970s

The ambitious ITO fails as the austere GATT forum begins

In the immediate aftermath of World War II, the United States attempted to forge an international institution to codify and monitor a set of specific trade principles. The promise of US aid compelled its cautious wartime allies to attend negotiations between 1946 and 1948 to create the International Trade Organization (ITO). After eighteen months of negotiations, the broad-ranging ITO, to be managed by an eighteen-member executive board, was central to the Havana Charter. Yet despite the persistent US initiative and post-war American enthusiasm for international institutions, the United States never ratified the agreement to form the ITO. Why not?

None of the prevailing accounts about this period provides a satisfying explanation. Analysts of US hegemony tend to overlook fundamental compromises made by US officials in negotiating the nature of the postwar international economic system. They also tend to neglect crucial trade-offs made between American policies for a liberal, multilateral economic system and those for the Truman Doctrine and Cold War. Scholars of international institutions overemphasize the weakness of the early GATT in formal, institutional terms and devalue the basic clash between regional European cooperation and liberal multilateralism. Finally, accounts highlighting the central role of US domestic politics do not adequately explain US leaders' decisions and actions taken to promote European cooperation and to contain the Communist threat. This chapter develops, instead, an alternative approach based on political leadership in its three basic forms in order to help explain the early development of the Western international trading system.

From 1941 until the Cold War took hold in 1947, US foreign policy under both Franklin D. Roosevelt (FDR) and Harry Truman emphasized the links between peace and freedom, including the integral role of international economic relations and trade liberalization. The integral role of trade liberalization in ensuring peace served as the fundamental intellectual foundation of their structural leadership with European leaders and in building support from the US Congress and domestic groups. During this period, US trade policy and leadership of international trade negotiations were among the highest-priority foreign policy goals, and they coincided with US diplomatic and security interests. Thereafter, the Cold War and, to a lesser extent, the domestic political constraints posed by the congressional elections of 1946 and the presidential election campaign in 1948 shifted the policy priorities. Republican control of Congress from 1946 reduced Truman's ability to count on congressional approval of his foreign policy agenda. Throughout most of the Cold War period, particularly beginning in 1948 with the Communist coup in Czechoslovakia, the Soviet blockade of Berlin, and the first trial of US Communist leaders, and followed by the Korean War in 1950, US foreign security and diplomatic goals were preeminent, and foreign economic policy and trade specifically were not presented as fundamental to US security.

Thus, the question arises as to whether advancing the GATT regime was seen as consistent or inconsistent with the overarching US foreign policy goals and vital interests. Broadly conceived, from the early to mid-1940s an open world trade system ranked very high in FDR's vision for establishing stable peace in the postwar period. More specifically, he sought both an expanded US role in world affairs and the gradual demise of colonial empires. International trade played an important role in each of these goals. Peace, for FDR, meant ending the oppressive economic conditions and beggar-thy-neighbor foreign economic policies that became so destructive in the 1930s. In his 1941 "Annual Message of the President to the Congress," FDR explained,

> In the future days, which we seek to make secure, we look forward to a world founded upon four essential human freedoms . . . [including] freedom from want – which, translated into world terms, means economic understandings which will secure to every nation a healthy peacetime life for its inhabitants – everywhere in the world.[1]

This basic idea grew from common understandings about economic dislocation as a cause of World War II, and thus the necessary paths to peace, for example as expressed in the UN Charter of 1946.

He further elaborated his strategy in the "The Atlantic Charter" of August 14, 1941, in which he pressed Churchill on the anticolonialism theme to declare as a common principle for future US and UK policies that "they will endeavor . . . to further the enjoyment by all States, great or small, victor or vanquished, of access, on equal terms, to the trade and to the raw materials of the world which are needed for their economic prosperity."[2] Churchill and top British officials argued for a trade regime focused on the goal of full employment and integration of the Imperial preference system. In order to gain acceptance of his policies in Europe more generally, FDR had first to either persuade or to strong-arm the British. Through the February 1942 Lend-Lease Agreement between the United States and the United Kingdom, a strong act of US structural leadership that bordered on coercion, FDR in effect required his primary war ally to agree "to the elimination of all forms of discriminatory treatment in international commerce, and to the reduction of tariffs and other trade barriers; and, in general, to the attainment of all the economic objectives set forth in the Atlantic Charter."[3] This understanding was subsequently included in each of the lend-lease agreements with the other allies.

It was precisely these foundational goals that formed the basis for the more substantial US planning for the post-war era. In setting the context for the 1944 Bretton Woods Conference and building upon article VII of the Master Lend-Lease Agreement of 1942, Secretary of the Treasury Henry Morganthau emphasized that the new international institutions would support "[the] creation of a dynamic world community in which the peoples of every nation will be able to realize their potentialities in peace."[4] This crucial relationship between commercial policy and peace was emphasized again in 1946 at the San Francisco conference aimed at creating the United Nations.

The critical steps in US structural leadership of a new international trade system based on the principle of nondiscrimination began in 1945. US officials were dedicated and persistent in their pursuit of this basic principle. First, the Reciprocal Trade Agreements Act was renewed by Congress for three years. Then, US officials invited governments to negotiate an agreement for reducing tariffs. In December 1945, the State Department circulated a key substantive document, *Proposals for Expansion of World Trade and Employment*, which outlined US ideas for organizing post-war international trade. In 1946, the United States published a draft entitled "Suggested Charter for an International Trade Organization of the United Nations," which represented an important instance of intellectual leadership by US officials. It was this set of ideas incorporated into draft articles generated by US officials that provided a foundation for the negotiation. Next, US officials attempted to facilitate and guide the eighteen-month-long series of meetings and negotiations required to create the Havana Charter. This series began with a preparatory committee meeting in London during October and November 1946, continued in New York in early 1947 and in Geneva from April to August, and culminated in Havana from November 1947 through March 1948.[5]

However, beginning at the same time in late 1946 and increasing by early 1947, leading US officials were caught off guard by newly perceived political-military threats in Eastern Europe and economic distress in Western Europe. Unexpected economic crises in Europe demanded that US officials shift their policy priorities and exert structural leadership in order to avert social and political breakdown in Europe. They were required to devote their intellectual resources and political strength to solving the immediate European economic crisis. The creativity, initiatives, and leverage previously directed at trade policies had to be redirected, weakening the previous priorities.

In response, the president introduced the so-called Truman Doctrine in March 1947, which was in turn elaborated and explained by Undersecretary of State Dean Acheson's speech in May and Secretary of State George Marshall's widely publicized address in June. Rapidly evolving US policy was aimed at both deterring the expansion of Soviet influence in Greece, Europe, and elsewhere, and coping with severe economic distress in Western Europe.

> The Marshall initiative and the policies that developed from it – for there was no plan at first – were at the same time continuous from the earlier American economic goals and a departure from them with respect to the means of implementation as expressed through lend-lease and the British Loan.[6]

US officials were also driven to create a comprehensive set of postwar economic recovery policies in order to address opposition in Congress and US publics to more bilateral aid or a continuation of colonialism, and opposition in Europe to rebuilding the German economy and open multilateralism.

As a result, US officials made major compromises in international economic policies. European economic cooperation, which was necessary for effective use of US aid and self-sustaining economic recovery, was promoted ever more rigorously, while US officials accepted precisely the special trading and payments arrangements they had opposed. "The U.S. objective of a global trading system was thus refocused onto a regional framework."[7] The rhetorical emphasis from the 1940s into the 1950s was that the regional economic system in Europe would require a temporary divergence from liberal multilateralism. Key US officials recognized the need for flexibility and compromise in the basic principles of broad international liberalism.

Nevertheless, even as the liberal, multilateral trade system was being overtaken by events, US officials attempted to stay the course. Indeed, President Truman's "Address on Foreign Economic Policy" at Baylor University in March 1947, just days before his speech in the Congress announcing the Truman Doctrine, argued forcefully that

> at this particular time, the whole world is concentrating much of its thought and energy on attaining the objectives of peace and freedom. These objectives are bound up completely with a third objective – reestablishment of world trade. In fact, the three – peace, freedom, and world trade – are inseparable. The grave lessons of the past have proved that our foreign relations, political and economic, are indivisible.

He mapped out in detail the US-led process of drafting a "world trade charter," highlighting its links to building a permanent peace and the ultimate American value of freedom in its three fundamental forms: worship, speech, and enterprise. US officials led intensive negotiations in Geneva through the spring and summer.[8] Punctuating the final negotiations at the Havana Conference of November 1947 through March 1948 was Truman's 1948 State of the Union address:

> We are moving toward our goal of world peace in many ways. But the most important efforts which we are now making are those which support world economic reconstruction. We are seeking to restore the world trading system which was shattered by the war and to remedy the economic paralysis which grips many countries . . . we have recently taken the lead in bringing about the greatest reduction of world tariffs that the world has ever seen. The extension of the provisions of the Reciprocal Trade Agreements Act, which made this achievement possible, is of extreme importance. We must also go on to support the International Trade Organization, through which we hope to obtain worldwide agreement on a code of fair conduct in international trade.

However, by 1948 US structural leadership for the ITO was also further undermined by tightening domestic political constraints. President Truman was increasingly engaged in a difficult presidential election race in the context of Republican control of both houses of Congress. Also, the ability of US executive branch officials to argue for the ITO on intellectual, substantive grounds was eroded as the modest GATT became official on January 1, creating a clear alternative. Part II of the GATT agreement included precisely the commercial policy elements of the ITO that formed the core US objectives for an international trade system.[9] Once this was established, the ITO became less urgent and the alternative to the ITO became increasingly acceptable to Truman. In particular, the emergence of the GATT helped to undermine any urgency for the ITO among congressional leaders. In this situation, policy makers should have foreseen that the GATT agreement would undermine support for the more ambitious ITO. The administration's ability to provide structural leadership for the ITO was undermined by its failure to manage domestic political interests, and congressional leaders in particular. In his Annual Economic Report to Congress for 1948, Truman explained that

> [s]till in process of creation is the International Trade Organization. . . . A major step toward this long-range goal is the General Agreement on Tariffs and Trade, recently concluded between ourselves and 22 other countries. . . . Like the proposed charter of the International Trade Organization, this agreement will help establish conditions under which world trade can flourish in less troubled times and under which the present reconstruction efforts can be carried forward.

Essentially, with less political space at home, US foreign policy leaders reverted to a much narrower international position that represented national more than multilateral interests. Even the president quietly abandoned continuing international structural leadership of the collective interests embedded in the ITO framework.

What began with intensive US–British negotiations during the war over a worldwide economic order was in fact radically refocused by 1947. Indeed, even before the economic and political crises in Europe triggered urgent reconsideration of the Truman administration's policies, the emerging international economic framework reflected "embedded liberalism." This was the basic compromise merging European insistence on recognition of the state's role in guiding employment and social welfare with the core principles of American liberal internationalism. Led by British negotiators, who were necessarily first and foremost concerned about domestic economic stability, the Europeans and other key states fought the US idea of a fully open, multilateral economic system. They would accept the commitment to a non-discriminatory system of international commercial and monetary relations only if it enshrined the welfare state. British and other European negotiators balanced US structural leadership with their own leadership based on the ideas then current in Britain particularly. In essence, the role of both European ideas and political leverage was enhanced because US officials needed their cooperation to build European unity and pursue the Cold War. Competing US foreign policy objectives required major compromise in the ITO negotiations.

Leadership by Truman and key officials of his administration, therefore, was both structural and intellectual in framing the proposals that were negotiated in 1945 and 1946. Their assertions of liberal internationalism were fundamental to agreements forged during the war, but increasingly compromised as the postwar environment was negotiated. In parallel to early British resistance to joining US visions for liberal multilateralism, other states increasingly opposed laissez-faire international trade arrangements. This gradually eroded the effectiveness of US structural and intellectual leadership, until US officials began to compromise over substantive disagreements.

Once the Cold War and European economic crises forced even more basic policy reassessment, the intellectual basis for US leadership shifted ground. Although Truman held his ground rhetorically and tried to maintain the public relations campaign for the ITO, in fact US structural leadership necessarily converged during 1947–1948 with the conceptual focus on European co-operation over liberal multilateralism. With the erosion by 1948 of the domestic foundation of US structural leadership for multilateralism, US officials quietly shifted to other pressing policy priorities, and the ITO was dead in the water. In effect, the United States got exactly what certain officials and congressional leaders most wanted – the GATT without the ITO – but liberal multilateralism was sacrificed on the altar of European recovery and regionalism.

In the end, of course, US allies had no choice but to follow suit and ultimately allow the Havana Charter to languish in their domestic legislative processes. US foreign relations documents from this period show that the British were not willing to move forward with the ITO until Truman had presented a convincing case to Congress, which he never did. Similarly, many other governments waited to learn the fate of the ITO in the United States. Once it failed there, they did not pursue it further.

By 1949–1950, Truman's public speeches focused on congressional approval of the Reciprocal Trade Agreements Act extension and the European Recovery Program. He still called for approval of the ITO, but now emphasized the need for technical assistance and foreign investment in those underdeveloped countries which gained little immediate value from tariff reductions. In 1950, National Security Council Paper no. 68 (NSC-68) argued:

> Our position as the center of power in the free world places a heavy responsibility upon the United States for leadership. We must organize and enlist the energies and resources of the free world in a positive program for peace.

"The American system" could only "survive and flourish" with a more rapid build-up of political, economic, and military strength and thereby of confidence in the free world than was now contemplated. In turn, the development of military power depended on the free world's ability to "meet its political and economic problems." In this context, nothing seemed more consistent with overarching US foreign policy goals and interests than the reduction of trade barriers and the creation of a worldwide trade system – that is, the ITO – among all US allies and friends, but it could proceed only as seen consistent with economic and political recovery in Western Europe. The ITO failed because US policy makers, beginning with the president, were unable to package the ITO with recovery in Europe. This was a failure of structural leadership based in part on the inability to innovate with the language and symbols of effective rhetoric about liberal internationalism. At the same time, it is understandable in terms of the ideological opposition of key US senators to major parts of the ITO, the urgent need for congressional support of Cold War programs, the Republican control of Congress, and presidential election politics in 1948.

US presidential leadership at home and domestic support for early trade policy

Since the creation of the GATT in 1947, presidential time, attention, and commitment have been instrumental in mobilizing domestic support for trade negotiations. When presidents and their key cabinet heads devoted time and energy to international trade, they were often able to overcome considerable opposition, whether from domestic industry, powerful interest groups, or a protectionist Congress.

The demise of the ambitious ITO in the late 1940s as the austere GATT was gathering momentum was, accordingly, first and foremost a reflection of presidential priorities. President Truman's attention was focused on international political military challenges. His preoccupation with economic recovery in Europe and the Communist threat deflated the potential for structural leadership by US officials in international economic policy. Truman mobilized his political capital to respond to the crisis in Europe with the Marshall Plan and more generally to combat the new international Communist menace. At that time, the nexus between the domestic economy and foreign policy was not as readily recognized or understood. Thus, attention was easily diverted away from international trade and refocused on traditional political and military objectives: building alliances and amassing arms.

The division of congressional opinion on the issue of trade added to the lack of presidential leadership in ratifying the ITO. The ITO embodied a formalized plan for liberalization that triggered two important ideological, political, and institutional concerns for key leaders and committees of Congress. First, some congressional leaders feared that the substantial institutional authority of the ITO would force the United States to sacrifice too much sovereignty. While the benefits of liberalization were recognized, Congress was not willing to grant the ITO legitimacy when the organization would restrict congressional control of trade policy. A key second concern was that the full employment and development provisions of the Havana Charter were too wide-reaching. For some members, these provisions represented excessive government intervention in the international marketplace.

The ITO did have a set of dedicated and influential supporters, however, which kept the debate alive in Congress. Key intellectual leaders in this regard, including John Dickey, Philip Reed, Oscar Heleine, Palmer Hoyt, Douglas Fairbanks, Jr., and John K. Galbraith, were convinced that the Great Depression could be blamed on protectionist policies. As US economic growth slowed and unemployment increased, they advocated an expansive trade policy that would reduce tariffs and enhance domestic economic growth. However, the proponents of the ITO lacked the resources and political support to balance the opposition by well-established advocates for domestic industry.[10] The interests of specific industrial sectors were pressed effectively on key members of Congress by, for example, former DuPont executive Elvin Kilheffer, the president of the Carnegie Endowment, Alger Hiss, and the president of Coty Cosmetics, Philip Cortney. Thus, at least in Congress, ITO advocates were outweighed by domestic industrial leaders.

Moreover, the president, Congress, and business never engaged the media or public on trade policy and the ITO in a sustained way. Thus, the survival or failure of the ITO was largely left to lobbyists and key members of Congress.

This resulted in part from the lack of a positive intellectual foundation for connecting economic prosperity in the United States directly with international economic relations. In the late 1940s, there was no general understanding that trade liberalization would benefit the domestic economy.[11] As a result, US citizens and groups remained hesitant to support a liberal trade policy. By the 1960s, they were increasingly aware of the benefits of trade liberalization and supportive of international trade negotiations.

Meanwhile, as US economic sectors and industries struggled to adjust in the aftermath of the Great Depression, government officials did not present a comprehensive strategy to spur domestic economic growth. The Truman administration, perhaps, could have galvanized support for the ITO with political leadership based on advocacy for trade liberalization as a solution for domestic economic problems. Officials might have argued that trade liberalization would establish the conditions required for renewed economic growth, in part by reducing the price of goods. Instead, public and elite debate over strikes, price controls, government intervention, and corporate responsibility failed to generate any substantive policy solutions for the domestic economy.[12] Without the guidance of a decisive governmental policy, neither the print media nor public groups ever had the opportunity to discuss the ITO.

A vital part of structural leadership is the ability to educate and mobilize political groups and congressional leaders in order to serve the larger good of the international regime. In particular, the ITO would have required President Truman not only to fight for industry and congressional approval, but also to accept the political costs of opposition by certain businesses and industrial sectors that were not likely to be persuaded by his efforts. The president most needed strong industry and congressional support for the Marshall Plan. Certainly he was convinced of the need for trade liberalization and of the importance of an international trade regime. Nevertheless, he likely calculated that he did not have the political capital to expend on mobilizing domestic support for the ITO, especially in a Congress controlled by the Republicans after the 1946 elections. From 1947, he was focused both on the growing Communist threat, and the fact that powerful industries and peak associations were lobbying Congress for more protectionist policies. Even business groups such as the Community of Economic Development (CED), which generally supported trade liberalization, were reluctant to commit to the sweeping breadth of the ITO Charter. The CED would accept the ITO only without Articles 11 and 12 on investment, which they feared could actually encourage developing states to nationalize the assets of US-based firms. Without persistent leadership to promote the organization and gradually build and enhance coalitions of support, the ITO could not gain the required support inside the United States.

In April 1949, Truman belatedly submitted the Final ITO Charter to Congress. The president had waited a year to make the proposal and, without consistent presidential backing, the charter had little hope of meeting congressional approval. The House did not hold hearings on the ITO for another year and the proposal never came before the Senate. In November 1950, the administration finally announced the failure of the ITO.

In sum, structural leadership requires investing the political capital to mobilize and sustain domestic, as well as international, support. In the late 1940s, President Truman was not willing to launch the full-scale campaign required to generate domestic support and provide US structural leadership for the ITO. As was outlined in Chapter 2, structural leadership requires the willingness and ability to generate domestic political support for ambitious agreements like the ITO. Furthermore, foreign security and economic policies must be reconciled. Once the ITO emerged in a form opposed by strong domestic interests, the Truman administration had to decide whether to pursue the required domestic support for both the ITO and the Marshall Plan in the same time period. This might have been possible had officials been able to explain how both were essential to US security, but administration (and international) support for the ITO broke down as policy makers determined that they might not be able to convince Congress of the need for both initiatives. The case clearly illustrates the delicate balance between competing US foreign policy goals and the management of domestic political support for US structural leadership.

Instead, the president dedicated his efforts and political capital at home to enacting the Marshall Plan, the main platform for US grand strategy in the Cold War. The plan, or the Economic Cooperation Act of 1948, required the allies to work jointly even after the war effort ended and argued that political success rests largely upon the establishment of sound economic conditions, stable international economic relationships, and the achievement by the countries of Europe of a healthy economy independent of extraordinary outside assistance.[13] Central to these economic goals were "the expansion of foreign trade" and the "progressive elimination of trade barriers" in order to create for Europe "a large domestic market with no internal trade barriers" similar to that "enjoyed by the United States." Most important to this book, the plan relied first and foremost on an institutional form – European unity and regionalism – that would continue to compete directly with important elements of the GATT.

Failure of the Dillon Round: setting the context, 1953–1959

Following the policies of FDR and the early Truman years, President Eisenhower also emphasized the crucial role of the economic foundations of national and international security. Indeed, it can be argued that he extended and deepened earlier ideas about the fundamental role of economic success and stability in national and international security. His version of containment, especially on a worldwide basis, clearly emphasized economic fundamentals more and military capabilities less. National Security Council Paper No. 162/2 (NSC-162/2) of 1953 explained that "[n]ot only the world position of the United States, but the security of the whole free world, is dependent on the avoidance of recession and on the long-term expansion of the US economy."[14] Because threats to economic stability or growth were seen to directly undermine national and international security, a sound, open international economy was essential to achieving what the United States considered its highest foreign policy objectives.

As he fought for essential congressional support in renewing the Reciprocal Trade Agreements Act (RTAA), due to expire in mid-1953, Eisenhower attempted to trump the powerful protectionist committee chairs from his own party with an urgent appeal to help him contain Communism. Building on his development of the containment doctrine, he warned that Asian Communism, and Communist China in particular, might threaten Japan's ability to export. In this context, he argued that trade policy could "dictate whether these areas remain in the free world or fall within the Communist Orbit."[15] His dedicated appeal helped convince key Republican leaders, but only created sufficient political space to achieve a one-year extension from Congress.

At a time when the US economy was by far the largest, most competitive, and insular in the world, with consistent trade surpluses, and with the Democrats in control of the House and Senate after the 1954 elections, it would have been reasonable to expect an easing of protectionist sentiments. In reality, however, the Eisenhower administration consistently confronted heavy protectionist pressures, and it can be argued that it did not truly and fully commit itself to overcoming them. In 1954, it successfully pressured the GATT for a waiver, granted in 1955, which allowed the US government to set quotas on certain agricultural imports, even including sectors such as dairy products that were not covered by domestic production limits. This set an important protectionist precedent for later European assertions to exempt their domestic agricultural support programs from the GATT.[16]

By 1955, the strength of protectionist interests in Congress and the limits to President Eisenhower's willingness to confront them led to the withdrawal of his proposal for the United States to join an important institutional initiative to formalize and strengthen the GATT.[17] The administration won a three-year renewal of the RTAA in mid-1955, but only after also making additional major concessions to the textile producers.[18] Also in 1955, the administration negotiated export restraints on Japanese textiles entering the United States for two years, and restrictions on cotton exports for five years from 1957.

By mid-1958, the administration finally won from Congress most of its requested authority for negotiating tariff reductions. Congress approved a four-year RTAA renewal with presidential authority to negotiate up to 20 percent tariff decreases. This established the political and legal basis required for the administration to pursue the first major GATT round since its establishment in 1947. Still, as is explained below, both the authority and the bilateral approach dictated by the RTAA would prove to be inadequate to the task.

The EEC versus GATT: conflicting US foreign policy goals

American leadership in the period prior to the Dillon Round of 1960–1962 was weakened by not only US domestic constraints but also the heightened leverage of new European regional groups. Domestically, protectionists and leading congressional Democrats emphasized the declining US trade surplus, which fell from $3.4 billion in 1958 to $1.1 billion in 1959.[19] Probably more importantly, however, the newly formed European Economic Community (EEC) was not yet able to co-lead in setting the agenda for the Dillon Round, but it was successful in exploiting American weakness in order to enhance its own position and policies. Whereas structural leadership by US officials, including important intellectual innovations and adaptations, had been the primary determinants of GATT success in earlier rounds, the Dillon Round illustrated that negotiations could fail if the United States could not overcome EEC recalcitrance. The meager results of the round would catalyze structural leadership by US officials to change the mechanisms of the negotiation process, and these changes would create a more effective and responsive GATT organization.

US foreign economic policy leadership during this time suffered because the Eisenhower and Kennedy administrations were unwilling to pursue tough bargaining with the EEC at a time when its very survival seemed in jeopardy and its success was crucial to US containment strategy. Since European unity and the success of the EEC were the predominant US goals, the two main European economic groups, the EEC and European Free Trade Area (EFTA), were effectively able to block major tariff reductions and the inclusion of agriculture.[20]

During the peak period of the Cold War, national security and foreign policy advisers were more prominent in US presidential administrations than trade advisers. Furthermore, "in the immediate postwar years, the chief economic advisers saw their policy sphere as overridingly domestic. . . . This situation meant that *foreign* economic policy could be handled primarily by the security complex," in other words the National Security Council, the Central Intelligence Agency, and the Departments of Defense and State.[21] From the time of the National Security Act of 1947 to the early 1960s, "the security complex used foreign economic policy to advance U.S. political-strategic interests."[22] This seemed logical at the time, but "[i]n almost every instance where there was a clash in priorities between economic policy and national security, the latter prevailed."[23]

Until the late 1950s, this arrangement seemed to work, because the overriding foreign security and economic priority was to support the rebuilding of European economies and polities, and to ensure cooperation among them. A key event in this regard was the Treaty of Rome in 1957, which established the EEC. The United States strongly embraced the idea of a united Europe, hoping that a responsible group of like-minded states would lessen the financial burden of the Marshall Plan and effectively aid underdeveloped countries. Europe served as both the main bulwark against Soviet and Communist incursion and the largest market for US products. Accordingly, in the 1950s the United States allowed the meaning of Article 24 of the General Agreement on Tariffs and Trade (GATT), which prohibited such protectionist trade groups, to be compromised because of its belief in the beneficial political effects of European regionalism.[24]

Nevertheless, senior US officials were also aware that a unified Europe could challenge American global leadership. Thus, the United States, while strongly supporting Europe, also sought to protect its central leadership role and to ensure that its voice would continue to influence the inter-European dialogue. That dialogue also included the main European states outside the EEC, as organized into the EFTA.

EFTA, or the "Outer Seven," centered on the leadership of Scandinavia and Britain. Like the EEC, the EFTA would seek to consolidate the power of its member states and gain greater leverage within the GATT. However, the presence of two competing European trade unions ran counter to American objectives. The formation of the EFTA undermined American objectives of unifying Europe, because "a rival to the Common Market was considered counterproductive to the Western harmony being promoted by the White House."[25] Douglas Dillon, Undersecretary of State and chief American nego-tiator, viewed the EFTA as a threat to the expansion of the EEC and a challenge to the principles of liberalization.[26] Thus, instead of providing US officials with a mechanism for balancing EC influence and enhancing their structural leadership, the EFTA was perceived to threaten a higher value.

The GATT forum, therefore, was intended in part to ensure that the devel-opment of these regional blocs in Europe meshed with American political and economic objectives. This strategic use of the GATT organization was intended to enhance US access to European markets and reduce tariffs that disadvantaged American exports, while at the same time fostering the growth of stronger political linkages between the United States and the EEC.

Still, in planning for the Dillon Round, the United States recognized it would be the first significant engagement between the United States and the EEC. For this reason, US officials sought to avoid acrimonious debate between the two parties and negative repercussions in other diplomatic areas. Thus, the United States made strategic choices in its structural leadership between pushing for greater liberalization and acquiescing to EC demands in view of more important political intentions. George Ball, a US negotiator in the Round, emphasized that the success of the Dillon Round "in his mind . . . had a more important political purpose, ensuring the survival of the US–European alliance."[27] Likewise, the White House recognized that

> [t]he commercial importance of the negotiations was matched by their political significance, since they constituted the first test of whether the US and the European Economic Community . . . would be able to find a mutual basis for the long-run development of economic relations critical to both areas.[28]

The Treaty of Rome dictated that EEC member states ("the Six") would determine a common external tariff (CXT) and Common Agricultural Policy (CAP) that would be applied to all trade with non-member states. In the early 1960s, therefore, the United States needed to balance two fundamental but conflicting goals: advancing the GATT as a tool to influence and shape the EEC CAP and CXT, while simultaneously enhancing the fragile political ties holding together the Atlantic Alliance. Throughout the Dillon Round negotiations, however, the executive branch lacked the domestic authority required for structural leadership of the negotiations. US officials therein failed to provide the structural leadership needed to direct the agenda and catalyze support for major reductions. Furthermore, they lacked the domestic support and international credibility to enact at home the liberalization measures which EEC officials accepted. In part because of these constraints, US officials were blocked in their main goals, and EC positions generally prevailed, including exclusion of agriculture from the negotiating agenda.

Prior to the Dillon Round, US negotiators pressed hard for new negotiations. In the December 1958 GATT session, they proposed a new round to begin in 1960, with the first phase of talks lasting from September 1960 until May 1961. US strategy was to hold GATT negotiations at the same time as EEC decision-making on the CXT, while using the GATT process as a lever to limit the level of the EEC barriers and to settle any grievances about European barriers which exceeded prior GATT commitments for the individual six countries. The six EEC countries had previously set, or bound, tariff levels on industry products on a country-specific basis, and the CXT exceeded the previously negotiated tariff levels on some products. GATT members, led by US officials, argued that the CXT violated GATT doctrine and damaged the ability of non-member countries to compete in EC markets. US officials argued for concessions, based on GATT doctrine, equal to their estimates of "broken bindings" on 1,100 tariff rates worth approximately $2 billion in exports. EC negotiators insisted that the level of the overall duty was on average lower than that agreed previously and granted concessions of not more than $1.6 billion.

US negotiators were committed to including the agriculture sector in the Dillon Round, specifically in order to mitigate both the levels of CAP restrictions and EEC autonomy in setting CAP regulations. US Department of Agriculture (USDA) officials, in particular, insisted on ensuring that the EEC markets remained open to American agricultural products. Despite US annual agricultural exports of about $1.1 billion to EEC states, the USDA insisted that the CAP violated the fundamental principle of comparative advantage and undermined the viability of future US exports. At the same time, existing quotas on American farm imports, export subsidies, and supported prices resulted in producers having a five-to-one surplus with the EEC. As emphasized in the work of Judith Goldstein, this very obvious presence of US agricultural protectionism reduced the fundamental credibility of US arguments and proposals.[29] Clearly, both the much stronger relative position of US agricultural exports and the obvious protectionist precedent set by the US GATT waiver of 1955 undermined the structural leadership that US negotiators could mobilize in pressing the EEC to reduce its heavy restrictions.

Moreover, the EEC realized that incorporating the demands of the six EEC countries into a concise, equitable CAP would be complex, and any commitments made during the Dillon Round would complicate the process. The EEC thus argued that the unfinished CAP meant that the Six needed to defer concessions in this sector until later negotiations. In successfully evading US demands, the EEC negotiators "began to flex their new trade muscle by resisting pressure from the alliance leader."[30] In the end, EEC negotiators agreed only to consider the effect of the CAP on non-member countries while formulating policies and regulations, and to negotiate at a later date in the areas of corn, sorghum, ordinary wheat, rice, and poultry.[31]

In the earlier GATT rounds, which included less important matters, US officials provided structural leadership in proposing the negotiating agenda and persuading officials of the benefits to be gained from making reciprocal concessions. The agriculture negotiations of the Dillon Round, however, marked a new situation. US leverage and credibility were not adequate to convince EEC officials on the priority of GATT concessions over their emerging CAP. The Six blocked a broad agreement and any trading of major concessions. The EEC also announced clearly that future agricultural negotiations would depend on its internal process. "Negotiations shall commence as soon as the EC Council of Ministers has decided to introduce the common policy for wheat [or] at the latest by June 30, 1964."[32]

US negotiators were also unable to provide structural leadership of the industrial tariff reduction phase of the Dillon Round. The traditional US item-by-item bargaining process for negotiating tariff reductions on a product-specific basis was no longer effective.

> The United States herself felt that she had no adequate weapons with which to penetrate the tariff barrier that was being built around Europe.

The machinery of the old Reciprocal Trade Agreements Act of 1934, regularly renewed since, was creaking. It had been designed for a different world.[33]

With an increasing number of states and negotiating issues, the bilateral strategy was too cumbersome.

Meanwhile, EEC negotiators challenged the structural leadership of US officials by proposing a 20 percent linear, or across-the-board, reduction in industrial tariffs. Just as US leaders had drawn on their domestic practices and institutions for their innovations in GATT negotiations, EEC officials promoted the same strategy applied earlier for reducing tariffs on intra-EEC trade. Furthermore, by offering a relatively large decrease EEC negotiators temporarily occupied the position of structural leader, thus challenging US officials to respond with equal tariff reductions.

Working under an extension of the US Reciprocal Trade Agreement in 1958, US negotiators could offer at most a 20 percent reduction of tariffs. However, in order to secure congressional approval, Eisenhower accepted a provision for the Tariff Commission to set "peril points" for domestic industries – to be exceeded only with presidential approval. Thus, US negotiators could not match key EEC proposals or meet the demands of their own basic principle of reciprocity without exceeding the peril points, which required that the president report his reasons to Congress. The president's hesitation to open this issue with a protectionist Congress meant that US officials were severely limited in their ability to negotiate.

The ability of US negotiators to accept the substantive proposals and innovation in bargaining process proposed by the Europeans was blocked most visibly by congressional constraints, but also undermined by the lack of presidential and executive branch political will. US structural leadership was also restricted by the perception of key executive officials that national security required favoring European unity over GATT. During this time, the US balance of trade and relative international economic position was also shifting unfavorably, thus triggering congressional leaders and certain industry groups to mobilize against liberalization. Ultimately, it can be argued that under these conditions Eisenhower's own beliefs, commitments, and dedication to international trade policy leadership were not adequate to overcome his reluctance to launch a campaign against protectionist industry groups. Certainly much more than Truman or FDR, he suffered internal conflicts between his long-term connections with US business and industries on the one hand, and his commitment to international economic leadership on the other.

Prior to the Dillon Round, key US officials still believed that, ultimately, US initiative and determination could ensure a satisfactory outcome in the GATT negotiations. The contest over industrial tariffs, however, illustrated the strength of the EEC challenge and its ability to block US goals effectively. The United

States simply lacked the requisite level of domestic and presidential support for structural leadership in offering the needed level of concessions. As issue linkage, or linking reductions in one area to concessions in other sectors, did not yet exist, if a country failed to offer adequate concessions in an issue area, there was less incentive overall to pursue tariff reductions.[34]

In the November 1961 GATT ministerial meeting before the end of the Round, members agreed that the item-by-item bargaining had stopped progress. As a result, they urged the United States to gain the necessary legislative mandate to use the linear cut technique in future negotiations. They recognized that American domestic weakness had slowed and almost ended the round, thus leading to a reversal of the traditional roles in the GATT wherein US negotiators were reprimanded. In the final months of the Dillon Round, US negotiators finally turned to President Kennedy for approval to use the linear cut. The urgency of this request was bolstered by the December 1961 report by the Department of State highlighting the threatening predictions that "chaos [would] ensue in our international trade, and the entire GATT arrangements [would] be in danger of collapsing"[35] if US officials could not complete the Dillon Round. This is one of the early examples of US officials attempting to create a perceived crisis upon which they could generate a turning point in the negotiations. They recognized that unless they could open political space for policy change in domestic processes and institutions, US structural leadership of the GATT negotiations would be impossible.

In fact, Eisenhower and his top officials eventually reached agreement with congressional leaders and provided structural leadership from 1958 in launching the Dillon Round. More important, however, presidential and US negotiators' leadership was substantially weaker in setting an effective agenda and establishing a productive negotiating process. After almost six years of struggling to gain adequate negotiating authority from Congress, the 1958 legislation locked the administration into a continuation of the traditional RTAA format for international negotiations. Furthermore, the president was specifically unwilling to dedicate additional political capital to directly confronting domestic constraints, particularly protectionist congressional leaders. Thus, the Eisenhower administration failed to forge and promote a cohesive trade strategy. As a result, American economic policy choices in the Dillon Round negotiations were inconsistent and ineffective. Eisenhower trod lightly, hoping to maintain the fragile balance of appeasing domestic industry as well as GATT member countries. He shunned the structural leadership required to drive the negotiating process and in the end upset both domestic industry and GATT members by failing to lead.

Thus, US negotiators were only allowed to do item-by-item, product-specific bargaining, mainly in a bilateral manner. No across-the-board, or linear, cut authority was allowed until the very end of the Dillon Round under President Kennedy. This was effectively the end of the old approach established by the 1934 Reciprocal Trade Agreements Act, which had been used successfully up to this point, but certainly not the end of reciprocity as a US principle and practice. Kennedy, who ran for election promising to remedy the balance-of-payments problem, made more coherent policy choices and thus changed public opinion and instituted structural change in a way that Eisenhower was unable to.

As the Dillon Round concluded, the GATT ministers realized that without significant changes in the negotiation format, the trade system was in jeopardy. In November 1961, they met in Geneva to map out new procedures and seek agreement on enlarging the scope of future negotiations to include agriculture and the demands of less developed countries. Negotiators realized that without US leadership and more focused efforts by other members, the trade regime would become increasingly irrelevant. Most important, however, to the success of the Kennedy Round were ambitious initiatives by US leaders to reclaim the central leadership position.

Leadership reclaimed? Launching and closing the Kennedy round

In Geneva in 1963, a new round of trade negotiations began in the context of the first period of détente in the Cold War. The GATT mechanisms, "fragile and constantly subject to attack," were weakened by the failed Dillon Round, but the success of the Kennedy Round would revive the liberalization process and the trade regime.[36] US structural leadership would be key to shaping the direction of, and maintaining the momentum for, liberalization. The main events and eventual success of the Kennedy Round resulted substantially from the structural leadership of US officials supported by their main European counterparts. Still, the EEC, both as an actor and as a crucial goal of US foreign policy, placed certain limits on American power in the Round.[37] In particular, the European states exercised an important degree of blocking power, which some analysts have in error confused with "leadership." Any consistent structural leadership by EC and European officials was not yet possible, owing to their specific, regional and national focus, and the difficulties in reaching consensus among members.

In view of the failure of the Dillon Round, the US president and key congressional leaders recognized the need to restore the legitimacy of the GATT mechanism, as well as to secure American leadership. The language of crisis and danger to the international trade system from recent past failure helped to mobilize congressional action for new trade legislation. Following passage of the 1962 Trade Expansion Act, US officials worked to gain international support for the new round in a series of bilateral meetings. Although most of the major trading states were reluctant to enter a new round in the wake of the Dillon failure, the persistence of US officials, supported by the experienced

British officials, who played a key entrepreneurial leadership role, and the continuing US ability to appeal for unity in the Atlantic Alliance, facilitated the beginning of a new round. In response to structural leadership by senior American officials, the GATT ministers met on May 16, 1963, and, coordinated by Director General Eric Wyndham White, began preparations for what would be called the Kennedy Round.

The Kennedy Round was negotiated over a four-year period from May 1963 through June 1967. The GATT membership of forty-seven at the outset grew to seventy-four by the end. The Round set precedent by increasing the depth of negotiated tariff cuts to an average of 35 percent on almost 55 percent of all dutiable imports, and widening the scope of GATT issue area coverage to include selected agriculture and non-tariff barriers (NTBs). The removal of the American Selling Price (ASP) and related European non-tariff barriers helped to catalyze future negotiation of NTBs. Also significant was the use of the linear strategy to negotiate concessions, which reduced bilateral confrontations and facilitated multilateralism.

Distrust among major member states – especially within the European Community – forced the United States to defend and reassert its right to lead. In September 1962, Pierre Drouin in *Le Monde* reacted to the US Trade Expansion Act by warning that it would be necessary now to be extremely vigilant.[38] Placed on the defensive, US negotiators needed to propose a negotiation agenda and reassert their structural leadership role. The EEC in particular challenged the previously unquestioned legitimacy of the United States to create an equitable liberalization agenda.[39] "The emergence of the EEC as a powerful actor was the major difficulty confronting the US in the negotiations. US leadership of the GATT was for the first time being tested."[40] Specifically, French attempts to assert bargaining leverage and challenge US leadership, and keep Britain out of the EEC, were a constant constraint for top US officials during the 1960s. Michael Blumenthal, the Special Trade Representative, observed that "[t]he pattern of French tactics has been to delay, to confuse the issues, and to work for minimum reductions in EEC trade barriers at the price of maximum concessions to the French within the EEC."[41] In fact, when the United States proposed the adoption of the linear cut strategy for the Round, French negotiators immediately attempted to substitute their own intellectual leadership with an alternative approach: *écrêtement*, which called for a leveling of tariff disparities in a harmonization plan that some EEC members believed would be more consistent with the principle of reciprocity. The plan involved a complex formula of assessing disparities and arriving at target rates for individual states and industries.

The *écrêtement* approach, as assessed by a working group prior to the May 1963 ministerial meeting, was eventually discarded, owing to its complexity. The working group concluded that the linear cut was the best strategy by which to reach major concessions, and a variation of the US proposal was adopted on May 21, 1963. Freed from the "handicap of bilateralism" that had slowed the Dillon Round, the GATT adopted a more multilateral approach that would later be formalized in the WTO doctrine.[42] Item-by-item bargaining was still used in particular cases when negotiations reached an impasse, but the linear cut formula was the norm throughout the Kennedy Round, and "led countries to offer reductions on large sections of their tariff schedule that they might otherwise have held back."[43]

Crucial steps to bridge the gap between US and French or EEC positions on the basic approach to negotiations were facilitated by British trade negotiators with long experience and the strategic opportunity to provide entrepreneurial leadership. British and US officials shared by far the strongest commitment to serious tariff reductions and success in the Kennedy Round, but British interests were focused more narrowly on industrial tariffs (which impacted their trade with EEC members), whereas US efforts emphasized the importance of including agriculture both substantially and from the outset.[44] Between the May 1963 and May 1964 GATT ministerial meetings, and particularly during major US–British consultations in February and April 1964, teams of senior British officials persuaded their US counterparts to modify their "rigid" formula for 50 percent reductions to a more flexible position that would allow for variation in the degree of reductions in both agricultural and industrial tariffs, and meet some of the French demands for harmonization. By both supporting US policy positions and pressing US officials to make key compromises based on their expertise and experience, British officials enhanced US structural leadership, the prospects for success, and their own influence over the negotiations.

The consistent exercise of US structural leadership in the negotiations was built in part on a campaign by Kennedy administration officials to develop a solid base of domestic political support. Officials attempted to create a sense of crisis by arguing that US leadership in trade built on core American values, and was essential to broader US international leadership and status. A key step was to explicitly link the ideas and goals of free trade with national and international security, in the tradition of President Roosevelt in the 1940s.

The Cordell Hull philosophy equating economic liberalization with international stability and peace remained influential among key interest groups in the 1960s.[45] Free trade advocates like Francis Bator argued before Congress, pressing the urgency of the situation: "Movement toward liberal trade is a steep climb up a slippery slope. If you don't move forward, you slip back. And if you slip far, you tumble – into an economic cold war where nobody trusts anybody and everyone stagnates."[46] Respected American leaders committed themselves to the liberal order and reiterated the need for creative, bold steps in the global arena. President Kennedy affirmed that without swift action the United States would lose its legitimacy in the economic sphere and damage its overall security position.[47] Michael Blumenthal argued that "the pervasiveness of ideology, the vision of peace and prosperity flowing from a free and open international economic system, offered US leaders a lever of power that dampened, even if it did not entirely suppress, demands for protectionism."[48] Moreover, because in the aftermath of the Cuban Missile Crisis of 1962 public and media attention was focused on the Cold War and pressing security concerns, the details of the negotiations and trade more generally were "not high on the list of public concerns . . . [and] governmental leaders had the leeway to press the policies they felt were needed."[49]

President Kennedy himself played a large role in building domestic political support and lobbying for greater trade negotiating authority.[50] He emphasized that because trade liberalization was "not partisan philosophy," the traditional Congressional battlefield divided by party was unacceptable. He argued forcefully that Congress should set aside prejudices and partisan politics that would undermine the instruments required for international leadership.[51] He hoped to gain increased negotiating authority from Congress to solidify US prestige and leverage in the new GATT round. By creating new policies and strategy, the US could advance key objectives of the Kennedy administration: trade liberalization and US international economic prestige. He had the same advantage as Eisenhower (from 1955) with Democratic control of both houses of Congress, but of course he was seeking authority from the members of his own party.

Domestic efforts culminated in the passage of the Trade Expansion Act (TEA) of 1962, which Kennedy termed "a bold new instrument of American trade policy."[52] This legislation granted the US executive an unprecedented level of negotiating authority, which provided the domestic basis required for structural leadership of GATT.[53] The office of the Special Trade Representative (STR) was created, and members were appointed who would act as negotiators within the Kennedy Round. Those negotiators were given authority to initiate a new round of negotiations and to offer an unprecedented 50 percent linear cut on tariffs. The TEA not only granted "new and flexible" authority to negotiators but also called for new techniques – such as the linear cut and issue linkage – that would change the content and strategy of the negotiations.[54] On the whole, "US preparations were based on the principle that the national interest required a major attack on trade barriers through optimum use of the broad TEA to reduce US tariffs in exchange for comparable concessions by other countries."[55]

In an era still charged with Cold War rhetoric, Kennedy called on the countries of Europe and North American to "pool . . . resources and resource-fulness in an open trade partnership strong enough to outstrip any challenge."[56] However, the United States also worried that political integration in Europe would undermine American power and that the EEC and CAP could disadvantage US goods and limit the GATT. After the Dillon Round failed to effectively shape and constrain the emerging influence of the EEC and the

CAP in particular, the Kennedy administration aimed to do so in a new round. In the president's 1963 State of the Union address, he noted that "[t]he winds of change appear to be blowing more strongly than ever."[57] In conversations with President Johnson, De Gaulle candidly asserted that the EEC and specifically France sought to "organize Europe – continental Europe – from an economic point of view and . . . perhaps also from the political point of view."[58] France thus furthered a "sense of urgency" in the US administration to "take new and more heroic measures before it was too late."[59] The United States recognized that the climate in Europe bred a desire "for release from a greater control over the exercise of American power," but US leaders hoped to help the EEC voice to "find expression in viable European-minded forms of economic organization and political cooperation."[60] President Kennedy and his leading officials believed that a new GATT round would serve the country's political, economic, and security interests by helping

> the US compete with the Six, prevent the Atlantic community from dissolving into separate trade systems, and lure the British and the rest of the Outer Seven into the Common Market. The Alliance would then spread around the financial burden of defense and aid programs that Washington had borne so long and which adversely affected the deficit.[61]

By the end of the round, Francis Bator argued that "this is a time of stress and redirection for the Atlantic Community. We can emerge stronger and more mature. Or we could dissolve into rival islands . . . but it is clear that this negotiation was an important test."[62]

As Cold War tensions diminished somewhat, beginning in 1963, there were new difficulties for and challenges to US leadership and management of its diplomatic and economic allies. US officials sought to preserve the unity of Europe in the face of a mitigated Communist threat and ensure the EEC's political and economic success. They remained hesitant to create unneeded conflict between the United States and the EEC for fear that heightened tension in the Kennedy Round would harm diplomatic ties. At the same time, US officials were increasingly concerned about the American economic position relative to Europe and Japan.

For the most part, in practice the US security policy complex still dominated the economic complex, and domestic economic policy remained the predominant focus. The US emphasis on political diplomacy over trade constrained the breadth and depth of progress possible in the GATT, because leading American officials clearly opted to compromise liberalization objectives in order to satisfy the demands of the EEC: "As Washington worried more about Soviet expansion in Europe, it was prepared to make a series of political tradeoffs to quell any US–EEC conflict."[63] Special Trade Representative

Blumenthal understood that the GATT negotiations had to achieve multiple objectives: "to do it successfully, to do it without causing too much damage in political terms, to maintain cohesion of our negotiating partners in Europe, which was very important to us, and still get some trade benefits."[64]

Throughout the round, therefore, the United States was forced to make strategic choices and modify its structural leadership in order to satisfy the EEC, while also ensuring that the Community would not negate all US efforts. In light of the moderate success of the round, the prevailing wisdom is that US negotiators were masterful in balancing the manipulation of alliances, the application of available leverage, and the use of negotiating tactics to reach key objectives. Indeed, some astute analysts consider the Kennedy Round to be the "first major negotiation and agreement between two equal poles of economic power across the Atlantic."[65]

However, although the round included certain EEC ideas and initiatives, their officials did not consistently exhibit structural or entrepreneurial leadership in shaping the negotiating agenda and process. The EEC was generally successful in delaying the process, but it was much less effective in shaping the agenda and outcomes. Whereas French officials were almost ambivalent in their preference between a successful round and a no agreement outcome, British negotiators were seriously committed to reducing industrial tariffs and forging a successful round. Thus, the EEC role generally had a twofold effect: strengthening the call to liberalize in sectors where the EC sought greater access to foreign markets, such as textiles and chemicals, and successfully slowing liberalization in sectors where the EEC wished to maintain domestic protection levels, such as agriculture. In these few areas, the European presence changed the overall outcome of the round, and in some sectors, notably agriculture and chemi-cals, it affected the scope of the negotiations. EEC abilities were significant in terms of blocking leverage in narrowing both the scope of expansion in the Kennedy Round agenda and the depth of tariff reductions.[66]

The failure of the EEC and European leaders to consistently sustain internal consensus was the most immediate and direct reason for their lack of structural leadership in agenda setting.[67] The EEC often lacked a coherent strategy for maximizing its role in the GATT, and fractious splits between France and the remaining members, particularly Germany, prevented the Community from forging unified policies and positions. The internal discord raised by French opposition to the potential entry of Britain into the EEC further constrained efforts to build consensus. In this political environment, member states assessed and anticipated the costs and benefits of EEC policies mainly in terms of national interests. French withdrawal from the community in 1965 attested to a European environment "devoid of generosity that earlier may have been ascribed to the Community."[68] This lack of unity and integrative bargaining strategy slowed the entire process, frustrating not only American objectives but also those of other GATT members.

The negotiation agenda included a commitment to achieve "substantial progress in the elimination or reduction of non-tariff barriers to trade."[69] Whether the final agreement embodied "substantial progress" in the area of non-tariff barriers is questionable, but, despite its limited progress, the Kennedy Round still opened the issue. In the chemicals sector, the EEC continued to link the 50 percent cut on all chemicals and related cuts in NTBs to the removal of the ASP. The EEC fought to abolish the ASP, established in 1922, which protected the infant American chemical industry from European producers. US officials were constrained in this dimension of structural leadership because the "powerful chemistry industry . . . felt strongly that the special protections provided by ASP should be retained."[70]

US trade officials agreed, but for different reasons. They sought to avoid eliminating the ASP because the action would necessitate congressional approval, and refusal by Congress to eliminate ASP could jeopardize American gains in the chemical sector. However, lacking any alternative and pressured by EEC insistence to end the ASP, US negotiators agreed to link European cuts in the chemical sector to the American elimination of the ASP.[71] Blumenthal and Herter noted that accepting a package deal linking US and EEC tariff cuts in the chemical sector to the elimination of the ASP "required considerable courage" in the face of domestic opposition.[72] In signing, the president made the commitment "to use his best efforts to obtain promptly such legislation as is necessary to enable the United States to eliminate the American Selling Price System."[73] However, as was feared by Blumenthal, when the proposal was brought before Congress in 1967 the ASP package was not approved. President Johnson could not impel Congress to abandon loyalties to domestic industry. In this instance, the EEC "effectively shifted the burden of failure in the chemicals sector to the United States."[74] This is a case where US external structural leadership was not matched by the required management of domestic industry opposition and mobilization of adequate congressional support.

Despite this failure, the US negotiators were able to contribute to progress in eliminating NTBs through structural leadership, based on consistently presenting new substantive ideas and pressing key states to establish an international dumping code. US officials sought to apply new ideas in the form of an innovation in trade policy – to add transparency to national antidumping proceedings – and "saw an opportunity, through such a code, to affect favorably the antidumping regulations which the EC was in [the] process of considering."[75] Leaders of most states, including the United States, were hesitant to change their national procedures and sacrifice policy autonomy to the GATT. However, they were moved by US structural leadership offers which held out credible promise of gains from establishing a more transparent regulatory process. This effectively galvanized leading members to create a code for NTBs that would later be considered the major achievement of the Kennedy Round.

In the Kennedy Round agenda, members also committed themselves to "provide for acceptable conditions of access to world markets for agricultural products."[76] Throughout the round, however, the EEC blocked progress in this area by refusing to offer significant concessions to exporting countries. Fearing increased internal EEC instability, a more difficult CAP development process, and the erosion of EEC negotiating leverage in other sectors, the EEC resisted pressure from the United States and other exporting countries. In bilateral meetings, US officials consistently failed to move EEC negotiators into a joint consensus on some agricultural liberalization. US negotiators thus faced "the prospect of having no agricultural negotiation rules by November 16, 1964."[77] They were well aware that farm lobbyists might undermine their required domestic political support if they decided their needs were unmet by the deal. US agriculture groups, backed strongly by the Secretary of Agriculture, Orville Freeman, emphasized the need to maintain and augment access to European farm markets. Throughout the negotiations, Herter and Blumenthal consistently emphasized that there could be no final Kennedy Round deal without liberalization in agriculture.

US willingness to make concessions in other sector groups, hoping to impel the EEC to offer greater cuts in the agriculture sector, indicates the expected leverage of the agriculture lobby to deny congressional support for an overall agreement. The choice to offer the EEC greater concessions in the chemical sector in 1967 was precipitated by the view that "it would be politically easier for the President to confront a divided if unhappy chemical industry than an angry farm bloc."[78] In mid-April 1967, US Ambassador Roth "expressed 'shock' at the meagerness of their [EEC] agricultural offers" and noted a "deep pessimism" in the US negotiating team.[79] In fact, Wyndham White frequently attempted to exert entrepreneurial leadership in chiding the EEC, alone, for "withhold[ing] from negotiations a whole sector of production" and for "frustrat[ing] any hope of cooperative action by other participants to develop more liberal policies."[80] In the end, agriculture was briefly mentioned in the final agreement as a result of US structural leadership and White's entrepreneurial efforts. Still, EEC blocking leverage mainly prevailed, as concessions in agriculture were much less than those in other areas – essentially only an understanding that there would be more substantive negotiations in the next round.[81]

As the US balance of payments worsened in 1965, congressional pressures, which had been dormant, spun out of control as domestic industry and agriculture sought compensation for the damage incurred by foreign imports. Key leaders in Congress attacked the uneven outcome of the negotiations, especially the lack of results in agriculture. Economic instability and domestic political splits then combined to decrease "America's external power [which] led to increasing incoherence in US policy and greater instability in the international economic regime."[82] In 1966 and 1967, the United States began to swing back towards protectionism, a trend that would continue into the next decade. Active structural leadership by the US president and senior policy makers might have balanced the protectionist pressures. They could have returned to the argument by President Kennedy that "[e]conomic isolation and political leadership are wholly incompatible."[83] However, President Johnson distanced himself from the foreign economic sphere, placing much more emphasis on creating a "Great Society" at home than on propagating Kennedy's "Grand Design." In comparison to Kennedy, he "was far less committed . . . to securing a successful outcome to the negotiations since his personal prestige was not bound up in them."[84]

In 1966, STR Christian Herter commented in the *New York Times* that "the original bold hopes for a sweeping away of trade barriers were doomed almost from the start of negotiations." While Herter was now "prepared to fight for the possible if the ideal was unattainable," the ambitious American agenda touted by Kennedy in 1963 had been seriously circumscribed by an EEC unwilling to compromise on key issues.[85] During this time, US officials sought to "avoid . . . the impression that the blame for no Kennedy Round or a mini Kennedy Round should be placed at the doorstep of the US."[86] Despite the structural leadership role of US officials at key points in the negotiations, they emphasized that the EEC's new claim to power also required leadership responsibility in the GATT system. The importance of the EEC was evident as June 30, 1967 neared, the date when the president's negotiating authority granted by Congress would expire. In May, the sector negotiations were in disarray, and the United States appeared to lack the domestic negotiation authority to overcome impasses brought about by the EEC. If adequate US–EEC consensus could not be built before the deadline, the US administration risked bearing the blame for a failed round. Still, top officials refused to extend the deadline because they sought to create a crisis environment, or focal point, in the negotiations through intense pressure in both domestic and international contexts to make the compromises required for an agreement. This decision effectively infused a sense of urgency that prompted concessions and a more conciliatory spirit. In a final effort to prompt concessions, US negotiators made the strategic calculation that the pressure of avoiding failure would be sufficient to catalyze last-minute agreement.

In sum, the Kennedy Round expanded the scope of both GATT coverage and future negotiations, allowing for meaningful inclusion of new issue areas in future rounds. By addressing agricultural protection and NTBs, a commitment was established to making deeper reductions in these areas through future negotiations, one that would help create momentum toward more substantive success in the Tokyo Round of 1973–1979. Establishing future commitments in this way forms part of an important continuing pattern in US structural leadership. Where substantive reductions in barriers cannot be achieved, firm understandings are agreed to pursue them next time. Substantial importance is attached to the idea of gaining agreement to broaden the range of content or issue areas covered by the regime, even if specific reductions in barriers cannot be reached in the round.

The Kennedy Round allowed the United States to reclaim structural leadership and legitimacy lost in the Dillon Round, but it also illustrated that US leaders would have great difficulty leading, if the EEC collectively exerted blocking leverage. The EEC/European blocking power had both prevented any significant reform in agriculture and substantially reduced the reductions in tariffs. Director General Wyndham White began his closing remarks on the round by focusing on how GATT was "set in motion" by US initiatives.[87] However, he concluded by emphasizing the importance of "co-operative action" to achieve greater liberalization. Thereafter, building consensus within the negotiations would require the leadership support of more players.

As more members sought to win benefits from the process, agreement became more difficult and the role of the traditional structural leader, the United States, in prompting concessions declined in relative terms. The process became more multilateral while it remained member driven. In particular, cooperation between US, European, and British officials in key sectors would be increasingly important to induce concessions from other members and to continue to gradually enlarge the consensus group regarding the scope and depth of trade policy liberalization. Still, as is shown by the next section, it would be a mistake to conclude that US structural leadership of the GATT was not sufficient to drive the process.

Entrepreneurial leadership by Wyndham White and the United Kingdom

US leadership in the Kennedy Round was significantly supplemented and reinforced by two additional actors. The entrepreneurial leadership of GATT director general Eric Wyndham White and British officials proved important at key points, particularly in terms of providing proposals and pressure for constructive compromises to avoid deadlock based on their negotiating experience and expertise. As an expert and respected director general, Wyndham White was able to innovate with entrepreneurial leadership based on a new process aimed at forging compromise among the four largest trading states. He coordinated a series of informal meetings with the lead negotiators for Japan, the United Kingdom, the United States and the EC. As the deadlines approached, the increased urgency of reaching a compromise, especially in chemical and agricultural groups, enhanced Wyndham White's ability as a "neutral" third party to create a focal point for bargaining, then suggest and at times even prompt concessions. Without an authoritative, entrepreneurial actor to present innovative policy solutions during impasses among the "Big Four," the intransigence in the toughest sectors could have solidified, eliminating the possibility of building a consensus and driving a successful outcome for the Round.

Often acting independently from the EEC and in parallel with the United States, British negotiators were effective in providing advice to both delegations at key points in the negotiations. Leading UK officials also played an entrepreneurial leadership role at times by balancing the leverage of US, French, and EEC officials and encouraging compromise at strategic junctures.[88] For very different reasons, the Japanese generally failed to assume any entrepreneurial leadership role in the process and offered only minimal episodes of structural leadership by joining a consensus group formed by the four powers.[89] Japan was thriving in its economic isolation and saw much of the negotiations as an effort to liberalize the international environment in ways unfavorable to its trading position. As a result, the Japanese had little incentive to exercise greater leadership.[90] Another key trading state seeking a notably protectionist agenda was Canada, which marshaled enough bargaining leverage to gain immunity from the linear cut strategy. Exempt from large, across-the-board cuts, Canada illustrated the weakness of the GATT and proved the exception to a general program of greater liberalization. US officials feared that Canadian failure to abide by the linear cut strategy "might endanger the Kennedy Round, in view of Canada's importance as a world trader."[91]

Finally, the industrial states sought gains on the theory of "reciprocity," but less developed countries lobbied instead for preferential treatment for their exports. The original agenda formalized a commitment to achieve "reductions in barriers to the exports of the less developed countries" and legitimized their claims for non-reciprocity.[92] However, the United States and other major trading states were able to sideline their complaints in the round, and the final agreement contained little substantive progress in affording them greater voice in the negotiations. They continued to be viewed as "free riders" by the developed countries and lacked the negotiating leverage to induce developed nations to act in their interests.[93]

Launching the Tokyo Round

The Tokyo Round of 1973–1979 was launched, in part, in order to address the important and contentious NTB and agricultural issues left unresolved by the Kennedy Round. A second, closely related reason was the perceived need to manage increasing domestic pressures to enact protectionist measures in national and international environments of weakening economic growth. The final reason was that US officials were once again concerned about the effects of the now expanded European Communities (EC) on the global trade system and US export markets. At a more general level, the second and third factors above were closely connected with concerns of senior US officials about perceived decline in US prestige and status as leader of the Western economic system.

Even as the Kennedy Round was closing, President Johnson created a Public Advisory Committee on Trade Policy to examine the effects and future of trade liberalization. By the late 1960s and early 1970s experts, the media, and interest groups were increasingly aware of the linkages between international and domestic economic problems. American officials, who were pressed consistently by interest groups and certain members of Congress to address the growing balance of trade deficit and the rising relative competitiveness of Japan and Western Europe, sought to renegotiate the terms of US participation and leadership in international economic affairs. Building directly from the prior administration, in 1970 President Nixon established the Williams Commission (Commission on Trade and Investment Policy) to study these increasingly difficult and controversial issues and to suggest policy changes.

The renegotiation of US international political leadership at this time was substantially driven by the assertiveness of the US Congress, particularly with respect to its perception of the proper balance between executive and congressional power in making trade policy. Congress rebuked the Johnson administration for accepting in the Kennedy Round an antidumping agreement and eliminating the ASP approach to customs valuation. In an unprecedented, though forewarned, attack on what it interpreted to be a violation of executive negotiating authority, Congress essentially refused to implement both of these elements of the Kennedy Round agreement. Furthermore, by the early 1970s and after the US elections of 1972 in particular, there was a sea change in the internal dynamics of both Congress and the political parties. As a result, Congress was increasingly assertive in its balancing with the executive branch over authority to set trade and foreign policy more generally.[94]

Internationally, governments were struggling to cope with the currency turmoil following the demise of the Bretton Woods adjusted peg exchange rate system in 1969–1971. US officials were also preoccupied with the Vietnam War, the Cold War and strategic nuclear weapons in particular, and the global position of the United States relative to the Soviet Union and China. The combination of these economic difficulties and political-military challenges led to growing protectionist attitudes worldwide. States were turning inwards to cope with the domestic implications of international instability. Traditional US structural leadership in international economic policy domains was not forthcoming and none of the other major Western states stepped in to fill the gap. In this environment, protectionism began to take root.

In February 1972, US officials initiated two separate Declarations on International Economic Relations: one with the EC and one with Japan. In these declarations each government pledged to "initiate and actively support multilateral and comprehensive negotiations in the framework of GATT beginning in 1973".[95] While US political leaders saw the further liberalization of trade as a necessary cure for slow US and European economic growth, they had a much less liberal attitude than prior to any previous GATT round.

Key congressional leaders had viewed the United States as "Uncle Sucker" in the previous rounds, having given significantly more than it had received.[96] This round, however, would be different. The United States was in just as much economic turmoil as the other major economies, and the European and Japanese economies were clearly competitive with the United States. Thus, the United States could no longer absorb short-term economic losses for the long-term benefit of the international trading system. Furthermore, after 1973 the Democrats, who controlled both houses of Congress until 1981, switched positions with the Republicans. Democrats became the skeptics toward trade policy liberalization, while Republicans were now the main supporters.[97]

With the first enlargement of the EC, including Denmark, Ireland, and the United Kingdom, in 1973, key US officials were once again concerned about the effects of a strengthened EC on the global trade system and US markets. In 1972–1973, therefore, US initiatives also responded directly to EC development, in order to ensure access to the new, enlarged market, and to maintain balance between the development of regionalism and the EC, and the broader international trade regime.

The Tokyo Round begins, 1973

The actual opening of the round in Tokyo from September 12 to 14, 1973 highlighted the most significant issues for the entire round. First, US and EC officials had conflicting opinions on the nature of the interactions between monetary and trade policies. The two negotiating teams had to agree upon a compromise formula before the declaration could be made. The other ministers unanimously approved the compromise. This was the first of many struggles by US negotiators to gain agreement from their EC counterparts which left the rest of the membership waiting for them to reach an agreement.[98]

A second important issue concerned the degree of special treatment to be extended to the least developed countries. The failure of the ITO in 1949 meant the loss of all the provisions specific to them, and this neglect of their special weaknesses and vulnerabilities with respect to trade policy liberalization had become a constant issue by the 1960s. The GATT traditionally enshrined the idea of reciprocity, in the form of reciprocal concessions, which had been adopted from longstanding US policy and practice. This became a fundamental principle for all future rounds.[99] While the governments of the OECD countries recognized that the least developed states (LDCs) needed special treatment, the officials of the more developed of the developing countries frequently refused to be denied the same special treatment or to extend those concessions to LDCs. Negotiators from the "developing" category were adamant, with some justification, that they not be excluded from the concessions given to the "least developed countries."[100]

Despite these differences, the developing and least developed countries as a whole generally were able to coordinate their negotiating positions and leverage. This was the beginning of their explicit, carefully coordinated efforts to forge coalitions to block the parts of agreements they most opposed. As discussed below, in 1978 the round almost came to another standstill because they refused to sign the agreement. Although prevailing accounts of this period strongly emphasize that the first important participation of the developing countries occurred in the Uruguay Round of 1986–1994, in fact they organized coalitions and created bargaining leverage by the 1970s. In parallel, however, the tension between the more and the least developed countries was already making it very difficult for their entrepreneurial leaders to design and build consensus around any single agreement.

In sum, there was sufficient US structural leadership to launch the round, but the Watergate scandal completely undermined congressional trust of the executive. As a result, the Nixon administration was unable to sustain its structural role or build consensus with the EC on the agenda for the negotiations. Rather as in the Dillon Round in 1960, structural leadership by the United States in 1973 sufficed only to open the process.

Conclusion

By 1948, President Truman no longer maintained the commitment, focus, and policy priority necessary to gain domestic support for ratifying the ITO. Had presidential attention and priority been devoted to ratifying the ITO, then the organization might have been rescued. However, the ITO debate coincided with increased domestic political pressure and ideological differences with key senators, as well as competing foreign policy goals that demanded presidential attention and leadership. Republican control of Congress after the 1946 elections and the 1948 presidential campaign both restrained the president's political space for policy innovation. Even more, the outbreak of the Cold War by the summer of 1947, the coup in Czechoslovakia and Berlin Blockade of 1948, as well as fears about the fall of Nationalist China (and the first war in the Middle East), commanded overwhelming public, congressional, and presidential attention. Amid such pressing international and domestic concerns, the ITO was gradually abandoned by the president.[101]

Furthermore, the design of the ITO was the outcome of intensive negotiation and compromises rather than what most US officials preferred. Thus, in the United States a curious coalition of "protectionists and perfectionists" helped to undermine political support. Congressional Republicans argued that across-the-board tariff cuts would flood the US market with low-cost imports. For their part, congressional Democrats were appalled that the ITO would allow

Great Britain to maintain its system of imperial preferences and that the charter's system of exemptions (including agriculture) and escape clauses violated basic American trade principles.[102] It also allowed substantial transition periods to the new system. Business groups were split, but by 1948 most opposed the ITO. Against the background of eroded support by congressional leaders and industrial groups, President Truman failed to merge his foreign security and economic goals and to press rigorously for congressional approval, focusing instead on the Marshall Plan and urgent political-military questions of the day. Importantly, this marked the beginning of a divergence between foreign security and economic goals, and the domination of trade policy and the US "economic complex" more generally by the national security complex.[103]

Since the formation of the GATT in 1947, American structural leadership. reinforced by substantive ideas and proposals from domestic sources and British and European officials, had been the essential catalyst – shaping both the scope and the depth of liberalization. However, during the 1950s and early 1960s, member states gradually gained greater bargaining leverage within the organization. While the changes would not fundamentally transform the bargaining structure of the negotiations until the 1970s, the Kennedy Round negotiations highlighted the expanding European role. In fact, the US campaign to launch the round was due in substantial measure to concern about access to European markets as the EEC, and the CAP in particular, were soon to take shape. The growing blocking power of the EEC was evident in the Kennedy Round. As its bargaining leverage expanded thereafter, the pressure from other GATT members and some EEC states would build for the EEC to become a co-leader in the process.

The early GATT rounds in the 1950s focused on introducing sets of new members, and with each new round of negotiations the trade system's breadth became increasingly worldwide. From a starting point of twenty-three original members in 1947–1948, it enlarged to forty-five by the Dillon Round, forty-eight by the Kennedy Round, and seventy-six by the opening of the Tokyo Round. At a certain level, then, this dimension points to consistent and cumulatively substantial progress in trade regime development.

At the same time, the trade system did not include adequate scope of issue area coverage to become relevant to the majority of its members. While accounting for a small overall proportion of trade in the system, especially in the 1950s and 1960s, developing states gradually increased as a proportion both of the total membership and of all trade within the system. Furthermore, key developing states such as India and Brazil were founding members of the GATT, and the officials of other, smaller states such as Australia, New Zealand, South Africa, and Israel were already important secondary players in this early period. Even as the organization moved away from a strictly bilateral concession to a more multilateral bargaining approach, the agricultural and development issues of greatest concern to developing states were essentially kept off the table throughout this period.

In general, despite the protectionist and precedent-setting agricultural waiver they pushed through GATT in 1955, on key occasions US officials provided structural leadership for expanding GATT issue area coverage, including many agricultural products. Particularly beginning in the early 1960s as the EEC and its CAP were emerging in concrete form, US officials aimed to maintain both the multilateral trading system and the access to European markets. A blend of clear national and broader interests drove continuing US initiatives and proposals, which kept the pressure on European negotiators to expand the trade system into agriculture. For the United States' own security reasons and priorities, however, US officials would not press them as hard as was required to make the system relevant to developing economies. This, in turn, made it more difficult to manage US domestic protectionist pressures and mobilize the support of key congressional leaders. Thus, particularly when they could maintain a unified position, and especially under constant French pressure to exclude agriculture, the major European states established blocking leverage on this issue.

At the same time, the scope of trade issue area coverage even during this early period was progressively expanded for the major trading states. Negotiations were consistently successful in reducing the tariffs on manu-factured products, to the point that US and European governments began resorting to non-tariff barriers (NTBs) as a means to forestall more sweeping forms of protection demanded by protectionist interest groups. Under the protectionist political pressures that emerged after national and international economic crises of the late 1960s and early 1970s, this use of NTBs and other trade barriers appeared to threaten, for the first time, even the basic principles of the trade system.

By the 1960s, the GATT gradually began to operate as a true organization with its own modest budget, personnel, and offices, and its membership continued to expand. Furthermore, GATT-based rules and procedures were tightened and made more precise by the Kennedy Round. In hindsight, it turns out that key episodes of structural leadership by US officials had driven the GATT negotiating process to achieve ever deeper levels of reductions in tariffs on manufactured goods traded by the major states.

However, the relevance of the system to actual trading practices appeared to be declining by the 1970s. Structural leadership by US officials, supported by the entrepreneurial initiatives of Director General Wyndham White and British officials, could not produce US–EC agreement on the most difficult issues in the Kennedy Round. Thus, the system gradually become less relevant to the trade and trade barriers of its membership. If the GATT-based system of rules and procedures could not be expanded in the breadth of its coverage to NTBs in the major trading states and agriculture for the developing states, then it was likely to become at best a secondary policy priority of even the largest trading states.

Leadership, rather than hegemony, shifted decisively over this period. First, Presidents Roosevelt and Truman drew upon the intellectual innovations of their officials and other thinkers in designing proposals for both the international trade system and the European Economic Community. These two presidents, their secretaries of state, and a few other key officials were the structural leaders most involved in negotiating the broad outlines of these institutions, first with British officials, and then with the other major Western governments. Formulating and negotiating the specific dimensions of key agreements, however, required persistent and flexible structural leadership by US officials, including substantial compromises. Both ideas and leverage from US sources promoting the liberal multilateral trade system had to be compromised in order to accommodate British and European insistence on the welfare state in an integrated framework of embedded liberalism.

Despite these substantial trade-offs, if the Cold War had occurred later, then US structural leadership might well have been sufficient to not only negotiate but also ratify the ITO in 1948–1949. In fact, even given the Cold War, the ITO might have become a reality if Truman had more tightly constrained the negotiating mandate of US officials leading to the Havana Charter, or dedicated more effort to building political support in Congress for his trade policy, or if the biggest European economies had not experienced major crises in 1946–1947. Instead, these factors together elevated European economic cooperation in the context of US security policy above the liberal trade system. This, in turn, enabled the ideas and proposals of European officials to influence US structural leadership in the negotiation of the terms of European economic cooperation and the initial GATT rules and procedures.

After years of effort, the Eisenhower administration finally succeeded by 1958 in developing minimum working levels of domestic political support with extension of the Reciprocal Trade Agreements Act (RTAA). Still, structural leadership of GATT negotiations by US officials was restricted or even lacking when the president was unwilling to directly confront protectionist industry and congressional leaders. US negotiators lacked the support of an active, engaged president and congressional delegation of authority required to build on European ideas and initiative in proposing a new, linear approach to GATT bargaining. The results of the Dillon Round were minimal, and it might well have collapsed entirely without the last-minute shift authorized by President Kennedy, which allowed US negotiators to provide structural leadership on the basis of linear tariff reduction.

Clearly, concerns of senior US officials about perceived decline in US prestige and status as leader of the Western economic system helped to drive the Kennedy and Nixon administrations to exert structural leadership in proposing new trade rounds. They did so in part as defensive reactions to the growth of the EEC/EC as an economic region. They sought to avoid the displacement of the international trade system by European regionalism, as well as to keep open US markets in Europe. In both intellectual and structural terms, US officials feared that regionalism in Europe would trump the liberal multilateral system. Structurally, US negotiators applied leverage, supported by Director General Wyndham White, to open new rounds, broaden GATT coverage, and deepen cuts in barriers. US officials did not propose or support substantial increases in authority for, or formal institutionalization of, the GATT as an organization. In fact, they defeated the proposed Organization for Trade Cooperation in 1955, which would have given specific enforcement and dispute settlement capabilities to the GATT. Still, they championed breadth of coverage and depth of liberalization, and later in the 1970s shifted their position to lead the effort to negotiate meaningful dispute settlement procedures.

The late 1960s and early 1970s generally were dominated by unilateralist and domestically focused US foreign economic policies. Nixon and Kissinger had security policy priorities and crises to manage, from Vietnam to strategic nuclear weapons. They were intensively focused on these national and international security challenges, and neither as interested in, nor adept at, foreign economic policy. Thus, their policy and practice lacked effective integration of security and economic domains.

The Nixon administration called for a new GATT round to reestablish US structural leadership of international economic issues. Their leadership, however, also emphasized a rebalancing of the associated economic and political costs as appropriate to the new capabilities of European states and Japan. More specifically, US officials also argued that trade liberalization would help both address weakening economic growth and manage protectionist pressures in the largest economies. Equally important, the administration sought to strengthen the trade system worldwide in order to balance the growth of regionalism and European influence which would result from the EC's major expansion. Finally, US officials also intended to resolve important issues not settled in the Kennedy Round.

The minimal structural leadership exhibited in gaining agreement for a new round among closest allies was short-lived, as the Watergate scandal began to engulf the president in the months before the Tokyo Round was formally launched.

4 The General Agreement on Tariffs and Trade, 1975–1995

From endangered species to unprecedented authority

This chapter traces, in three parts, the main forces underlying and driving changes in the GATT-based global trade system from the late 1960s through the mid-1990s, with emphasis on the period 1975–1995. In particular, the first section maps out how key member states and the system more generally diverged markedly from established rules and procedures beginning in the mid-1970s. Despite the successful launch of the Tokyo Round in 1973, long-term observers and analysts of the system have noted that "new protectionism" emerged in various forms throughout the period of the Tokyo Round and into the 1980s. Next, the second section assesses how and why the Tokyo Round was completed in 1979 in the midst of a tumultuous era in international politics and economics. The main thrust of the chapter, the third section, explains the principal failures and successes of the extended Uruguay Round from the US attempt to launch it in 1982 through its completion in 1993–1994. A concluding section briefly analyzes the several failed and successful attempts at developing the trade system during this period in the context of structural and entrepreneurial leadership.

The protectionist landslide, 1969–1976

As a result of the acceptance of GATT principles among all major trading parties, and the successive rounds of multilateral trade negotiations, tariff levels had markedly declined by the 1970s. However, accelerating in the 1970s and continuing into the 1980s, states in the trading system invented or emphasized other ways to protect their domestic economies. This protectionism led to a decline in the role of the GATT regime in shaping trade policy as compared to the 1960s. Most notably, many NTBs were implemented during and after the Tokyo Round. This section examines this "new protectionism" from the late 1960s through the mid-1980s. It analyzes the episodic nature of US trade policy leadership and the evolving role of joint US–EU leadership, as well as the broader political and economic context. The question is, why did trade liberalization assume only a background role, while key trade rules, and at times even arguably basic principles, were often neglected during this time?

This particular case of failure to advance trade liberalization defies simple definition. Prior to the Tokyo Round initiation in 1973, the basic question was why it required six years to begin negotiations considered to be a continuation of the Kennedy Round. The main answer is that the United States and leading European states were simply diverted by other political and foreign policy priorities. First, trade liberalization in general and toward the GATT in particular has rarely, if ever, been the preeminent goal of US foreign policy. As is established in Chapter 3, trade policy must compete for attention and priority with both political-military strategy and other diplomatic and economic goals.[1] Priorities during this period in both security and economic matters at times clearly took precedence. Leading US foreign policy makers were preoccupied with the Vietnam War, managing US relations with China and the Soviet Union, and strategic arms limitation efforts with the Soviet Union. By the early 1970s, they were dedicating considerable time and effort to opening a diplomatic dialogue with China, managing conflict in the Middle East, and negotiating the return of Okinawa to Japan. The trade policy initiative capturing the highest-level US government attention was pressing the Japanese for voluntary export restraints (VERs) on their textiles.

In the economic sphere, the collapse of the Bretton Woods agreement between 1969 and 1971 and the fears generated by fluctuating exchange rates captured considerable attention from foreign policy makers. After World War II, the United States had pressed hard for the policies required to strengthen the European and Japanese economies. By the late 1960s, the United States' relative economic position and policies toward Japan and Europe had shifted decisively, and its officials were looking for ways to shift the costs of leadership. During this period, all the major economies faced balance of trade problems, and adjusting exchange rates was often the policy of choice to manage their trade balances. In 1967, slow economic growth, conflict in the Middle East, and mounting unemployment forced the British to devalue their currency, sterling. Events in 1968 forced the British to close the London gold market. In 1969, the French franc was devalued by about 11 percent, and the German mark revalued by 9 percent. As all the other leading currencies were being adjusted, the dollar alone remained to defend the Bretton Woods system. The responsibility for maintaining the Western monetary system fell upon the US Federal Reserve. US officials seemed to understand their options to be either supporting the broader system to the detriment of the US economy, or boosting the US economy at the expense of others.

In fact, US foreign and domestic economic policy options were limited by this time. During the Kennedy years, there was a surplus in the balance of trade; however, it was not enough to cover the military abroad, capital invested abroad, and loans and economic assistance abroad. Most important, President Johnson aggressively pursued the Vietnam War from the mid-1960s, and he was unwilling to compromise on his Great Society programs at home. Between 1966 and 1970, military expenditures alone increased by $7 billion. As Nixon assumed the presidency in 1969, there were substantial underlying inflationary pressures in the US economy. At first, Nixon applied short-term policy measures to improve the balance of trade, but in 1969, economists were already predicting that the trade deficit could reach $5 billion by 1972. In fact, the trade surplus ended in 1971 and the deficit stood at $2.7 billion by 1972.[2]

Nixon's dramatic attempt to restore the faltering economy was the "New Economic Policy," announced on August 15, 1971. It highlighted a wage and price freeze, suspended the convertibility of dollars into gold, and imposed a 10 percent surcharge on all imports to the United States. The administration claimed that because the European and Japanese economies had caught up with the US economy, the new policy was the only way to maintain fair competition. US officials hoped to coerce the Europeans and Japanese into making trade concessions by imposing the surcharge. The European and Japanese response was to argue that the US surcharge was a blatant attempt to transfer its economic problems abroad.[3]

Critics also saw problems with linking monetary policy to trade policy and trying to solve domestic economic problems with foreign economic policy. They argued that Nixon had complicated and overburdened the negotiating process. In the face of true competition from Europe and Japan, and growing domestic economic problems, Nixon effectively withdrew from structural international economic leadership until 1972. Instead, he attempted to distribute to other economies as much as possible of the costs of adjusting to radically new international economic conditions. This was a major shift from American policy over the previous twenty-five years, and the other major trading states were taken by surprise.

In order to cope with their own economic difficulties, European governments turned inwards to protectionism and regionalism. As the United States negotiated export restrictions (VERs) with the Japanese, the Europeans unilaterally established tariffs against Japanese textiles. They focused their joint efforts on furthering the European Economic Community, particularly the expansion of the original six to nine members with the entry of Britain, Denmark, and Ireland in 1973. In the aftermath of these events and the Arab oil embargo and production cuts of 1973–1974, the first truly worldwide economic recession of the postwar period occurred in 1975.[4]

Even after the Tokyo Round had been formally launched in September 1973, this case of failure to follow GATT rules and, at times, principles continued, because US officials were not leading and major European states focused on EC development. Indeed, some trade experts and officials, at least in Western countries, reacted to the "new protectionism" with elements of "new international trade theory," and structural leadership in trade disintegrated as the Nixon administration became immersed in the Watergate scandal. The Tokyo Round was paralyzed and the trade policy behavior of key states world-wide appeared to be crisis driven. Pressured by France in particular, the EC was adamant about maintaining its CAP in order to protect agriculture against foreign competition. Other GATT members, led by the United States, tried again to liberalize European agriculture after unsuccessful efforts in the 1960s. US negotiators intended to link agricultural and industrial liberalization together, thus ensuring that the EC would have to compromise on agriculture in order to receive other concessions. EC and European officials argued that agriculture must be negotiated separately.

In April 1975, a temporary settlement was reached "that allowed for the possibility of discussing agriculture under the umbrella of the general goal of reducing protective measures."[5] However, as Roderick Abbott, an EC nego-tiator, told US negotiator Alan Wolff in a private conversation, the "US would have to press the EC hard if such negotiations were to be successful."[6]

US trade officials hoped to gain concessions from the EC at the economic summit at Rambouillet, France, in November 1975. However, President Ford made no serious effort towards agricultural liberalization. As Abbott warned, without strong US structural leadership the EC position would not budge. This battle between the EC and the United States over agriculture completely stalled the negotiations in the first half of the round. European leaders abso-lutely refused to compromise. Furthermore, the US STR's structural leadership was contingent on his ability to maintain a delicate balance of US domestic political interests.

Although the US and EU officials exerted the most leverage, they were not the only identifiable players at this time. Initially, Japanese prime minister Takeo Fukuda, whose domestic policy agenda strongly emphasized economic reform and growth, also offered to have his government play a leadership role in forging policies for international economic recovery and stability. Japan had become the world's second largest economy, and its economic growth rates were the highest among the major economies in the aftermath of the 1975 worldwide recession. As its exports continued to flood Western markets, senior Japanese officials faced ever-increasing protectionism from the United States and Europe. They were threatened by both US and European governments with even more barriers to their exports if they could not offer significant steps in opening their domestic markets to Western products.

Therefore, Japanese negotiators expressed their willingness, in principle, to move beyond their traditional passive and defensive role in GATT negotiations. Specifically, they set out to contribute as entrepreneurial leaders by creating policy options and bargaining packages to help reduce the differences between the US and EC ministers.

In practice, however, Japanese officials were seriously handicapped by domestic constraints in providing even entrepreneurial, never mind structural, leadership. During the entire first half of the trade round, Japan's internal economic and financial ministries were consumed in fierce struggles over negotiating issues. As long as the ministries could not work out consensus agreements, the government could not make major policy decisions and formulate technical negotiating positions on key issues. Of course, ministry bureaus and commercial organizations responsible for promoting domestic agriculture fought for continuing defensive positions on this key trade liberalization issue.

Ultimately, the role of Japanese negotiators increased at most to the level of mediation, which failed to move US and EC officials. A further difficulty in playing any effective entrepreneurial leadership role was that on the agriculture issue at the heart of US–EC conflict, the Japanese were at least as opposed to reform as EC officials. Late in the round, Japanese officials were significant by their absence from any effective leadership role in the GATT process when the most important decisions were taken.

Some LDCs, but particularly certain developing members, played an important new role as a blocking coalition during this round. LDCs and most developing states were effectively excluded from substantive involvement in prior rounds because their issues, especially agriculture, were consistently pushed off the agenda. Additionally, most lacked the financial resources to support the negotiators necessary to participate in all of the relevant discussions. Furthermore, as the major states turned increasingly toward new forms of protectionism, the GATT forum appeared to lose even its importance as a constraint on the trade behavior of the United States and European states. Developing and least developed states thus began to block agreements at key decision points. Indeed, even as the developed states finally resolved all of their issues, the developing and least developed states further extended the round. By the end of 1978, when they refused to sign the agreement, it seemed that the entire round might collapse.

Structural leadership by US negotiators based on a substantive innovation broke the impasse. They designed a protocol to the controversial customs valuation agreement for the developing states and guided partially successful negotiations on it. It created a graduation system in which developing and least developed members could take five years to implement the obligations of the agreement.[7] This appealed to leading developing countries, but not the LDCs; indeed, only India, Brazil, Korea, and Argentina signed the final agreement.

Negotiators for both developing and developed countries were concerned about the failure to attract LDC participation. Officials from the LDC governments complained especially about the lack of consultation with their officials regarding the main negotiating issues. Negotiators from most OECD states argued that they had given the LDCs a free ride. Although the LDCs were not given the opportunity to voice their opinions, neither were they asked to give concessions in the negotiating process. They had been seeking increased access to markets, while not offering substantial concessions.

All of these factors led to protectionist attitudes in countries worldwide, as no clear leader emerged for the trade liberalization process. Underlying ideas were shifting with regard to the nature and causes of both protectionism and the required responses thereto. The United States was still inclined to press for a new round, but was willing to do so only on the basis of a new understanding. The European states, Japan, and the United States must share the costs of leadership. As is explained in Chapter 3, in February 1972 the United States initiated two separate Declarations on International Economic Relations: one with the EC and one with Japan. In the declarations, each party pledged to "initiate and actively support multilateral and comprehensive negotiations in the framework of GATT beginning in 1973."[8] As US officials understood the European and Japanese economies to be increasingly equal to that of the United States, they expected these countries to fill the leadership gap. Their governments, however, were not sufficiently motivated to lead, in part because they had been accustomed, for three decades, to relying heavily on US international political leadership. Instead, they focused on steps to cope with recession and other immediate domestic economic difficulties.

The initiation of the Tokyo Round coincided with even deeper domestic problems for the US government, which ultimately paralyzed the US presidency and resulted in President Nixon's resignation in August 1974. The Watergate scandal compelled Nixon to forgo any serious work on policy while he scrambled to salvage his presidency. Congress established its committee to investigate Watergate in February 1973, and by June, John Dean was testifying that Nixon was involved in the cover-up of the burglary. The president's three major speeches on Watergate spanned the period April 1973 to April 1974. Thus, the administration had the domestic and international authority through the spring of 1973 to maintain the agreement for meeting in September to open a new trade round. By the summer of 1973, however, just prior to the GATT meeting, the president was not only losing all congressional support but also becoming increasingly vulnerable to charges of criminal involvement in the Watergate scandal. To make matters even worse, by October Vice President Spiro Agnew had resigned in disgrace after months of intensive media and political pressure, owing to charges of tax fraud.

Indeed, despite the international agreement to meet in Tokyo to launch the new round, even as the round opened in September, the US administration lacked authority from Congress to make trade deals. Thus, the domestic basis for US international structural leadership was lacking. Nixon pressed Congress in April 1973 to approve the Trade Act, initially hoping to grant most favored nation (MFN) status to Communist countries, but this triggered controversy in Congress and led to the Jackson–Vanik Amendment, which granted MFN status to the Soviet Union only as long as it allowed Jews and others to emigrate. The Trade Act included a "fast-track" system with increased executive authority, but Congress maintained initial and final approval. Before the Tokyo Round, Congress had never approved a trade agreement negotiated by the executive unless it had given advance authority. Congress was loath to give power to an executive that it did not trust, but it hoped that the Trade Act would allow negotiators to bargain more effectively in the NTB area.[9]

The US domestic crisis finally came to an end with Nixon's resignation in August 1974. President Ford engaged directly to help push the Trade Act through Congress. In a speech of December 1974, he emphasized the crucial role of US structural leadership and the consequences of its absence: "The world today looks to the United States of America for leadership. We have provided this since the end of World War II. We did not provide it prior to World War II." The bill was passed, and signed by the president on January 3, 1975. Finally, three years after the original US initiative to gain agreement from the EC and Japan to begin the Tokyo Round, the US executive had the authority to negotiate. In response, the EC promptly approved the Commission's negotiating mandate in February.

Less than one year later, however, US officials were again preoccupied with domestic politics. With presidential elections forthcoming in 1976, the administration devoted little attention to the round. Prior to the elections, US structural leadership was severely weakened by a relatively new president who might not even be elected in 1976. As a result of their reliance on US structural leadership of the GATT negotiating process, "[t]here could . . . be no significant developments in the negotiations until the President had been elected."[10] Uncertainty prevailed about future US trade policy. Other key states were not willing to take risks in bargaining with a US administration that might not even survive to deliver on its commitments. Lacking the domestic base and authority for structural leadership, US trade officials were forced to place their initiatives on hold.

In sum, to this point in the round both the EC and the developing countries had played an important role in the negotiations. Their roles, however, lacked any significant leadership toward advancing the overall process, because they were driven heavily by value-claiming strategies and proposals in pursuit of relatively narrowly defined national interests. The EC was constrained by the frequent inability of its members to formulate a single agreed negotiating position and the severe pressures caused by economic crises, both international and domestic. The Japanese were a much quieter force in constraining US initiatives; nonetheless, they were loath to open up their borders to manu-factured goods. EC and Japanese officials each separately told US negotiators in private that they would make concessions only under intense US pressure. This pressure, however, was not forthcoming, since US structural leadership was lacking.

The LDCs and developing states proved to be a powerful blocking force. US structural leadership was not sufficient to engage the LDCs or their issues in particular. If US negotiators had pressed their EC counterparts even more concertedly to compromise on agriculture and the OECD states had allowed more substantive LDC issues onto the agenda, perhaps the round would have been substantially more successful. Still, US officials were pressed hard from both sides, with most members insisting on substantive agricultural liberalization and the EC rejecting meaningful reform.

New protectionism

A new and fundamental element of the Tokyo Round was the reduction in non-tariff measures (NTMs). Under the increasing pressures to compete – with East Asian exports, for example – and to adjust to the collapse of the Bretton Woods exchange rate system in 1971 and commodity price shocks in the 1970s, states turned to new ways to protect their domestic economies. By the mid-1970s, GATT members, particularly the developing countries, were deeply concerned about the trend toward a wide array of restrictions on trade and domestic support measures, such as subsidies. In this climate, key GATT members focused on non-tariff measures, which had never been negotiated. There was substantive agreement that NTMs were a major element of protectionism. Through intensive research and discussion, the NTMs were grouped into five separate categories: quantitative restrictions (later known as import licensing procedures), technical barriers to trade, government procurement, customs matters, and subsidies and countervailing duties.

Many issues needed to be overcome in these discussions. One of the main problems with regulating NTMs was perceived threats to national sovereignty. Key member states had certain non-tariff practices embedded in national constitutions. Legislating changes in constitutions is a high-visibility, controversial, and resource-intensive project. Members were therefore seriously concerned that governments might not support the reforms agreed to in the Tokyo Round, or might not succeed in implementing them. The negotiators attempted to develop ways to change NTMs that would not be perceived as threatening. This required substantial study, certain innovations, and entrepreneurial leadership to design a new framework and facilitate its acceptance.

As is highlighted above, the Tokyo Round was undertaken in the context of widespread protectionist pressures. Particularly after 1975, the first truly worldwide recession since the 1930s, states focused on protecting their domestic interests. GATT director general Olivier Long was especially concerned. The 1976–1977 annual report of GATT emphasizes that:

> [t]he spread of protectionist pressures may well prove to be the most important current development in international economic policies, for it has

reached a point at which the continued existence of an international order based on agreed and observed rules may be said to be open to question.[11]

Even with the end of the Tokyo Round impasse in 1977, Director General Long remained deeply concerned. His final report on the Tokyo Round emphasized that "[p]rotectionist pressures gained momentum, particularly in 1977 and 1978, and those in national Administrations favoring liberal policies were finding it increasingly difficult to hold the line."[12]

Senior US officials and members of Congress had long viewed the United States as the main victim of international protectionism. Post-World War II US policies allowed Europe and Japan to discriminate against its products in order to stimulate their economies. However, as the US loss of relative economic position became clear by the 1970s, domestic interests pressed for protection. Similar pressures were rising in the EC. As the Community grew in number of states, key domestic interest groups determined that it was increasingly important to lobby for their positions. The most important domestic group was the farmers, particularly those in France. With the United States and the EC, by far the most important players in the trade rounds, each pursuing mainly their own interests during the mid-1970s, it was impossible to complete the round.

The origin of co-leadership, 1977–1979

In February 1977, President Jimmy Carter asked Robert Strauss to be his Special Trade Representative. With Senator Russell Long's strong encouragement and assurances of support, Strauss accepted the position. The previous two administrations had focused heavily on trade experience in their STRs. Strauss was instead known for his political skills, toughness, and success as campaign manager for the president. It was his sense of politics and strategies of persuasion, as well as his close working relationship with the president and key leaders in Congress and the administration, that primarily enabled his structural leadership on behalf of the United States in completing the Tokyo Round. The president's trust in Undersecretary of State Richard Cooper was also crucial to Strauss's ability to win presidential support. Strauss regularly asked Cooper to participate in key meetings with the president because his endorsement helped win Carter's support and approval.[13]

One of his first acts as STR was to press hard on top Japanese officials for an agreement regarding their electronics exports. During the London economic summit in May 1977, Strauss secured an agreement from Prime Minister Fukuda on a quota for television imports.[14] This deal was critical to provide some relief to domestic producers of color televisions, which in turn reduced industry and congressional pressures. His ability to bargain effectively with very reluctant top Japanese officials was enhanced by their understanding that Strauss could speak authoritatively on behalf of President Carter, as well as his connections with senior members of the Japanese government. Similarly, his close ties to leading members of Congress, including Senators Long and Ribicoff, and their perception that he could speak authoritatively for the president helped him manage domestic interests and gain congressional approval. Each of these factors was essential to presenting an image of strong US structural leadership in trade policy.

In addressing EC officials, Strauss built on a growing reputation for tough bargaining and his close working relationship with German chancellor Helmut Schmidt. During an initial meeting in Brussels to determine a formula for reducing tariffs, Strauss was given a paper with tariff proposals from Roy Denman, representing the EC. Strauss took one look at the paper, pushed it back, and said, "You could have written this a year ago. It doesn't represent any progress."[15]

In fact, Strauss had no idea what the complicated formulas meant. He just instinctively knew that whatever the EC was proposing would not go far enough. Denman later complained to Deputy STR Wolff, "That Prussian [Strauss] can't come over here and dictate to us."[16] Strauss had found the key to forging negotiating leverage with the Europeans; he was following Abbott's advice on the need for strong US pressure and structural leadership. Later in the same meeting, Strauss pushed the EC negotiators to agree to make negotiating offers by January 1978, which created an important foreign policy deadline to help force decisions to be taken at the domestic level, especially in Europe, and probably opened political space for key negotiators to force compromises among competing ministries.

On the same trip, Strauss opened the core issue, agriculture, where he had the least leverage, because winning any compromise from European states also required significant US concessions. US agricultural policy proposals lacked the credibility of true structural leadership in that they continued to offer only the elimination of tariffs and export subsidies, rather than getting at the heart of the matter: domestic support programs. In particular, US domestic interests were split deeply between likely winners and losers from liberalization and stronger international rules. Competitive export interests such as feed grains, poultry, wheat, tobacco, and oilseeds were traditionally balanced politically against the entrenched import-competing interests represented by sugar, dairy, rice, cotton, wool, and meat.

As a result, Strauss knew that he needed to be very direct with the Europeans. He asked them what they could not live without. This was a clear case of structural leadership to forge the required consensual basis for joint leadership at the multilateral level. US–EC negotiators had to agree on maximum concessions possible within the limited bargaining authority of EC negotiators. EC officials needed to maintain the fundamentals of the Common Agricultural Policy, thus Strauss assured them:

> You have my word there will be no attack on common agricultural policies.
> Now we could try to open it, to penetrate your markets more. We have got
> to do that, but we are not going to attack the structure itself.[17]

In a major concession to the Europeans, and a clear example of structural
leadership, Strauss agreed to negotiate agriculture in parallel with the industrial
negotiations. It would not be explicitly linked to reductions in tariffs on
industrial products as the US government had originally intended.

If it could offer substantial liberalization of agriculture, the EC's leadership potential was substantial in this situation. Like the United States, it was
constrained by election cycles, protectionist interests and procedures, and
especially the CAP. Additionally, however, the EC officials and key European
governments confronted serious difficulties reaching common positions on
international trade issues. Officials of major member states in particular held
deep concerns about the ability to compete with Japanese industrial exports.
Even once a common position was agreed, individual members at times
continued to pursue their own agendas behind the scenes, thereby threatening to undermine the EC's common negotiating position on the most difficult
issues. Leading US negotiators understood the need to maintain direct contacts
with top officials from individual European states. Often, US officials found
EC officials, especially the EC Commissioner for Foreign Affairs, to be more
committed to successful negotiation of tough issues than key member states.
For the Commission and the EC more generally, negotiating the GATT in the
1960s and 1970s was likely the single most important source of their authority
in the foreign policy domain.

Throughout the 1970s, EC member state officials tended to focus increasing
time and effort on European matters. Their regional focus contrasted with
crucial US global interests, which no longer automatically placed European
unity as their highest priority. Furthermore, as US foreign policy and leadership worldwide was still constrained in the aftermath of the Vietnam War,
European leaders sought ways to substitute common foreign policy through
the EC for what they perceived as US weakness or withdrawal. Finally, even
pursuing their interests beyond Europe, EC states were less reliant on the
international trade regime because their trade relations with developing states
generally were governed by separate agreements. This meant that European
states, in contrast to the United States, often were more reluctant to change the
status quo. It also established a degree of EC structural leverage over smaller
developing and least developed states that had preferential access to European
markets.

For the same reasons, however, European officials became substantially more
central to US structural leadership in GATT. For the first time, EC and European
negotiators were better positioned to gain the endorsement of negotiating
approaches and initiatives with certain other key members and organizations.

From other leading states, such as Canada, to approval in the OECD, and key developing states such as India and Brazil, EC structural leadership was crucial at times in helping to broaden the consensus group of states supporting proposals. Along with US officials, who provided the principal structural leadership required to close the round, the EC co-led in agenda setting and in persuading other states to participate and negotiate until agreement was reached.

A simple but effective process was created. First, EC–US negotiators struggled to forge a common position. Next, US officials provided crucial structural leadership in negotiating this position with the Japanese officials. In bargaining terms, the strategic sequencing was that the politically most important two trading entities would reach agreement, then rely on the co-leader with the greatest structural leverage over Japan to negotiate its entry into the small leadership group. Japan had risen to be an economic superpower, and by the 1970s it was taking substantial steps to open its domestic markets. Still, the United States and the EC encountered serious difficulties in developing Japanese markets for their finished goods, and Western officials confronted serious concerns at home about competitiveness relative to Japan.

In November 1977, STR Strauss sent Richard Rivers to Tokyo to negotiate with the Japanese. In hindsight, it is clear that this was intended to be a probing move designed to test the boundaries of their negotiating space. Officials of the finance ministry, among others, resisted or rejected each of his negotiating points.[18] However, a week after Rivers left Tokyo, Prime Minister Fukuda reshuffled his cabinet, selecting people who were more flexible on the main issues.[19] It was not until external pressure, and especially US structural leadership, escalated the stakes publicly in late 1977 that modest concessions were made on both tariffs and NTBs.[20]

By January 1978, Strauss claimed that the negotiations were 80 to 85 percent complete, but his original ambitious deadline had not been met.[21] France was delaying the process by refusing to talk to American negotiators. Japanese officials still were not making their final offers, because they believed American negotiators were holding back. They perceived the US negotiating strategy to be predominantly "claiming," or excessively focused on US domestic interests, in part as a result of the constraints imposed by Congress.[22]

Most of the US–Japanese agreements actually occurred in the context of the Bonn Summit Conference in July 1978. The Japanese had finally worked through their interministerial conflicts and were prepared to discuss compromises. Their negotiators appeared at Strauss's hotel room to present him with a proposal. "So with that lever, we negotiated on the side all during the Bonn Summit Conference."[23] At the end of the conference, both US and Japanese officials were pleased with the outcome. While the United States did not gain any major concessions from the Japanese, for the first time US officials had established import quotas for products that had been completely banned. Japanese officials played no significant leadership role for the rest of the round.

At this critical juncture, however, Strauss's ability to win European support to press for final completion of the round was paralyzed by a US legislative restriction. Under section 331 of the Trade Act of 1974, the president was authorized to waive the law requiring the imposition of countervailing duties on subsidized imports over the anticipated four-year negotiating period. If the waiver was not extended before it expired on January 3, 1979, the duties would be automatically imposed without proof of these items causing material damage to domestic suppliers. Strauss and his allies failed to get a bill extending the waiver passed before Congress recessed in October 1978. Congress was not scheduled to reconvene until mid-January 1979. The EC absolutely refused to finish negotiations until the United States had resolved the waiver issue. Once again, negotiations were stalled. Finally, late in March 1979 Congress passed the necessary legislation, the Trade Agreements Act, to extend the waiver.

Concurrently, the developing and least developed countries exerted blocking leverage by refusing to sign the preliminary agreement at the end of 1978. Ministers from the group of most involved industrial states, including the EC, the United States, Japan, Switzerland, New Zealand, Canada, the Nordic countries, and Austria, had signed the "framework of understanding" setting out what they considered to be the elements necessary for a balanced package at the end of the round. Ministers from developing states reacted in protest against their exclusion from this agreement, but also because they concluded that there was little of value and relevance to their trade policy requirements.

As compared to the past, the central negotiating coalitions in the round were pursuing positions based at least as much on ideology as on substantive interests. The most advanced and experienced developing states sought formal establishment of special and differential treatment, whereas the least developed and other developing members perceived that they had little to gain on substantive issues once real concessions in agriculture were excluded. However, there were also deeper North–South ideological issues driving their positions. Stimulated by the unprecedented success of the OPEC cartel in 1973–1974, the related campaign for a new international economic order, and their new assertiveness through the United Nations Conference on Trade and Development (which is actually an organization), most developing and least developed members began seriously to consider boycotting the agreements in principle.

Basing their position more specifically on the argument that they were not given adequate representation during the negotiation process, and led by India, Brazil, Korea, and Argentina, they held out for further concessions. US negotiators led the way in appeasing them as much as possible. An important complication in reaching agreement was the deep split between leading developing states on the one hand, and the least developed members on the other. The more economically advanced developing states argued forcefully against being required to make reciprocal concessions when they were still struggling with widespread poverty in their societies. They would not allow the least developed states to reap all of the benefits of special treatment while they would be treated on the same basis as much more economically developed states. This would prove to be a fundamental issue of central importance to all future GATT-WTO trade negotiations. While still struggling domestically with Congress, Strauss and his top negotiators worked intensively to develop a solution acceptable to all the developing states. In a clear example of substantive innovation, they formulated a new, compromise approach based on a phase-in period: "Over the course of several months we negotiated a protocol to the valuation agreement . . . which would allow the developing countries to take five years to implement the obligations."[24]

The system of graduation thus appealed to the more developed states within the "developing" category because they would be given additional time to liberalize. The negotiators for least developed states, however, would not budge. They resented their complete exclusion from trade negotiations and had less to lose in the no agreement situation. In moving to close the round, by 1978–1979 the inner group of industrial states, including the EC, the United States, Japan, Switzerland, New Zealand, Canada, the Nordic countries and Austria, all signed the "framework of understanding" setting out what they considered to be the elements necessary for a balanced package at the end of the Tokyo Round, as already stated. Thus, at the end of the round only India, Brazil, Korea, and Argentina signed the agreements.

The US negotiators simultaneously managed these major challenges at home and abroad. In the end, structural leadership by US officials, joined by EC negotiators and European officials, was crucial to producing a final agreement. A more detailed dispute settlement process was certainly one of the few most important outcomes of the Tokyo Round. Despite strong EC opposition, which effectively blocked a much more substantial agreement, the new procedures established a more precise mechanism for enforcing the trade rules. More generally, this dispute settlement agreement elaborated key elements of the existing rudimentary system, from the requirement for consultation between the parties to a final written report from the panel. When they perceived violations of particular GATT rules, member states could also turn to the specific dispute settlement procedures associated with several of the key agreements from the round. As it turned out in practice, however, the crucial limitation in the process was that a losing party could ultimately refuse to join a "consensus" in GATT's Council, the standing group of all members. In this way, the Council could be prevented from giving its required approval of panel reports and creating a legally binding finding under the GATT.[25]

On April 12, 1979, Alonzo McDonald signed the Tokyo Round agreement for the United States. The structural leadership provided by Robert Strauss and President Carter, among others, joined with that by key Europeans, won sufficient support. Together, along with minimum Japanese agreement, they overcame developing state and LDC opposition to conclude what appeared at the time to be the most successful trade agreement to date. President Carter, in particular, provided consistent and direct support to the negotiations in terms of strong rhetorical support for trade liberalization. Both directly and through Under-Secretary of State Richard Cooper, the president supported Strauss, which established his strong negotiating authority with the European and Japanese ministers. With both the president's commitment and Strauss's connections in Congress, domestic opposition was managed and eventually congressional approval was granted.

Tokyo outcomes

The Tokyo Round clearly ended with mixed results. The most important failures were in agriculture, safeguards, and inclusion of the membership in the final agreements. It failed to resolve the ever-present problem of agriculture, and it stopped short of providing a clearly needed agreement on "safeguards" (emergency import measures). At the end of the negotiations, only four developing states and no least developed members actually signed the final agreements. The large majority of the GATT's newest members and its over-all membership of ninety-nine countries by 1979 opted out of much of the agreement. Furthermore, because the new codes were established as separate agreements which most members did not adopt, the trade regime was no longer universal among the GATT membership in its basic legal structure. One more level of rights and obligations had been added within the system, and the challenge of maintaining a coherent whole became ever greater than before.[26]

Probably the greatest failure of US structural leadership in the round involved the lack of substantive progress in reducing the elaborate EC and US systems of domestic agricultural support and protection. Why were President Carter, USTR Strauss and other US policy makers willing to accept an agreement without significant reform of the EC's CAP? As is explained above, EC states gave somewhat less priority to the GATT than the United States, both because they increasingly emphasized regional European matters and competitive-ness, and they had separate agreements with many developing and least developing states. They also confronted serious difficulties in reaching decisions on their common negotiating positions, and French officials were especially opposed to flexibility in agriculture. Still, negotiating reductions in agricultural support, including its dense system of non-tariff barriers, was a main goal of the round. Why was Strauss not able to negotiate any serious reduction in agricultural support, especially given his close connection with German officials and the strong support of Britain, Australia, New Zealand, and others? Earlier, this was explained mainly in terms of the blocking leverage established by the EC, but of course US domestic farming interests receiving government support also sought to block reform.

Even more surprising than the failure to reform the EC's CAP and agricultural subsidies programs in general was a major concession by the United States in its countervailing duty law. Toward the end of the round, under joint pressure from the EC and other states, officials of the Carter administration agreed to insert a proof of injury clause into the countervailing duty laws.[27] This raised the threshold sharply for US industries seeking relief from subsidized foreign agricultural and other imports. Instead of simply petitioning the US government for countervailing duties to offset the value of the subsidies, US industry would have to demonstrate injury as a result of the subsidies. Among other industries, this would prove very costly to US agricultural producers competing with European exports subsidized under the CAP. The much higher threshold for relief would effectively concede major US market shares to European exports, which would in turn ratchet up the pressure from US producers on government officials in the future, because of declining market shares.

The outcome over time of not restricting agricultural support was a major increase in European agricultural subsidies in the 1980s and a parallel relative gain in their market share of agricultural exports, which displaced US and developing state products. This, in turn, set up an even more intense conflict to be fought out over agricultural protection in the 1980s and 1990s. In the context of intensive bargaining efforts to develop compromises, this US concession may have been a gesture of US structural leadership intended to elicit important compromises and agreement from the EC and other states such as Japan with high levels of agricultural support. At the same time, in retrospect, and considering the longer-term effects on the Uruguay Round, it appears to have been a substantial US concession with very little received in return. The CAP remained in place, and agriculture was the most important failure of the round.

Nevertheless, one important achievement was the replacement of linear tariff reduction with harmonized rates. Inequities in the linear model appeared soon after its introduction. States with peaked tariff schedules, including the United States, were able to forestall significant cuts in particular industries. The harmonized system mandated significant cuts at the top, and by accepting the new structure the United States reduced its own tariff rates by an average 31 percent. The United States accepted a disproportionate burden of this liberalization, but the total reduction did not reflect allowances granted to powerful US domestic industries. The final schedule limited damage to apparel and automobile manufacturers, and exempted footwear and television producers entirely.[28] Again, this illustrated the willingness of US negotiators and senior officials to make important compromises in order to induce key agreements. Despite the exempt industrial sectors, domestic interests were compromised, and US and European officials provided structural leadership in this regard.

The agreements reached regarding NTMs and dispute settlement were significant expansions of GATT coverage and enhancements of precision in rules and procedures. By attacking NTMs, the trade regime was finally positioned to address new protectionism, the core political issue of international trade. As the results of the Kennedy Round were implemented, the unprecedented openness of the system to industrial exports required substantial adjustments, and states needed time and political space to adjust. The new codes broadened the role and reach of GATT, which in turn provided a basis for beginning to manage strong protectionist pressures in the system.

Even further, the new dispute settlement system was perceived as more authoritative both in national political contexts and in international trade relations. Until this agreement, states were expected to follow the rules and even more the principles of GATT, but there was no clear, practical mechanism in the system for enforcement. The more fully elaborated dispute settlement procedures were a milestone toward establishing GATT, and later the WTO, as an increasingly authoritative international organization. In sum, the Tokyo Round results were substantial and significant because of the new issues tackled, particularly the non-tariff measures, as well as the more specific authority given to the GATT through its member states in the form of the dispute settlement process.

How did negotiators finally close the round? First and most important, strong and effective structural leadership by Strauss, backed solidly by President Carter and Richard Cooper, among others, gradually moved the process to a conclusion. Strauss adeptly incorporated US private sector groups in the process as a means of developing their support and commitment to concluding the round. Through persistently and carefully cultivated relationships with congressional leaders, he played a leading role in the passage of the Trade Agreements Act of 1979. He also made effective use of cross-issue linkages to move the Europeans towards the key compromises.

The second factor was the emergence of joint US–European and EC structural leadership as a necessary element in the negotiating process. Closure of the round would not have been possible without the underlying international liberalization commitment of key European states, the sporadic co-leadership of top EC and US officials, and the support of Helmut Schmidt and other important European leaders. As is explained in earlier chapters, key observers of international trade negotiations have argued, incorrectly according to this study, that EC co-leadership was essential from the Kennedy Round. On the other hand, astute analysts such as Raymond Vernon, Andrew Moravcsik, and Patrick Low have emphasized the lack of European leadership through the

1980s due to the regional and national focus of even the largest European states. Vernon, for example, contrasts the limited nature of European interests with the U.S. ambition to lead the non-communist world.

> Europe, on the other hand, viewed its interests in terms that were [much more specific] and more narrowly defined, and accordingly, much less concerned with the problems of building and strengthening a global system. This European view persisted into the 1980s, dampening any expectation that Europe would take the lead in any new global initiatives in the trade field.[29]

Moravcsik's extensive assessment of the European integration process from the 1950s to the early 1990s emphasizes the fundamental role at key junctures of each European state's own national economic interests. Even more specifically, Low emphasizes the "defensive" and "accommodating" nature of European positioning in international trade negotiations: "Looking back over the GATT's history, it is hard to identify any initiatives that the European Community has taken to promote and strengthen the multilateral trading system."[30] There is certainly truth in each of these assessments, but, as explained in this chapter, the Tokyo Round cases highlight the mid- to late 1970s as the period of fundamental transition. The GATT process could only function with joint US–European structural leadership. By 1973, US leadership was still sufficient, as long as key European leaders could be coaxed to abandon blocking positions. Of course, it is also the case that launching the round in 1973 was a less difficult project than most of the other cases covered by this book. There were relatively few specific and substantive commitments required of states in the 1973 agreement.

By 1977–1979, US structural leadership remained clearly more important, but on its own it was not sufficient to win the agreement of other key GATT members, for example through the OECD, or to guide the agenda formation and negotiating process, and carve out a modest compromise in the agricultural issue area. "We had a partnership with Europe, and the fact is you need a partnership with the European Community to move major trade talks forward. It will not be moved with a partnership with Japan."[31]

The accession of the United Kingdom to the EC proved very important to the Community in this regard. Most specifically, the United Kingdom provided the Community's principal negotiator, Roy Denman. He had headed the EFTA team in the Kennedy Round, and thus brought to bear long experience in international trade negotiations. More important, even prior to the arrival of the Thatcher government in May 1979, the weight of the United Kingdom with the EC helped to shift the balance against the French ability to block any agricultural reform. "The French were a problem. . . . We knew we could never get the French government's support, but we hoped that we could move them toward neutrality."[32] In this way, the UK role in providing entrepreneurial leadership was crucial, along with that of Helmut Schmidt individually, who was more open than the French to agricultural reform and international liberalization.

Despite the deep fears of European officials and companies about competitiveness relative to the Japanese, as signaled by increasing trade deficits with Japan, the EC was gradually becoming a powerful international trading and negotiating entity. Leading US officials understood that any agreement had to begin with the US and the Europeans. EC and European leaders understood that they had to choose between maintaining a blocking strategy, thus breaking down the negotiating process as a whole, or assuming a co-leadership position. This was the fundamental reason that the round failed to address agricultural protection in general, and the CAP in particular, in any meaningful way. More difficult to explain is the US willingness to sharply tighten its countervailing duty laws with the proof of injury clause, which had the effect of advancing subsidized European agricultural exports. This certainly demonstrated the structural leadership of US officials in their will and ability to make serious compromises and manage US domestic interests for the sake of advancing the Tokyo Round.

Japan's overall role in the Tokyo Round conformed to a well-established pattern.[33] Its officials had the potential by this period, especially based on their relative external economic position, to play a structural leadership role jointly with those of the United States and Europe, but domestic divisions and specific sectoral interests could not be overcome. The nature of their bureaucratic and political processes, in addition to their defensive policy positions on key issue areas of trade policy liberalization, has required strong external stimuli to catalyze foreign economic policy shifts. In this regard, issue linkage and a negative ruling in the GATT dispute settlement process in particular, but also US pressure, more generally have been the key factors causing Japan to act.[34] Indeed, Japanese officials are consistently inclined to react rather than lead. Furthermore, even such combined external pressures will only trigger the required political decisions late in the negotiating process and once they are absolutely required. "Negotiating with the Japanese really involves the Chinese water treatment. It takes a great deal of persistence and patience."[35]

The least developed and developing state members played a key role during this round, mainly as a blocking coalition, which reduced the extent of overall US–European structural leadership. Although most scholars focus on the role of the LDCs beginning in the Uruguay Round, the Tokyo Round marks the emergence of their substantial political influence. Their effective exclusion from the negotiation process led to blocking behavior. US officials continued to operate with much of the same pyramiding, or consensus-building, strategy as employed in earlier rounds. Serious consultations with the officials of any non-OECD members, with the partial exception of a very few leading traders such as India, Brazil, Argentina, and South Korea, only occurred after the United States' the EC's, and the largest European states' negotiators had won the agreement of Japan, Canada, and other key Western states such as Switzerland, New Zealand, Norway, Sweden, Denmark, and Austria. "The only time we went to the GATT for a formal meeting was when we truly had something to put forward and had the advanced countries at least willing to support it."[36]

At the end of 1978, almost all least developed and developing members were refusing to sign the agreement, and complete failure seemed possible. An important factor underlying the new blocking power of these states was that one of the deputy director generals of the GATT was from a developing member state. He played a key entrepreneurial role in conveying information to their representatives. Reasonably timely and complete access to information helped these states draw attention to areas of major interest to them, particularly tropical products and special treatment. Despite its clear limitations, the agreement on tropical products was one of the first to be negotiated. It was also important to institutionalize special and differential treatment for the first time.

The Uruguay Round

The Uruguay Round (UR) of the GATT was in all likelihood more ambitious and more successful than any previous multilateral trade negotiations (MTNs). Even in 1986, at the round's launch, no one fully anticipated how extensive it would become.[37] Episodes of structural leadership by US officials were crucial from the outset. Although necessary, however, their structural leadership was not sufficient in 1982 to launch the round. A new round could only be launched with the active joint structural leadership of EC and US officials in gradually building the required consensus among the other key members. US leaders in trade policy only discovered (or rediscovered) the necessity of US–EC cooperation, and of considerably greater entrepreneurial leadership by other officials in an effort to win over additional parties, as a result of their failure to win agreement for a new round in 1982. This case of failed trade policy and politics in 1982 and the subsequent US-led campaign to convince the EC is explained in the first subsection below.

The second subsection maps out US and European structural leadership, which broadened the circle, particularly from 1985, and finally established the minimum coalition necessary to launch the round in 1986. Further subsections assess the two failed attempts to complete the round, first in 1990 and more importantly in 1991–1992. In each case, the breakdown of US–EC cooperation and leadership was the central cause of failed negotiations. The final subsection examines the successful closure of the round once the US–EC split was mended. Indeed, by 1993–1994 members could take stock of a truly unprecedented accomplishment in terms of the scope and depth of the agreement, as well as the precision of trade regime rules and the authority of the new WTO.

The increased scope of the negotiations in terms of issue areas was most apparent in agriculture and services, but also the trade-related aspects of intellectual property rights and foreign investment. Agriculture had been a fundamental problem in earlier rounds, and its substantial inclusion for the first time marked a turning point in MTNs.[38] The services, as an entirely new domain, required special efforts in terms of structural, entrepreneurial, and intellectual leadership.

Furthermore, late in the round a new international trading body was proposed, to replace the GATT: the World Trade Organization (WTO). Initially proposed by Canadian officials, this body was intended to have more far-reaching decision-making powers, to improve the image and reputation of the negotiating body, and to add a much more authoritative dispute settlement procedure.[39] Overall, by the early 1990s the emerging outcome was both "unexpected" and successful.[40] The UR was unprecedented in the breadth of its negotiating agenda, the number of developing and least developed state parties (GATT membership) and coalitions, the specificity of agreements and authority associated with functions proposed for the organization itself, and the complexity of balancing such a large number of cross-issue trade-offs.

American hubris and hurry? The failed launch in 1982

Proponents of a new GATT round in the early 1980s encountered difficulties from the beginning, as most states were not convinced of its necessity and some were strongly opposed. Starting in 1981 with the election of Ronald Reagan as president, however, US officials were the first to clearly perceive and enunciate the need for new negotiations. They forged plans to launch a new round and began the process of persuading other member states of its importance. Increasing protectionist pressures were evident worldwide as several major states endured economic recessions. In the US Congress and key departments of government, key officials understood the political imperative of addressing strong anti-Japanese sentiment among some industrial sectors and protectionist groups. High-level officials voiced fears that compliance with the international trading regime was falling sharply, despite the Tokyo Round agreement. An unusual degree of governments' trade measures appeared to violate international trade rules and procedures.

US structural leadership was key in the progress toward the launch of the UR, and "had it not been for the tenacity of the Americans, the negotiations would never have taken place."[41] This US initiative was based on President Reagan's simple but strongly held free market beliefs, and spurred on by the administration's perception that it was necessary to relieve congressional pressures to restrict imports. US negotiators and top officials were unusually coherent in their understanding of liberal principles, especially as promoted clearly and forcefully by the president, and their pursuit of an assertive trade liberalization agenda. Once the administration had worked through the most visible and controversial issue of US trade politics at that time, the rapid rise in Japanese auto exports into the United States, trade officials turned to the new round.

In the "hubris" of a new administration and USTR, US officials announced to the Western world the need for a new ministerial meeting.[42] With the leadership of the new USTR, former senator Bill Brock, officials developed an ambitious set of negotiating objectives that exceeded both the trade regime's traditional domain and its recent emphasis on non-tariff barriers. US negotiators would seek: (1) liberalization of all agricultural trade; (2) a new basis for relations between developed and the more advanced developing countries; and (3) a new attack on barriers to investment and trade in services.[43] Key business groups seemed especially interested in the final area and active in proposing the liberalization of services, and USTR officials built on their ideas and initiative to generate negotiating proposals and political support in Congress for the round.[44]

This belief in the necessity of new negotiations was most conspicuously not shared by the crucial partner in multilateral trade negotiations, the European Community (EC). EC and European officials were much less excited about the idea of a new round of negotiations than the US administration, which became clear at the Western economic summit of 1981 outside Ottawa.[45] Unlike the United States, the EC was "not particularly interested in supporting new initiatives in GATT, and had none of its own to propose."[46] In fact, the US drive to integrate the developing states more fully into the trade regime raised European concerns that the negotiating agenda would conflict with its priority for advancing its internal market. In particular, the EC sought to avoid disrupting its preferential trading relations under the Lomé Conventions with many developing countries.

Furthermore, it was even more worried about how the US emphasis on liberalizing agricultural trade would affect its Common Agricultural Policy. French officials in particular, but with support from Germany and Italy, insisted that there would be no agricultural reform, whereas Britain, led by Margaret Thatcher, pressed for liberalization of the CAP. Despite this cleavage between key member states, EC and European leaders gradually realized that they could not afford either to allow the United States to blame them for the failure to launch renewed negotiations or to abandon their leadership position in trade at a time when the international regime seemed increasingly irrelevant.

The first official moves toward a new GATT initiative were meetings in 1981 of both the Group of Seven (G-7, comprising Canada, France, West Germany,

Italy, Japan, the United Kingdom and the United States) and the Consultative Group of Eighteen (G-18). The G-18 was an invention, an example of structural leadership, of US negotiators specifically designed to facilitate systematic broadening of the consensus group for key trade issues. After discussions about the worldwide slowdown in economic activity, each group concluded that a new initiative for trade liberalization was required.[47] Largely on the basis of US structural leadership exercised in coordination with EC leaders, it was determined, in turn at each meeting, that there should be a ministerial meeting in 1982. It would be the first to be held in almost ten years. This led to the official declaration at GATT's annual session to hold the next meeting in Geneva at the ministerial level, which triggered a rush of activity in member states to develop positions on the negotiating agenda.[48]

At the Geneva Ministerial, the draft declarations and work program included many unsettled points that the trade ministers found difficult to resolve.[49] US negotiators were especially adamant about the need to focus on services.[50] In an important attempt at structural leadership based on key new ideas and issue areas, they pressed their case in forceful arguments to include these new subjects, especially intellectual property rights.[51] There was some limited success in the form of a preliminary text on intellectual property and services. There was substantial reluctance and suspicion about the nature of US motives, however, and initially the EC joined the developing states in opposition. In the end, US structural leadership prevailed on the basis of specific substantive arguments, in parallel with the entrepreneurial efforts of key officials, and US and EC negotiators reached agreement on several points.[52]

The Geneva Ministerial, however, did not proceed as the ambitious US delegation expected it to. In fact, key opponents of the round, particularly France, India, and Brazil, were deeply suspicious of new rules for the services. From Senator Brock's vantage point, "key states just naturally reacted against US proposals because they were coming from the United States."[53] At the same time, these states were concerned about US intentions with respect to liberalizing the service sector and how it might affect their future international competitiveness. Governments worldwide were deeply concerned about the economic recessions in key countries and the newly emergent debt crisis.

Bargaining deadlocked, moreover, on the agricultural issue almost at the very beginning.[54] This paralysis was caused primarily by the EC's refusal to accept the arguments for agricultural reform, a position that would gradually dominate the overall negotiating process. Agriculture should not have been, from a more technical viewpoint, such a problem, since it constituted only 3 percent of the EC's imports and about 8 percent of exports.[55] The massive internal payments and support system was also causing problems for the EC as an institution and for some members in particular because of its heavy financial burden; in 1982, for example, the CAP expenditures made up 60 percent of the EC budget.[56]

In practice, however, the EC stood firm against US structural leadership and the entrepreneurial efforts of other states, groups, and officials, emphasizing that it would allow the round to fail rather than compromise on agriculture.[57] It gained bargaining leverage from this position as the negotiators realized that they could use the agricultural sector to slow progress and manipulate negotiations in their favor.[58] In response, Australian negotiators walked out of the Geneva Ministerial meeting in protest over the delays and inconclusiveness of agricultural talks, which were crucially important to them.[59]

In the end, a new round was not launched. US officials achieved much less than intended, but they also held unrealistically high ambitions and dedicated too little time to pre-ministerial meetings, bargaining, and preparations.[60] There were deep problems within the declaration, and it was a "hasty and not deep[ly] considered attempt."[61] Though Geneva was clearly a failure, some elements of progress were made. Before the meeting, most member states had not favored launching a new round. The meeting persuaded many ministers that it was vitally important to confront protectionist inclinations and numerous disputes in international trade worldwide.[62] Though few wanted a completely new round, most began searching thereafter for ways to reduce conflict and enhance predictability in trade relations. Negotiators became much more open to entrepreneurial initiatives from key states and GATT officials and committees on how to strengthen the trade system.

United States Trade Representative Brock sized up the ministerial as avoiding "tragedy" and making "limited movement in the right direction."[63] GATT committees were tasked to begin work on a variety of subjects and to renew efforts on others. It was gradually recognized that negotiations were required in new issue areas such as the services.

On the other hand, Senator Brock readily admits that the United States could have prepared other states much more fully for its initiative. US officials simply did not take the time to conduct adequate preparatory efforts, beginning with bilateral meetings with key EC member states, then gradually broadening the circle to Canada, Japan, and other major trading states. Without the groundwork being in place, the US proposals found key members' negotiators insufficiently prepared for serious negotiation. Negotiators for many members needed to offset expected losses in newer areas such as the services with specific commitments toward gains in other issue areas such as textiles. Essentially, US structural leadership and substantive proposals were not adequately supported by efforts to build joint US–EC structural leadership and then reach out one by one to other key members.

Striving for consensus, 1982–1985

From the close of the 1982 ministerial to the official launch of the UR in 1986, US officials worked intensively to build support and agreement on their key issue areas. On average twice a year, they arranged informal gatherings of trade ministers from about twenty-five countries, both developed and developing, to identify areas of possible consensus.[64] Actively drawing on the intellectual contributions of others, including their own business-sector constituents, US negotiators integrated research findings into their proposals. In this way, they reinforced and facilitated the arguments for including new areas in the negotiations. This is precisely the concerted effort to both promote and prepare for the launch of a new round that would have been required in 1981–1982 to gain adequate support for the US position. A minimum winning coalition would have included at least the EC states, Japan, Canada, Australia, Brazil, and Argentina. Moreover, on the domestic front the United States began to regularly consult and mobilize its own business community on the proposed issues.[65]

President Reagan attempted to size up the support for a new round of GATT negotiations at the G-7 economic summit in June 1984. The formal statement from the meeting declared that the states should "continue consultations on proposals for a new trade negotiating round in the GATT,"[66] which represented progress toward the US position. However, the EC would still not agree to set a date for the start of the round, mainly because of objections from France. German and Japanese officials were informally willing to voice support for reform, but they were not yet prepared to explicitly accept agricultural reform and the new round.

EC negotiators were unwavering in their insistence that they not be forced to reform the CAP. Though not strictly opposed to the start of a new round, they placed preconditions on what was negotiable. After formally announcing that it supported a new round in 1985, the EC declared that "the Council is determined that the fundamental objectives and mechanisms both internal and external of the CAP shall not be placed in question."[67] France warned that it would invoke "vital national interest" to veto any proposal for explicit restrictions on export subsidies.[68] The French were prepared to discuss agriculture if, and only if, the goal was not liberalization. The EC claimed that it would instead conduct international agreements for individual products, i.e. cartelization, which was not supported by any other state.[69]

By July 1985, US officials were convinced that at least half of the GATT member states were ready to begin a new round. With the understanding that they had the support of a majority of members, they announced that "since the Council is incapable of taking a decision," the United States would request a meeting of the GATT's highest body, the sessions of contracting parties. By making this apparently procedural request, US officials were exerting structural leverage by forcing a crucial test of support for the new round. A special session called at the request of one member country needed the support of at least one-half of the GATT membership.[70] By the end of August, the required number of countries agreed with the proposal to convene a special session. This was the decisive, or focal, point in initiating a new round.

US structural leadership of the system had been tested and accepted. In a classic case of pyramiding to the point where opponents were isolated, states remaining opposed to the round did not push their opposition to the extent of demanding a vote, and decisions throughout the round were always taken on the basis of consensus.

It is likely that agreement on the need for a new round also stemmed from another element of structural leadership: repeated US threats to focus future US trade negotiating efforts elsewhere if GATT members did not agree on a new round. US officials made it perfectly clear that if a new GATT round were not launched, they would negotiate bilaterally and regionally. Negotiating bilateral agreements with Canada and Israel, the United States "could abandon a multilateral process it would not benefit from."[71] The Reagan administration threatened the use of bilateral negotiations with any states that were willing,[72] and, as states do not wish to be left out, it is likely that this threat increased the willingness of key states to seriously consider launching a new round.[73]

This strategy was especially designed, in part, to convince German policy makers of US seriousness and ability to focus the main US trade policy efforts elsewhere. The single most important and direct means to persuade French leaders was understood to be active German support. To the extent that German leaders would more actively and intensively lobby their French counterparts to agree to a new round, US officials believed that the French and EC position could be shifted.

Thus, from 1982 through 1985 the US catalyzed key domestic constituencies for a new round, pressed trade liberalization as a core idea, educated other delegations about new negotiating issue areas, and threatened skeptical states with US bilateralism and regionalism. In this way, it helped to create the environment for the launch, which in turn allowed US officials to convince the main European states, and thereafter to forge a winning consensus group. Without a doubt, the United States was the main structural leader for launching the UR, but it only became possible once the EC was willing to join in the leadership process.[74]

Success in 1986 and failure in 1988

The Uruguay Round finally began in Punta del Este, Uruguay, on September 15, 1986. At the meeting, the ministers adopted a declaration to launch the eighth GATT Round. It included a standstill and rollback provision to prevent GATT-inconsistent, trade-restrictive measures from being introduced during the round, and designated fifteen negotiating groups.[75] The standstill provision had been advocated since at least 1982 by US officials at annual economic summits and at the start of GATT meetings. Overall, the newly launched Uruguay Round was seen to have three main tasks: (1) to update the rules and disciplines of GATT; (2) to open markets and extend the scope of GATT in content or new areas; and (3) to broaden the size of its membership base, primarily among least developed and developing countries. The ministers agreed on a deadline of December 1990 for completing the round.

The main issue areas established for the UR negotiating agenda clearly reflected the main US proposals and policy preferences.[76] US officials worked diligently to shape the agenda from the outset,[77] and they were well prepared from at least 1985 in comparison to other countries.[78] US negotiators were intensively involved in each issue area from the beginning. The negotiating process could not advance without US leadership, as "no one was willing to move without US positioning."[79] Others waited until the United States had presented its goals and proposals before responding with their own. In this way, the United States set the pace of the negotiations, leading by example, actively engaging and trying to persuade members of the merits of its proposals.[80]

In addition, the USTR enjoyed substantial presidential and domestic support for its structural leadership at this time.[81] The combination of the president's dedicated ideological support for trade liberalization and his management by delegation approach meant that the USTR was given substantial slack, or maneuvering room for conducting negotiations.[82] In part for these reasons, the period from 1985 to 1989 marked especially intensive US efforts to forge a new set of international trade agreements and institutions.

US negotiators originated several important proposals during the Punta del Este Ministerial in 1986. First, the controversial and difficult trade-related aspects of intellectual property rights (TRIPS) issue area was pressed mainly by the United States, but also in coordination with the other largest trading states. It was clear to both US and other negotiators that powerful US industry lobbies would strongly oppose any agreement without major advances in services and intellectual property. Not surprisingly, the US negotiator offered the first comprehensive proposal in services, and its most involved officials remained the principal structural leaders in this area. The initial US proposal was influential in terms of ideas, or raising "many issues that were to govern the negotiations throughout most of the Uruguay Round."[83] The process in trade-related investment measures (TRIMS) was similar, but with far more Japanese involvement in supporting US proposals.

US structural leadership at this time was constrained in two respects. First, the US ability to lead depended on the position of the EC. US leadership was critical, but if the EC failed to follow the US lead, then consensus building slowed substantially.[84] By this time, the influence and capabilities of the EC had grown to a point where their structural leadership was also essential in moving the key members towards consensus.[85] In launching earlier rounds, agreements were reached with EC support of US leadership, but in launching the UR, even more intensive and extensive US–EC interactions were essential.

Broadening the circle to ever larger groups of members in "consensus" required close US–EC coordination and strategy.[86]

Second, in negotiating their proposed agendas, US officials understood that compromises were required and losses were inevitable because, as Charlene Barchefsky explained, "policy-making by a dictator doesn't work in trade policy."[87] For developing states, compromises by leading states are crucial to remaining engaged in the negotiations. In addition, however, ministers and lead negotiators from small and medium-sized states in the trading system expect to provide entrepreneurial, if not structural, leadership in the negotiating process. Several of the most engaged and entrepreneurial negotiators in prior rounds were from Latin American states. This was recognized, for example, in the preparatory committee's decision to hold the opening of the round in Uruguay.[88] Furthermore, the critical services negotiating group was chaired by a Colombian, and by the Punta meeting other negotiators from smaller member states in Latin America and elsewhere were consistently substantive players.[89] Indeed, Uruguayan minister Enrique Iglesias, who later became president of the Inter-American Development Bank, played a crucial entrepreneurial leadership role as chair of the Punta Ministerial.

With hindsight, the mid-1980s were a milestone in the development of EC foreign, as well as internal, economic policy. From the perceptions of relative decline in international competitiveness with Japan and North America, to the specific demands of the UR for a leading EC role and common EC trade liberalization policies, there was heavy pressure on EC and European leaders to reach crucial decisions collectively.[90] They were pressed hard to enact protectionist policy measures in order to offset fierce external competition, while they also understood the critical need to provide trade policy leadership for the UR. In fact, without the UR, the internal EC process of CAP reform would have been even more difficult, if not impossible. In particular, the Punta Del Este declaration of 1986 was

> more specific and detailed on agriculture than on any other subject for negotiation. Whereas textiles and some other subjects were each dealt with in a single sentence, three paragraphs were devoted to agriculture. They established a much wider negotiation than had ever been attempted on a global scale.[91]

Although EC negotiators reluctantly accepted that text, even by 1988 they were not yet prepared for substantive negotiations on agriculture. The more pressure key GATT members applied for CAP reform, the more EC officials emphasized the limits on how far they would be able to go in reshaping the CAP. In fact, despite the demands of US and Cairns Group negotiators for a ban on subsidies – that is, the CAP – the declaration called only for a "phased reduction in the negative effects and dealing with [the] causes" of distortions in agricultural production.[92] EC structural leverage, based in part on the EC's status as a leading food importer and exporter, enabled the EC to shape the agenda to its advantage and delay the fundamental compromises required. Confrontation on the agricultural issue was delayed until the Montreal Mid-Term Review in 1988, the next major stage of the Uruguay Round.[93] As is explained in Chapter 3, the US concession to require its industries to prove injury as a result of subsidized imports, along with major successes in European agricultural export expansion thereafter, further hardened both EC and US commitments to their well-established positions on agricultural reform.

In the period prior to the mid-term ministerial, most activity was focused in the fifteen separate negotiating groups. They mapped out proposals from the parties and formulated negotiating plans to meet the objectives of the Punta del Este Declaration. In addition, major coalitions formed to coordinate nego-tiating strategy and enhance bargaining leverage, including the Quad (ministers from the United States, the EC, Japan, and Canada), the Cairns Group, and the De la Paix Group. These sought to identify areas of substantial overlap in policies related to the fifteen negotiating areas which could be formulated into unified negotiating proposals. This process was considerably easier for single-issue coalitions such as the Cairns Group of agricultural exporters or the De la Paix, which advocated enhancement of the GATT as an organiza-tion (and its dispute settlement) as well as tighter regulation of unilateral protection, than for overarching groups. The latter often included ministers representing sharply conflicting positions on certain issues, including for example the Quad members on agriculture. US and Canadian proposals for deep cuts in most agricultural barriers and subsidies conflicted with EC and Japanese insistence on maintaining high levels of subsidies and tariffs. Building on a process used in various forms since the 1960s, GATT director general Arthur Dunkel held "Green Room" meetings of a dozen or more ministers (or their immediate representative) from the largest trading states and those most concerned and involved in particular issues. During most of the round, the states most often represented, in addition to the Quad, were Switzerland, India, Mexico, Singapore, Brazil, South Korea, Hong Kong, Australia, Argentina, and South Africa.[94] Dunkel relied on his entrepreneurial leadership role to guide these sessions, particularly to probe the points of potential flexibility and test potential solutions in the areas with the most difficult disagreements.

Green Room sessions became an essential element in the round. Even when they did not produce immediate progress toward agreements, the par-ticipants learned where they needed to focus intensive research, bargaining, and consensus-building efforts. They, in turn, met with the negotiators from the states they represented, for example in their geographic region, or those in their immediate networks of communication and coordination, to brief them on the meeting. When significant progress was made toward consensus on an issue, the Green Room participant was generally expected to take the leading position in working to extend that consensus outward to other ministers in his or her immediate contact group(s), as organized by region or issue area. This is a delicate political process blending both the potential structural leverage inherent in the minister's "inside" role as a Green Room participant, typically on a continuing basis, and the more entrepreneurial roles of persuasion and education of the other group members. A minister is exerting structural leadership to the extent that the minister presses colleagues to join his or her state and the others represented in the Green Room in a consensus group because of the cost of exclusion from the agreement. On the other hand, the minister is leading more in an entrepreneurial capacity when attempting to win over additional ministers from his or her own contact groups on the substantive merits of the issue areas.

By 1987, US officials calculated that the negotiations could be accelerated by gaining a commitment to hold a ministerial meeting by late 1988. In particular, they intended to force a turning point in the process, an agreement on agricultural liberalization, by invoking the Punta del Este Declaration on the possibility of implementing deals made prior to completing the overall round. In a clear assertion of structural leadership, in June 1987 the US administration announced a new, "double zero" negotiating proposal in agriculture to end all domestic support and export subsidy programs by 2000. The aim, by dramatically expanding the agricultural liberalization agenda to include domestic support, was to avoid past failures in negotiating serious reform in agriculture. Of course, the US initiative was also exerting leverage in attempting to refocus the timing and expectations of the negotiators so as to bring more intensive pressures on the EC members, and France in particular. With deep concern about the implications of the new US approach to the CAP, the EC adopted a firm position against any early agreements. In essence, on agriculture it seemed that once again US initiatives and leverage would be pitted directly against EC blocking capabilities.

It was not surprising, therefore, that the Montreal Ministerial in 1988 was dominated by tough bargaining. The preparatory negotiating group developed a lengthy list of recommendations and issues for the ministers to decide. There were several different negotiating areas that required fundamental and difficult decisions. The Montreal meeting made some useful progress, reaching a degree of agreement in five of the nine negotiating subjects on which major ministerial decisions were required: tropical products; dispute settlement; trade policy reviews; future ministerial meetings; and agreements in tariffs and services.[95] The other four areas, however, were hotly disputed and the negotiators could not agree.

The difficulty in agriculture was quite simple: the United States and the EC, each backed by an important group of aligned states, were not prepared to shift from their incompatible positions. Both sides sought to reduce the high and increasingly visible budgetary costs of farm protection, but their approaches diverged sharply. The EC proposed a partial and gradual reduction of barriers in agricultural trade, whereas the United States demanded nothing less than total liberalization in ten years. The Cairns Group, in an attempt at entrepreneurial leadership, proposed a compromise of 20 percent reductions in domestic and export subsidies in the near term, with the expectation of additional reform in the longer term. Neither US nor EC negotiators accepted the compromise proposal.

Most important for the United States was winning relief from the escalating EC subsidies for grain exports, which had led to a reduction in world grain prices, considerable loss of markets by US exporters, and congressional legislation of a countervailing US export subsidy program. With the clear backing of both President Reagan and Secretary of State George Schultz, USTR Yeutter and Secretary of Agriculture Richard Lyng insisted that no agreement in agriculture was preferable to a bad one.

The EC's complex and evolving internal decision-making processes could not produce a substantive reform proposal. It was further complicated by the regular national election cycles in key states and an important internal EC shift of negotiating responsibility in agriculture to the main institutional advocate for the sector. In September 1988, the EC presidency announced that its Agricultural Council would lead the UR negotiations on agriculture. This substantially elevated the role of the main institutional advocate for agricultural interests and the CAP, thus reducing the political space for compromise.[96] It became an either–or game; compromise was not possible, at least in the short term.[97]

Moreover, the likelihood of a major breakthrough was further complicated by the US presidential election and the near-term changeover to a new administration. Yeutter and Lyng had only a few weeks remaining in office. Their authority declined because EC negotiators had the option of waiting to determine whether the newly elected Bush administration would moderate US demands.[98] US and EC officials simply could not carve out acceptable compromises and draft language. It appeared at the time to be a costly failure for the trade system, as well as US structural leadership, as it "gave the round a psychological defeat, when it needed victories, and it halted momentum in agriculture just when it needed to be accelerated."[99]

This failure, however, resulted from not only the US–EC interactions, but also an assertion of leadership from the ministers of five Latin American states. US and EC negotiators suggested that the ministers approve the useful package of results achieved in most other areas of negotiation, and instructed their negotiators to go back to work on agricultural questions. This proposal was flatly rejected jointly by Brazil, Argentina, Chile, Colombia, and Uruguay, which all declared that if there were no agreement on agriculture, then they would accept no agreement at all. They believed that agriculture could be resolved if the United States and EC could muster the necessary political will, which had not yet been forthcoming.[100]

The South American countries were successful for two main reasons. First, US officials could not oppose a coalition advocating what were essentially US negotiating positions, as supported by important US export interests and President Reagan's own beliefs. Second, the coalition was legitimated by "its perfect consonance with the culture of an organization founded on the belief in free trade in all goods as far as possible."[101] Their veto effectively placed "the onus of justifying opposition to liberalization squarely on the shoulders of the other parties."[102]

This was a milestone in the use of bargaining coalitions by developing states. With hindsight, their initiative appears to have been an exertion of blocking leverage by these few ministers against US and EC structural leadership. More to the point, however, their joint action was entrepreneurial leadership because it aimed to pressure and facilitate substantive US–EC agreement in agriculture. Essentially, they attempted to substitute their own leadership when the US and EC failed to lead. Indeed, they also reinforced the Cairns Group's insistence on effective agricultural liberalization. The five countries, in effect, declared that no agreement at this point was better for the UR and overall trade system than one that carved out the most political and difficult issue of all.

Thus, discussions in Montreal came to an abrupt halt. In the textiles negotiations, no real progress was made, in part because the developing states refused to compromise before there was tangible progress in other areas, particularly agriculture. US negotiators indicated flexibility with regard to textiles, including significant possible movement toward the developing state position.[103] The EC Commission, on the other hand, was bound by the tough stance of its southern members – mainly Greece, Italy, and Portugal, which had large textile industries. Here as well, key developing states refused to compromise until the EC and others would bargain.[104] In safeguards, the disagreement was mainly along North–South lines. Developing and least developed states pressed for provisions to protect their export markets, and EC negotiators were unwilling to make significant compromises, in part because they lacked a single negotiating position. Lastly, in the intellectual property rights, or TRIPS, area, negotiations made some progress. For the first time, several developing states showed readiness to negotiate on standards.

In sum, the Montreal Ministerial failed for two major, interrelated reasons. First, the structural leadership inclinations and incentives of EC officials were outweighed by domestic political constraints and politicians in key member states, as led by France, as well as the members' inability to forge a coherent, common EC negotiating position. The EC negotiators needed both additional negotiating authority from their members and a degree of flexibility and maneuvering room to integrate gains and losses across agriculture, textiles, safeguards, and other areas. Second, US and EC negotiators had not adequately worked out a strategy for co-leadership based on prior understandings and agreements in the most difficult issues. Neither individually nor collectively were they positioned to make the ministerial a real focal point in the process. Without a credible position on agriculture and other core issues, they simply could not lead in creating the focal point: a sense of crisis with intense, time-urgent pressure for the ministers to reach agreements.

The failure at Montreal was immediately perceived in the Western media as a breakdown that threatened the international trading system. This, in turn, helped to build exactly the sense of urgency, even perception of "crisis" in some states, required to mobilize political support in key countries and decision making in the EC. Both US and EC policy makers understood that they would have to make substantial compromises in order to complete the round. To ensure agricultural reform, the United States took the initiative, in February 1989, to accept a "ratcheting down" instead of the complete elimination of subsidies. This structural leadership from the Bush administration's new USTR, Carla Hills, and Clayton Yeutter, who had become Secretary of Agriculture, emerged surprisingly early. The United States received in return EC agreement that specific reforms would be made in the three areas: border protection or barriers, internal support programs, and export subsidies. EC officials agreed to "progressive substantial reduction" in subsidies, an unprecedented commitment, while insisting that none of the three areas could be reformed in isolation from the others. These policy shifts created promising bargaining and possible agreement space. Building on the crisis environment, it seemed possible to create a focal point for completing the mid-term review fairly promptly.

GATT director-general Dunkel called a small-group meeting in Geneva from April 5 to 8, 1989 with ministers from the United States, the EC, Canada, Australia, Brazil, and India. Under his entrepreneurial leadership, the Geneva Accord was reached on the basic conditions and process for a final agreement. The round was to be completed under the pressure of a one-year deadline. By April 1990, either the four special problem areas of agriculture, textiles, intellectual property, and safeguards were to be resolved or all other areas of agreement would be void. In other words, unlike the Tokyo Round, it was "all or nothing." Making the progress achieved in the more developed eleven negotiating areas contingent on resolving the problem areas was an important, explicit application of cross-issue linkage.[105] No state could collect the gains it most wanted in its favored issue areas without conceding enough ground to allow agreement in its most difficult areas, with emphasis on the four special problem areas.

Failure to close the round in 1990

In the aftermath of agreement in Geneva, the political pressures on negotiators naturally dissipated. The negotiating groups continued their work, aiming to meet the revised, July 1990, deadline for establishing the basic outlines of agreement in all areas. The final process of completing the agreements would culminate with a ministerial meeting in Brussels during December. However, when the GATT Trade Negotiating Committee (TNC) met in July, the EC rejected the working draft text on agriculture. This, in turn, made ministers reluctant to really engage with their final offers on the other difficult issues, and it became clear that the entire process was more complex and difficult than anticipated, at least in requiring completion by the end of 1990.

In the weeks before Brussels, US officials held talks with members of the Cairns Group, especially its Latin American members, as well as other developing states, to encourage them to force negotiations on agriculture from day one in Brussels and threaten a walkout if necessary. At pre-ministerial meetings in Geneva, Washington, and other capitals, there was a general understanding on the need to force the EC to yield on agriculture. In return, however, US officials believed that the developing states would, and should, be willing to make concessions. Specifically, they asked for concessions on TRIPS, TRIMS, services, and in market access areas such as textiles and clothing. Although states such as Argentina hinted publicly at their readiness to compromise on these issues given meaningful results in agriculture, none of the members appeared to have fully committed themselves to US proposals.[106] The ideas, such as a walkout similar to that in Montreal, were planted. Most important, the United States could count on a substantial group of supporters in the agricultural issue area. Essentially, a blocking coalition was organized on an "if necessary" basis in order to reinforce US structural leadership.

Another US strategy to increase the pressure on key states to offer compromises and reach agreement at the forthcoming December ministerial was the threat to resort to bilateral negotiations if the efforts in the multilateral field failed. In a direct assertion of structural leadership, US negotiators spread the word widely that they were ready to expand trade relations regionally, while fighting a subsidy war with the EC.[107] Secretary of Commerce Yeutter said:

> [I]f all the reform that is achievable is the amount that is encompassed in the EC proposal, then it simply isn't worth it. I'd rather simply forget the whole thing and go about protecting our interests in our own way,[108]

namely by creating the United States' own agreements elsewhere. The United States had recently entered into a free trade agreement with Canada, and talks were under way at the end of 1990 to extend that agreement to include Mexico. Moreover, in September 1990 the United States announced its plans to create the Enterprise for the Americas to explore a hemisphere-wide trade zone between countries of North, Central, and South America.[109] The United States was serious in its intentions to pursue free trade, and this conviction helped to raise the stakes at Brussels, since no member wanted to be denied the future benefits of increased access to US markets or to lose existing export sales in the United States.

There was also discussion in media sources about escalating trade wars if no agreement was reached or if the round failed. Carla Hills declared that "I will have petitions on my desk stacked to the ceiling the day the round breaks up. We will have trade wars over all sorts of silly things." Even *The Economist* warned, in an alarmist mode, that the consequence of a failed agreement would be that the "GATT will itself collapse," risking "a 1930s[-style] trade war."[110] Furthermore, President Bush and leading trade officials were vividly aware that the Democrats controlled both houses of Congress (throughout his presidency), just as President Reagan was constrained by a Democratic Congress during the last two years of his administration.

As a final tactic to force agreement at the Brussels Ministerial, US officials explicitly threatened that fast-track trade authority, which was due for extension in March, would not be renewed. By exercising this threat, US negotiators were attempting to create a focal point in the negotiations, since there could not be a GATT round without the United States. By structuring and presenting the negotiating situation as "now or never," they aimed to pressure the EC into negotiating and compromising in agriculture. Indeed, most negotiators believed that a collapse of the process could result from a failure of the US administration to gain a renewal of fast track, and all but the French believed this to be a bad thing.[111]

For the December 3–6 Brussels Ministerial, the GATT's TNC prepared a draft almost 400 pages in length for review, final negotiation, and approval. It contained little, however, that could be considered as final, and the situation seemed ripe for tough bargaining over the Dunkel text.[112] Although some parts of the text provided a reasonable basis for negotiations, others were very divisive, with multiple formulations of different wordings. To solve this, groups were established under particular ministers to deal with services, rules, TRIPS, TRIMS, agriculture, textiles, and market access. Some progress was made in most of these areas, including the four most complex issue areas of agriculture, textiles, intellectual property (or TRIPS), and safeguards. Each of the four ministers guiding these problem areas provided substantial entrepreneurial guidance and leadership, but once it became apparent that agriculture was deadlocked, the serious negotiations ended.

The Brussels focal point occurred on Thursday, December 6, when conflicting US and EC positions on agriculture seemed irresolvable. In a new thrust of unilateral structural leadership, the United States proposed a 75 percent reduction in domestic support programs and a 90 percent decrease in export subsidies over ten years. The EC could only agree to reduce domestic programs by 30 percent. The chair of the negotiations, Swedish agriculture minister Mats Hellstrom, proposed a compromise solution. It was accepted by the United States and the Cairns Group as a basis for negotiations, but rejected by the EC, which then scrambled to resolve internal dissension and forge a compromise position.[113]

At the same time, tens of thousands of farmers from various EC states protested in large demonstrations. French and German officials were confronted with the largest, most frequent, and most intensive protests, including several that threatened to become violent. EC officials attempted to draft an offer to submit to the agricultural negotiating group, but they lacked both the authority to make reasonable compromises and an adequately unified position. Even Director General Dunkel declared that "not one political decision has been taken" by the EC. US trade officials bemoaned the EC's stance and claimed that the EC was "an economic behemoth that has no capacity to make political decisions."[114] Without a doubt, the difficulties the EC experienced in Brussels and earlier were caused by its inability to assume leadership over its own agriculture programs, and this failure paralyzed the process.

The final attempt at reconciliation broke down late on December 6 after the agriculture compromise was formally rejected by the EC, Korea, and Japan.[115] A group of ministers from Latin American states withdrew from all negotiating groups to protest the EC's rejection of agriculture proposal.[116] Just as in Montreal, the other informal groups that had been meeting were halted because of failure in agriculture. The Brussels meeting adjourned without agreement, as the United States and the EC failed to meet the deadline, and "other countries saw no reason to show their hands as long as their leading trading partners did not do so."[117]

On the next day, the UR was adjourned indefinitely, leaving its fate uncertain. Still, although the UR had failed to meet this deadline, as set at the outset four years earlier in Punta del Este, this collapse was neither fatal nor as important as others earlier in the evolution of the GATT. There were certainly multiple factors leading to the key events in Brussels, but agreement between the United States and EC was a necessary and, in all probability, sufficient condition for completing the Round. Agriculture was the "make or break" issue, just as it was at the 1988 Montreal Ministerial, and it would continue to paralyze the process for years to come.

In the months leading up to Brussels, however, it had become increasingly apparent to key ministers, excluding those of the EC, Japan, and Korea, that if any agreement had been reached, it would have failed to meet even the basic goals of Punta del Este in 1986.[118] In fact, it can be argued that the failures at both Montreal and Brussels saved the Uruguay Round and the multilateral system from arguably the worst of failures: "a fraudulent success, distorted by a new sacrifice of the ever-postponed expectations of agricultural and textile trade liberalization."[119] The Bush administration's decision to agree to adjourn indefinitely in 1990 can be contrasted with the US approach in previous rounds, which accepted relatively weaker agreements in order to maintain cohesion and incremental development of the regime.[120] Even if it was not part of a coherent strategy at the time, one element of structural leadership is recognizing when the failure to agree is preferable to a weak agreement. According to Andy Stoler, the US negotiators "knew the meeting was doomed to fail and realized that they were not going to get a good services agreement," and therefore "it was fortunate that the UR was halted and restarted."[121] US officials did not miss an opportunity to bind the CAP within the GATT, because the EC failed to offer anything beyond its previously agreed CAP reforms.[122] No agreement was better than a bad agreement, and this would have been a bad agreement, especially because of the CAP.[123] Thus, it can be argued that the overall trade regime was better off without such a flawed agreement.[124] On the other hand, the challenge to US and EC officials thereafter was to manage the declining credibility of the regime worldwide and prevent substantial erosion of its authority and effectiveness.

Just as with prior collapses, those outside the process tended to be more alarmed by the failure and skeptical about the overall prospects for the round. Indeed, some outside observers seemed to predict the end of the GATT. The most involved negotiators and policy makers, however, were deeply invested in the round and committed to its completion.[125] By agreeing on a "suspension," they gave Director General Dunkel the power to assess when and how it would be worthwhile to restart the process in Geneva.[126]

In order to restart the negotiations, Dunkel had to have agreement on a new work program. For this purpose, he assumed the role of entrepreneurial leader, pursuing extensive consultations with governments worldwide, both individually and in groups, in order to map out their goals, positions, and minimum requirements. By February 1991, he reported that there was a consensus in favor of completing the round, and that he understood what it would take to restart negotiations.

Most important, however, was a breakthrough on agriculture only about two weeks after Brussels. US officials had declared as preconditions for returning to the round that the EC agree to reform each of the three main areas: (1) domestic supports; (2) border protection; and (3) export subsidies.[127] The crucial EC shift occurred in two rapid steps. First, key German officials, believing that the entire round was at stake, changed their position after the collapse at Brussels.[128] Then German Chancellor Kohl met with President Mitterrand of France one week after Brussels, and they agreed on the need for reform. This represented a "remarkable turnaround in one week."[129] EC negotiators then bypassed the Agricultural Council, which had taken over the agriculture negotiations within the GATT, and accepted Dunkel's proposal to restart agriculture negotiations on the basis of a framework for binding commitments.[130] They agreed to reform all of the above three areas. The timing, if not the nature, of this policy shift was clearly caused by the high-visibility failure of the GATT process. Structural leadership by US negotiators triggered deep concern among top German officials about the broader implications of failure at Brussels, which in turn proved decisive in breaking down French opposition to compromise.

Failure to close the Uruguay Round in 1991–1992

In Geneva, officials of the GATT and leading states recognized that the negotiations had to be reorganized to focus efforts and pressure on the most difficult areas. After months of negotiations, the fifteen groups were merged into six new ones: (1) agriculture; (2) textiles; (3) TRIPS; (4) market access (tariffs, non-tariff measures, natural resource-based products and tropical products); (5) "rule making" (safeguards, subsidies, GATT articles, the Tokyo Round codes, and TRIMS); and (6) institutions (the Final Act, dispute settlement, and the Negotiating Group on the Functioning of the GATT System, FOGS).[131]

Once the EC position on agriculture shifted and Dunkel determined that the round should be restarted, US officials focused on reestablishing their own domestic political base: congressional fast-track negotiating authority. US executive negotiating authority expired in March, but by May 1991 the administration won from Congress an extension of fast-track authority until March 1993.

Fundamental changes in the international context were also causing governments worldwide to reassess their understanding of economic growth and development, including the role of trade policy liberalization. With the reunification of Germany, the end of the Cold War, and the collapse of the Soviet Union from the late 1980s into the early 1990s, many developing and least developed states to began to abandon inward-looking economic policies and adopt more liberal and market-oriented ones. In this context, the example set by the dynamic, export-led growth of the East Asian tigers was increasingly persuasive to many developing states. Developing and least developed states not already members began to investigate membership. Those inside GATT became much more interested in even the most controversial issue areas, such as services and TRIPS. Indeed, developing and least developed states began to apply leverage gained from their own liberalization efforts to help advance their access to the largest trading markets.

The EC began its own CAP reform process, in part due to demands from Spain and Portugal, which had joined in 1986, for an improved agricultural policy, and from other members for reducing the budgetary burden of the CAP.[132] The EC's effective and entrepreneurial agriculture minister, Ray MacSharry, led the development of a crucial preliminary proposal. The MacSharry plan drew criticism from most European governments and the French in particular, although it was widely understood that reform was necessary.

French officials attempted to assert structural leverage by playing the CAP against the GATT, arguing that CAP reform should follow a GATT agreement.

They emphasized that reforming the CAP required knowledge of import levels to be determined in the GATT process. In fact, however, they mainly sought to prevent US and other negotiators from using CAP reform as a springboard for demands that would lead to further agricultural reforms. France refused to permit the Commission to negotiate under a new mandate, effectively blocking the progress of both. USTR Carla Hills insisted that it would be "premature" to debate agriculture prior to CAP reform, and continued to wait.[133]

While France and certain other member countries were insistent that CAP reforms and UR negotiations should not be linked, the two processes were closely interconnected. The CAP reform process was pressed forward in part by the need to unify and maximize bargaining leverage for the EC in the UR. For EC negotiators in Geneva, the reforms provided greater credibility and authority. In particular, they created the credible commitment required by GATT members insistent on major agricultural reform that the EC would be able to make the compromises believed to be essential to the success of the round.

France lost critical support in this process when Germany backed the MacSharry plan. Kohl told Yeutter, "[I]t has become apparent that Germany has a great deal at stake in the Uruguay round and a great deal to lose if the talks fail."[134] By October, the German minister declared that the path to successful conclusion of the UR was now clear and that the coalition between France, Germany, and Ireland would no longer block agreement in agriculture.[135] France finally gave the MacSharry plan qualified support on October 20, 1991.[136] The plan was not formally accepted, but was gaining critical headway. Thus, the EC believed that ministers had given sufficient flexibility to negotiate in Geneva, raising hopes for the year-end deadline to conclude the UR.

The United States welcomed the MacSharry plan.[137] In fact, Yeutter declared that it was "truly mind-boggling as compared to anything that has been contemplated there [in the EC] for the last 20 or 30 years [and] could lead to new international agreement on trade."[138] Still, the official US response was to "wait and see," pending formal approval by the EC Council.

By December 20, when the GATT TNC met to receive the overall negotiating text, agreement seemed to be within reach. It adjourned for three weeks to provide time for governments to consider the draft.[139] Some states accepted it quickly, including certain members of the Cairns Group. Then the EC halted the process when it rejected the draft on December 23, arguing that the agricultural section undermined the foundation of the CAP.[140]

As Dunkel convened the TNC in January 1992, the urgency of reaching agreement was heightened by the US presidential election year, which would command the time and efforts of key officials in the Bush administration. It is generally understood among trade negotiators that US officials are increasingly unlikely to make politically controversial compromises, and therefore to provide the requisite leadership, as the election approaches. Furthermore, Congress's legislative timetable left just three months for the round to be brought to a successful conclusion. Still, the negotiations in Geneva remained paralyzed by the US–EC conflict over agriculture.

It turned out that French politics, even more than the US presidential elections, would prove to be the decisive constraint. After the Socialists regained control of the assembly (1988), President Mitterrand appointed Michel Rocard as premier. Rocard followed Mitterrand's centrist politics, but in 1991 Mitterrand replaced Rocard with Edith Cresson, who became France's first woman premier. After a poor showing by the Socialists in local elections, Cresson resigned (1992) and was replaced by Pierre Bérégovoy.

As the EC's Agriculture Council approached its formal decision on May 21, which approved the MacSharry plan, protests by French farmers escalated and some turned violent. Areas of rural France were off-limits to all government ministers, owing to the likelihood of catalyzing demonstrations, and even violence.[141] The intense opposition generated by the CAP reform helped move the French government to put the ratification of the Maastricht Treaty to a referendum, even though this was not required by the constitution.[142] The government ended up launching a quite late and tense political campaign, and only barely won approval of the treaty on September 20. Clearly, under these circumstances the EC was not going to make the compromises required for a trade deal in agriculture.

Thereafter, US officials assumed the lead. On September 25, President Bush sent an urgent letter to the Europeans calling for a resumption of talks. Despite the traditional concerns about US ability to lead in the midst of elections, US officials apparently calculated that the positive impacts on votes from a successful round would outweigh the negative ones.[143] President Bush surprised many ministers with his strong rhetorical support for completing the UR.

As a result, US and EC officials tried to resolve differences in Brussels on October 11 and 12. Nevertheless, the EC rejected the US proposal for limits on soya production and the level of subsidized exports. Subsequently, the United States declared that the "position of the EC has retrogressed so the gap is as wide as it was previously."[144] On October 21, the United States threatened sanctions over the soya dispute.

On November 3, 1992, William Clinton was elected president of the United States. The election meant a new negotiating team and possibly shifts in policy emphasis; some US officials indicated that the transition could delay negotiations by another year.[145] Most important, the extension of US fast-track trade authority expired in early March, which would leave little or no opportunity for the Clinton administration to engage.

In early November 1992, Dunkel called an emergency meeting of the TNC. On the basis of his consultations with governments, he declared that there was a deep sense of crisis, with a very real danger of the round failing. The TNC then appealed directly to the EC and US to fulfill their leadership responsibilities as the two major powers in the multilateral trading system, and called on Dunkel to exert pressure on both Brussels and Washington.[146]

In response, the US and EC officials met at Blair House in Washington, DC, and reached a compromise on November 20. The two-part agreement included soya (oilseeds) and a bilateral pre-agreement on the agriculture chapter of the Draft Final Act.[147] A joint US–EC statement claimed that "we have achieved the progress necessary to assure agreement on the major elements blocking progress in Geneva."[148] They announced that in the market access negotiations, they would maximize tariff reductions by reducing high tariffs, harmonizing low tariffs, and eliminating tariffs in some key sectors. In the services negotiations, they would take a common approach on financial services, improve their offers, and expect others to do the same. Essentially, the Blair House agreement represented cross-sector linkage for the EC, in particular, whereby agricultural concessions would have to be balanced by "concrete results" in other trade areas such as financial services and market access.[149]

The initial reaction of most states to Blair House was enthusiastic. Though agricultural exporters were disappointed by proposed weakening of the Draft Final Act's requirements, they accepted that the settlement was crucial to the round. The TNC was then reconvened on November 26, agreeing to Dunkel's proposal that substantive negotiations be restarted in order to achieve a successful political conclusion of the Uruguay Round before the end of 1992.[150]

In fact, the apparent breakthrough was not decisive. French officials announced that Blair House represented only a pre-agreement, because it required endorsement by EC ministers. They claimed that the Commission had exceeded its mandate and agreed to measures incompatible with the CAP. Although a threatened French veto was averted, the Commission's ability to negotiate in Geneva was weakened. Canada, Indonesia, Japan, Korea, and other members continued to oppose tariffication. The US and EC schedules of agricultural commitments, reflecting the Blair House agreement, were not submitted until late December. Major differences existed between them, and with other states, over market access negotiations. Moreover, with the agricultural issue resolved in principle, and the two largest participants pressing to complete the round, other participants, such as India, began to assert demands that they had withheld earlier.

Despite these complications, the Bush administration worked intensively to conclude a deal before its departure on January 20. The key US and EC trade officials met in London on January 2 and reached an outline for agreement on the core issues.[151] Negotiators Warren Lavorel and Hugo Paemen then continued bargaining until the process collapsed at the very last minute, on January 18.[152] At a meeting of the TNC on January 20, Dunkel reported that closure was possible if the required political decisions could be taken. It soon became apparent, however, that not all the necessary decisions could be made before the end of US fast-track authority on March 2. Although the Clinton administration promised to quickly request an extension, the process would clearly take a few months, and there was no certainty about the eventual outcome in Congress.

Furthermore, in the French general election all the leading candidates announced that they would reject the crucial Blair House agreement. Additionally, Dunkel's term as director general was ending. After thirteen years as director general and his persistent determination to close the round, a new leadership group would be taking over at the GATT.

Completing the Uruguay Round, 1993–1994

Despite the concerns about failure to complete the round in 1992, an effective set of new trade policy leaders quickly emerged in 1993, and key states and coalitions appeared to be poised to work intensively for agreement. On March 11, 1993, the thirty-seven states of the De la Paix Group sent a letter appealing to President Clinton, to the presidents of the EC Council and Commission, and to Prime Minister Kiichi Miyazawa of Japan "to display leadership at this critical time and to give the Round the priority it so clearly deserves."[153] They emphasized that the basic elements of the agreement were in place, but that the membership could do little without resolution of the US–EC impasse. They called for US negotiating authority to be renewed and pledged their own commitment to the round's success.

During his first visit to Brussels, new USTR Mickey Kantor agreed to a proposal by EC negotiator Leon Brittan for intensive bilateral talks in pursuit of Blair House-like Euro-American agreements to once again revitalize the bargaining.[154] In April, US and EC negotiators settled a bilateral dispute on government procurement. This improved both the transatlantic context for GATT bargaining and the prospects for ongoing negotiations in this area among parties to the Tokyo Round, in parallel with the UR.[155] Kantor and Brittan also clarified the procedure to resolve the final outstanding issues, the "trigger strategy" or pyramiding that had been used effectively in the agricultural negotiations. A bilateral solution would be formulated, which would then be presented to each of the next two largest trading powers, Canada and Japan. The two negotiators planned that this package, with endorsement by the Quad, would be ready for the Western Economic (Tokyo) Summit in July. If successful there, the G-7 would next attempt to persuade the additional seven or so most involved and influential ministers. Finally, the larger group of about fourteen members would seek to gradually convince all the other GATT members, building toward a broad consensus, in part through use of the GATT's TNC. At that point, the overall size of the consensus group of ministers would be sufficiently large to persuade the most reluctant members that it would not be in their interest to veto the decision.[156] This "pyramiding" strategy of persuading state by state to build a gradual consensus was the foundation of the US–EC co-leadership process.

The critical element in US domestic politics was fast-track trade authority from Congress, which President Clinton was granted in an extension from June 30, 1993 until April 15, 1994. The final date was specifically determined to provide sufficient time to complete the negotiations, while keeping intense pressure on the negotiators to reach agreements and accelerate the closure process. Allowing for the necessary notice to Congress, it would require the completion of substantive negotiations by December 15, 1993 – the deadline USTR Kantor was given by the president to complete the round.[157]

A crucial foundation of Kantor's structural leadership in GATT was his well-known close working relationship with the president. As with Robert Strauss's relationship to President Carter, Kantor was appointed USTR after serving as head of President Clinton's election campaign. He had the access and ability to communicate directly and quickly with the president, as required to advance the negotiations. At key points when he argued for creating "the elbow room to get the Round done," the president would provide the required authority and support.[158]

In Geneva, Peter Sutherland became Director General of the GATT. From early in the selection procedure, Sutherland was evaluated by both Brittan and Kantor as highly effective and determined. He was known for being outspoken and dynamic, as "active, tough and engaged," and for pushing people into hard-to-reach decisions.[159] Indeed, within a few hours of his confirmation he declared in a press statement that the Tokyo Summit meeting, already labeled as important by the United States and the EC, was to be crucial to a quick conclusion of the round.[160]

Each of the government leaders or heads of state most involved had their own reasons for expecting the summit to produce specific achievements. The prime minister of Japan sought validation as a world leader to help consolidate control of his government, and this heightened his natural responsibility as the host to make the meeting successful. As this was President Clinton's first major international meeting, Clinton aimed to establish himself as the foremost international economic policy leader, both at home and worldwide. The Canadian prime minister, Kim Campbell, sought specific outcomes from the summit to help attract and persuade voters in the forthcoming national election. Finally, European leaders aimed to announce specific agreements that would be seen as addressing their most pressing domestic issue: economic recession.[161]

At the meeting, the leaders agreed to wording reflecting the overall framework for market access negotiations, declaring it a "major step to the immediate resumption of multilateral negotiations in Geneva."[162] They announced their determination "to achieve with all [their] partners a global and balanced agreement before the end of the year."[163] The Quad members emphasized that the Tokyo package was based only on discussion among themselves, and that they were now eager to meet with other countries. This endorsement of a specific framework provided renewed authorization for the lead negotiators to pin down substantive agreements. It also enabled Director General Sutherland to announce a precise schedule of deadlines for the key negotiating groups on market access for goods and services, and for institutions.

Despite this significant new momentum from the leading states and the director general, the bargaining process was once again delayed by US politics and policy priorities. By the summer and fall, the round was directly competing with US ratification of the North American Free Trade Agreement (NAFTA) with Canada and Mexico. USTR officials pursued negotiations simultaneously on the UR and the NAFTA agendas, particularly during July and August. NAFTA was completed first, in August, but key officials recognized that, especially with Democratic control of Congress, the vote in the House would be very close. The agreement triggered many concerns and criticisms. Most Republicans would be favorably inclined, whereas a majority of Democrats were not. For this reason, the side agreements on labor and environment signed in mid-September were central to the administration's strategy for winning the support of House Democrats inclined to oppose the agreement.

President Clinton placed high priority on both the UR and NAFTA as key elements of his worldwide trade strategy, which also encompassed bilateral and regional initiatives with Asia (China and Japan most prominently), Europe, Africa, and the Middle East. By the fall, however, policy makers and negotiators determined that they could not simultaneously devote sufficient effort and priority to NAFTA ratification and UR completion. Furthermore, as the NAFTA negotiations continued, it became clear that political support was eroding. Completing the UR would likely require delaying NAFTA by another year, and this might well close the window of political opportunity. In turn, the administration calculated that if NAFTA failed, the political environment for trade liberalization would likely not be favorable for accomplishing the key US objectives for GATT.[164] Moreover, NAFTA was an immediate concern for many US lawmakers, since they saw it as affecting their constituents' lives even more than the UR. President Clinton certainly preferred to avoid congressional rejection of a major administration initiative, NAFTA, and thus the NAFTA ratification process received first priority. It was obvious at the Brittan–Kantor UR talks in both October and November that the US negotiators were focused elsewhere.[165]

At the same time, the policy emphasis on, and publicity for, NAFTA served to reinforce the credibility of US threats to focus intensively on bilateral and regional negotiations instead of GATT if the global negotiations broke down. In this way, US officials could join effective pursuit of "alternatives" with legitimate frustration over the long-delayed GATT process. NAFTA was a tangible and credible US "alternative" to GATT, and as such it captured serious attention from key European officials.[166] Among key domestic constituents and congressional leaders, US officials also were "under pressure in the context of a stalled UR to demonstrate that trade liberalization could work."[167] The Clinton administration could win a major trade policy achievement, which also served by late the following year (1994) as the platform for pursuing the ambitious western hemispheric free trade area.

The Europeans also had to consider seriously other major US alternatives in the Asia-Pacific region. Throughout 1993, the Clinton administration actively promoted free trade in the Asia-Pacific region, which included the world's fastest-growing economies. It pursued an ambitious series of negotiations with Japan, China, and the states of Southeast Asia for bilateral and regional trade agreements. Most visibly, President Clinton convened in November the first summit of leaders of the eighteen economies in the Asia Pacific Economic Cooperation (APEC) forum. This strategy seems to have worked, since European leaders, and particularly those in Germany, became increasingly concerned about the effects that both NAFTA and APEC would have on their markets, as the states involved represented half of the world's trade. In Germany, Europe's largest exporting economy, officials work hard at persuading their French counterparts to make compromises in the Uruguay Round.[168] Thus, the visible US preoccupation with NAFTA and its APEC initiative in particular provided heightened pressure to close the GATT round,[169] but it was not clear that the UR negotiations could finish in time.

Indeed, the enhanced structural leadership potential for US negotiators could only be delivered when the administration was able to focus its efforts on the GATT. The absence of instructions from the Clinton administration and the resulting rigidity in the US negotiating positions were paralyzing the process.[170] US negotiators could not even construct a proposal based on the scheme agreed at the Tokyo Summit. All unresolved questions were set aside until the US government had finished NAFTA ratification. Specifically, it again was necessary for the two largest trading powers to come to agreement on the crucial unresolved issues before the other governments could become involved.[171]

In the end, the US House of Representatives ratified NAFTA on November 17, 1993 by a vote of 234–200. Despite the negative votes by three-fifths of the Democrats, the president's own party, the overall vote seemed promising for congressional passage of the UR. Democrats in Congress are less opposed to global trade agreements because the effects are not as directly visible to their constituents most concerned about the effects of trade. The immediate effect of congressional approval was that it finally allowed the top negotiators and the Clinton administration to refocus on the UR. The promise of congressional support for a GATT agreement further increased Kantor's structural leverage for bargaining with the EC.

USTR Kantor restarted bilateral negotiations with the EC's Brittan, which continued for three weeks and paralleled multilateral negotiations in Geneva. A marathon negotiating session on the night of December 6 decided almost all issues of bilateral dispute in agriculture and market access for industrial products. Indeed, this latest adjustment of the Blair House pre-agreement even won French agreement. On December 7, Kantor and Brittan presented the results to the GATT members and gained their support.

Kantor and Brittan bargained bilaterally from December 10 to 14, 1993, just one day before the ultimate deadline.[172] Gradually they reached agreement under the intense pressure of continuous meetings and a firm deadline rapidly approaching.[173] Nevertheless, four issues could not be resolved. They agreed to disagree on financial services, maritime transport, civil aircraft, and audiovisuals (the most important to the United States). The final text provided for negotiations to continue on specific timetables in the unfinished areas, except audiovisuals.[174]

In early 1994, the member states met to formalize the agreements. The TNC then met several times to outline the conference to be held in Marrakech, Morocco. On April 12–15, the Final Act of the Uruguay Round GATT negotiations was signed by all the trade ministers.[175]

Conclusion

The 1970s were clearly a period of decline in the overall effectiveness of the trade regime, in which new protectionism surged and threatened to undermine previous accomplishments in trade liberalization. Even after the launch of the Tokyo Round in 1973, a lack of US and EC structural leadership and cooperation threatened even the basic maintenance of, or adherence to, the trade regime. Governments of both the United States and the EC constrained the first half of the Tokyo Round by their struggle over agriculture, and a core group of LDCs joined together to play a new role as a blocking coalition. The negotiation process was also fundamentally constrained by uncertainty regarding the future direction of US trade policy.

Why and how, then, did key leaders engineer a reversal in the direction of the trade regime? Credit for the initial recovery is owed to US structural leadership, supported by key episodes of entrepreneurial leadership by other key officials. By advocating and advancing understanding of a protocol to the valuation agreement with the developing states, the United States led in breaking the paralyzing conflict and revitalizing the trade negotiation process.

The intensive phase of Tokyo Round negotiations began in 1977. The driving force of revitalized negotiations was Robert Strauss, the Carter administration's Special Trade Representative, and President Carter's persistent commitment to the principles of liberalization and the round. Although Strauss was inexperienced in trade policy, his creativity, political connections and capabilities, and ambition were essential to closing the round. By forging a quite modest US–EC compromise in agriculture, he was able to ensure that the issue finally gained formal status on the agenda. This, in turn, aligned EC and US leadership, swinging their combined weight behind the pyramiding process. EC co-leadership was crucial to broadening the circle of consensus. Although by the end of 1978 developing states and LDCs still refused to sign the agreement, chiefly because it offered so little for them, Strauss and his top negotiators managed to reach a workable solution and close in 1979 what prevailing explanations and accounts evaluated as the most successful trade agreement to date.[176]

In the end, the Tokyo agreement helped to reestablish the basic political and legal credibility of the GATT principles. During the negotiations, the number of members increased substantially and the agreement sharply expanded GATT's coverage of issue areas. Membership increased from seventy-six in 1973 to ninety-nine in 1979. NTBs, agriculture, textiles, and clothing were added to the GATT agenda for the first time, although little else was accomplished in agriculture, and the dispute settlement process was significantly expanded. Seven of the nine stand-alone agreements included relatively specific commitments or codes covering dumping, government procurement, standards, and subsidies. In these areas, international trade regulations and procedures were made measurably more precise. The GATT's independence as an organization and authority to act were enhanced by dispute settlement procedures included in these codes, but only for the members accepting each code.

Despite the useful formalization of special and differential treatment for developing states, the round failed to produce an agenda and agreement of relevance to most of them, especially with the lack of substantial reforms in agricultural trade policies. Most importantly, much international trade by GATT members continued to contradict the basic intentions, if not the technical provisions, of the regime. Indeed, the lack of any substantial reform in EU, Japanese, US, and other agricultural support systems further complicated the challenge for future trade policy liberalization. Furthermore, the domestic political constraints on agricultural reform in the United States would be heightened by the major US concession. By changing its countervailing duty laws to require industries to prove alleged injuries from subsidized imports, it enabled subsidized European agricultural products to sharply improve their US and other market shares relative to US and developing country exporters. It can be argued that this example of US structural leadership, going first and farthest in terms of concessions, had the counterproductive effect of making future US and US–EU structural leadership in agriculture more difficult and less likely. It certainly complicated the context for bargaining over agriculture, as explained in the next chapter, between the United States and the EC.

In essence, the causes of the Tokyo Round enhancements to the trade regime lie first with the structural leadership of President Carter and his cabinet officials, most prominently USTR Strauss. Despite his failures and critics, Strauss worked with a rare combination of structural and entrepreneurial skills, and he adeptly leveraged his close connections with President Carter, other executive branch officials, and congressional leaders, as well as key German, EC, and Japanese officials, to win agreements. Maintaining the support of Congress was a major accomplishment given that the Democrats clearly controlled both houses from 1977 through this period. Also central, however, was the co-leadership of EC negotiators in lining up each additional state in the consensus group.

Where the Tokyo Round failed most notably, particularly in agriculture and deeper NTB reductions (and tighter rules for dispute settlement), it was precisely the specific areas blocked by EC negotiators' persistent refusal, backed by the other most protectionist states in agriculture (including the Japanese), to accept US initiatives for greater breadth or depth of liberalization. In other words, US structural leadership was limited to achieving only what the major EC state officials would support and join as co-leaders. Defection by almost the entire developing state membership did not stop the final agreement. The United States could not force the EC to accept the minimum requirement for winning over developing state officials for even limited participation. Even creating an "à la carte" trade regime of inner and outer members, which ran against broader US goals and preferences, was accepted by US officials as the price of winning EC compromise and co-leadership. Where EC negotiators would not extend their co-leadership in structural terms, their US counterparts could not forge agreement, even when it meant that most members would opt out.

Officials of the new Reagan administration were convinced by 1982 that a new round of GATT negotiations was necessary. This conviction was not shared by the EC, however. One of the main US goals was a complete liberalization of agricultural trade, an idea that it pushed in the 1982 ministerial. US officials also sought improved relations between developed and developing countries and a repudiation of the barriers to trade that had grown since the close of the Tokyo Round. They pushed these issues forward almost single-handedly until the launch of the Uruguay Round in 1986. Although open to new negotiations, the EC and other members made bargaining, especially in the area of agriculture, very difficult during this period. Under the force of active US structural leadership, key European officials gradually shifted in 1984 and 1985 to support the new negotiations. Thereafter, agreement among a majority of the member states was achieved by July 1985.

At the launch of the Uruguay Round, it was clear that cooperative leadership by at least the United States and the EC was essential to any successful outcome. In particular, compromises and sacrifices by these leaders were important to maintaining the participation of the developing states. This recognition of EC importance, however, resulted in the EC staking out a position of opposition to any early agreements. Tension internal to the EC prevented it from taking a single, effective negotiating position. For the first time, a core group of five developing states demonstrated a clear entrepreneurial leadership role, but its initiative was stymied by the EC's blocking position. For this reason, the attempt to close the round relatively early, in 1990, failed.

This study has emphasized the US–EC split over agriculture because this cleavage often dictated whether the EC negotiators were mainly playing a blocking role or, instead, coordinating and co-leading with the United States. With the EC blocking, US officials could still act, or support others to act, as structural and intellectual leaders, especially in the fourteen issue areas outside agriculture. In this situation, however, US structural leadership, supported by the entrepreneurial and intellectual leadership of other key officials, from Canada for example, and groups, was not sufficient to drive the pyramiding process. From its failed attempt to launch the negotiations in 1982, to the 1986 launch and the subsequent cases in the round from 1988 through 1994, only close US–EC coordination and structural co-leadership, supported in turn by entrepreneurial leadership by Canadian and several other negotiators, could incrementally build the consensus group necessary to forging agreements.

In the few cases when the EC had a sufficiently unified position and the acquiescence of key European heads of state or heads of government, the structural leadership of its negotiators proved decisive in reinforcing the pyramiding process. In 1992, the EC accepted an entrepreneurial initiative by Dunkel to recommence agriculture negotiations on the basis of a framework for binding commitments. In an important example of structural leadership and substantive innovation, EU Agriculture Commissioner MacSharry led the development of an important preliminary proposal. US and EC trade leaders met in October to negotiate the proposal, and then met again in January 1993 and outlined an agreement. A successful conclusion of the Uruguay Round was reached through US–EC cooperation, based in part on US leverage against France through Germany's more flexible position on agricultural reform. US–EC leverage was a critical case of joint structural leadership applied through pyramiding and strategic sequencing to gradually, incrementally build the required consensus group. Fast-track trade authority, but only under specific time constraints and deadlines, from Congress further accelerated this process by setting a focal point on the deadline. The focus on agreements seen as addressing economic recession helped to pressure members, especially the EC, to conclude the round. NAFTA, passed in 1993, directly competed for US trade policy priority with the GATT, but the Uruguay Round nevertheless was successfully closed in April 1994.

Despite nearly continual US–EC and US–French conflict over agriculture, the final success grew from the overall coordination and co-leadership by US and EC officials across most of the other fourteen negotiating areas, as well as the entrepreneurial leadership efforts of many other state and GATT officials. Particularly in agricultural reform, it was a "battle of the sexes" in terms of intensive competition over outcomes, while their joint higher goal of advancing the regime prevailed nevertheless.

This study certainly has not been able to do justice to the critical entrepreneurial efforts in particular of trade negotiators from Uruguay to Canada, Singapore, and many other states. This round, more than any before, required the sustained, dedicated, and skillful entrepreneurial leadership of negotiations from a wide range of ministers and negotiators. The majority had their base in the developed states, but many others had long experience representing the governments of major developing states or smaller developing and least developed states. During the Uruguay Round they worked as neutral, expert facilitators of negotiations as heads of formal GATT committee or in more informal capacities. In addition, officials from several Latin American states were strongly represented in these capacities as well as among negotiating coalitions that were central to the creation of key turning points or blocking actions.

From the services to TRIPs, TRIMS, and most other areas, at most key focal points in the negotiations US and EC negotiators worked in close interaction with largely overlapping positions and proposals. This study emphasizes the degree to which EC and European leaders often blocked substantive agreement on agriculture, which in turn frustrated the officials of least developed and developing states, but this was the key exception. In most other areas, US and EC negotiators generally worked together, and with other key ministers, to educate, persuade, and pressure other key ministers to move toward their common or overlapping positions. For this reason, both parties had much at stake in reaching an overall agreement. Especially for the EC and European leaders, it was this stake, along with other elements of US leverage, that drove eventual compromise in agriculture.

Furthermore, over the period of the UR, the EC finally became not only the common market envisioned in 1957 but also a deeper and broader European project. Clearly, by 1993 the EU represented a substantially enhanced presence in Europe and in the international economy. Not surprisingly, at certain points in time it also assumed increasing structural leadership capabilities that proved critical in further developing the international trade system.

5 Foundations for the future

Can the WTO become relevant to development and its least developed members?

This chapter examines the 1999 Seattle and the 2001 Doha, Qatar, WTO ministerial meetings, as well as the 2003 Cancún Ministerial and the 2004 summer negotiations. Why did the Seattle meeting fail and the Doha session succeed in launching a new round of WTO-based global trade negotiations? Why did the Cancún Ministerial fail and the summer 2004 negotiations succeed in reaching a preliminary Doha Round agreement? Although the analysis incorporates previous scholarly work, it mainly presents new principal arguments and key details. Through the integration of primary materials and extensive interviews with trade ministers, ambassadors, and WTO personnel, it aims to contribute to the evolving analysis and understanding of the WTO, international bargaining, and multilateral institutions.

The failure to launch a new round of multilateral trade negotiations in Seattle is often attributed to very visible American mistakes. Most often mentioned are the failure of the Washington State Police to prevent street demonstrators from blocking a main building in Seattle for an entire day, USTR Charlene Barchefsky's decision to simultaneously chair the meeting and represent the interests of the United States, and President Clinton's controversial remarks on the opening day of the meeting about linking trade sanctions with violations of international labor standards. Many people remember the demonstrations and associate the meeting's failure with them. Journalists and experts also attribute the failure to the increase in WTO membership and particularly the demands of the least developed countries. Each of these elements forms part of the multitude of errors, difficulties, and barriers to launching a new WTO trade round at Seattle, but all together they represent only part of the puzzle of what exactly happened before and during the ministerial.

Could anything else have gone wrong with the Seattle Ministerial meeting?

An important and little-understood element of the 1999 ministerial was the decision by top US officials to host the meeting. President Clinton made his intentions clear in his speech of May 18, 1998 at the ministerial conference in

Geneva celebrating the fiftieth anniversary of the GATT-WTO: "I am inviting the Trade Ministers of the world to hold their next meeting in the United States in 1999."[1] He also called for a new round of trade negotiations during his 1999 State of the Union address. Unofficially, the meeting had been scheduled in Hong Kong, but that changed when acting USTR Rita Hayes insisted that it be held in the United States.[2] The city of Seattle eventually won the competitive bidding among US cities to host the meeting.

This turned out to be a serious miscalculation, to the extent that the administration sought to launch a new round because it created a ready-made opportunity for groups opposed to, or critical of, economic and financial globalization to highlight the WTO as part of the problem, if not a main villain. US officials might not have been able to predict the extent of the protests, but, as explained below, there were clear indicators that the meeting would provoke considerable opposition by a wide range of interest groups. This decision is little known outside the relatively small community of trade negotiators, but it forms an essential part of the evidence revealing a lack of US preparedness for, and realism about, a high-visibility ministerial meeting.

Certainly President Clinton and some of his most senior officials understood that antiglobalization protests were on the rise. They had experienced them firsthand in Geneva in 1998 during the Ministerial meeting:

> Inside the grand palace housing the WTO, proponents of trade agreements celebrated fifty years of trade liberalization. Speakers from around the world argued that world trade has grown sixteen-fold since 1950, because of GATT's rules. They noted that the people of the world have benefited from that trade with more and cheaper goods as well as a better quality of life. Outside that grand palace, however, some ten thousand protestors disagreed. While some individuals quietly protested, others threw rocks and overturned cars.[3]

The 1998 protests were of a previously unseen magnitude. More important to explaining Seattle, however, was that senior US officials and Ambassador Barchefsky, in particular, were eager to complete bilateral negotiations (permanent normal trade relations, PNTR) with China in order to finalize Chinese accession to the WTO. While the PNTR negotiations with China were successful – indeed, a major policy accomplishment of the administration – reaching the agreement consumed the time, energy, and resources necessary to adequately prepare for Seattle. Cabinet-level officials, their key personnel, and the very modest USTR staff do not have the resources to intensively pursue the completion of more than one such major policy initiative at a time, and priority was given to PNTR. Regional trade initiatives, including what became the African Growth and Opportunity Act of 2000 and the Caribbean Basin Initiative, further constrained their already scarce time and resources.

Completing the PNTR agreement certainly tied down the USTR and some of her top officials in the months prior to Seattle when their structural leadership and full-time, intensive planning, coordination, and international coalition- and consensus-building efforts were required to make the meeting successful. The lack of adequate time and preparations by senior US officials cannot be emphasized enough.

Furthermore, the PNTR agreement with China, completed on September 19, 1999, angered labor unions in the United States. As a result, the White House apparently directed the USTR, Charlene Barchefsky, that the United States would only accept a WTO agreement with commitments to respect core labor standards. In particular, by late 1999 the Gore presidential campaign was well into the election cycle and a labor clause was likely considered necessary for his bid against Bill Bradley for the Democratic nomination.[4] Still, it is clear that Bill Clinton also was acting on the basis of long-held beliefs in the importance of combining an "open trading system" with "decent labor standards."[5] In the same way, the president was also attempting to integrate his own beliefs about trade and the environment, the needs of his vice president's campaign, and US positioning for the Seattle negotiations. Only two weeks prior to the Seattle meeting, the president and vice president jointly announced new policy initiatives to integrate environmental considerations into US trade policy and international negotiating strategy, as well as an initiative for US technical assistance to developing countries.

Additionally, the lack of "fast-track" negotiating power reduced the credibility and structural leadership that President Clinton and USTR Barchefsky could bring to bear. It could be argued that the administration did not press as early or as effectively as it might have for fast-track authority in 1997 when President Clinton requested it of Congress but did not call for a vote. Particularly in the aftermath of the Republican successes in the congressional elections of 1994 (and again in 1996) and their majorities in both the House and Senate throughout the next six years of the administration, they did not press hard for either fast-track authority or the Free Trade Area of the Americas initiative. When a vote was forced by Newt Gingrich in order to embarrass Democrats prior to the mid-term elections, it was overwhelmingly defeated in the context of the presidential scandal. If the president had set fast-track as a top priority and won the authority from Congress in 1997, and particularly his main supporters for trade liberalization, the Republicans, possibly his top political advisers would have calculated that it was worth the risk to make a serious commitment to launching a new WTO round in Seattle.[6] Regardless, once the presidential scandal made headlines in 1998, and the impeachment process continued into the spring of 1999, President Clinton and his advisers certainly understood that the timing was not right for major trade policy initiatives requiring formal congressional action. Indeed, it was precisely those Republicans in Congress pressing impeachment who were also some of his key supporters for trade liberalization.

A final element undermining US structural leadership – President Clinton's remarks about trade sanctions and labor standards on the opening day of the Seattle meeting – completes another piece of the puzzle. Why did President Clinton intentionally go well beyond both the administration's position (and his speech prepared for delivery at the meeting) on WTO support of labor standards?[7] In a controversial interview for the *Seattle Post-Intelligencer* just before his departure for Seattle, he argued that core labor standards should be developed by the proposed WTO working group and then included in every trade agreement: "and ultimately I would favor a system in which sanctions would come for violating any provision of a trade agreement."[8] Clearly, his remarks were directed more at key domestic audiences, and the protestors in Seattle and organized labor in particular, than at the gathered trade ministers. The trade sanctions argument was known to be a non-negotiable item for key developing members such as Brazil, India, and Thailand, as well as many least developed states. Predictably, it was considered by the majority of trade ministers to be a "bomb" dropped on what was already an extremely difficult and tense negotiation. For President Clinton, in domestic politics electoral goals had to be his priority by November. Thus, no agreement was better than one that did not link trade and labor standards.[9] From 1998, he was pursuing other important areas of foreign policy leadership, from intervention in Kosovo to peace negotiations for Northern Ireland and the Middle East, but not those requiring direct congressional approval. For all these reasons, US structural leadership was seriously weakened even before the ministerial began. It lacked sufficient initiative in proposals and the negotiating draft, coordination and co-leadership with the EU, and domestic political authority and credibility.

The European agenda

Besides the lack of US structural leadership and prior reparations in 1999, the European Union was, in most ways, also unprepared to lead the meeting. It is clear that the agenda for a new round was associated more with Leon Brittan, the EU's trade negotiator, individually than with the European Commission as a whole. From the very first ministerial meeting under the new WTO, that at Singapore in 1996, Brittan led in pressing for a new, millennium round " 'by the end of the century,' but without any direct support from the US, Canada, or Japan, and with strong opposition by India, Brazil, and most other members."[10] US officials did not appear really to want to launch the round.[11] Some negotiators argue that a new round was a "vanity project" for Brittan. In any case, Brittan traveled to key states worldwide in an extensive campaign for a new round that would have financial services (or foreign direct investment) and competition policy as the core agenda items. Despite his clear dedication and persistent efforts for a new round, his agenda lacked any serious integration of the "collective" interests involved and he failed to listen adequately to his colleagues at home and abroad. Thus, his leadership was flawed in fundamental ways. Brittan had a hard time getting along with his own personnel, which further complicated the ability of the EU to provide leadership.[12] Finally, only about six weeks before the Seattle meeting, Brittan was replaced by new trade negotiator Pascal Lamy, who was abruptly handed responsibility for the EU's high-visibility and controversial leadership position.

The EU and US positions still diverged sharply by the Geneva Ministerial Conference in 1998. Jacques Santer, president of the EU Commission, argued for starting a new "millennium round" and encouraged WTO members "to embrace this approach."[13] In his major address, President Clinton proposed that members:

> should explore what new type of trade negotiating round is best suited to the new economy . . . [and] whether there is a way to tear down barriers without waiting for every issue in every sector to be resolved before any issue in any sector is resolved.[14]

Reflecting the deep concerns of many members about beginning a new round before full implementation of the Uruguay Round agreements, WTO director general Renato Ruggiero emphasized that "our first responsibility is the implementation of existing commitments. . . . Full implementation is essential to the credibility of our system – and its potential to carry the weight of future responsibilities." This was an important, entrepreneurial assertion forewarning of deep and broad opposition to a new round until the key implementation issues had been addressed much more substantially.

Agriculture was the crucial sector for many developing states and therefore an essential requirement for launching a "development" round. As usual, the EU was adamantly opposed to offering any major agricultural concessions outside of what it might agree through internal reform of the CAP. Furthermore, the EU had not yet forged a single negotiating position to form the basis for trade-offs with the United States and the Cairns Group. The EU "came to observe, not to talk."[15] By the late 1990s, there was also more direct and extensive cooperation between the EU and its major allies in blocking agricultural reform, Japan and South Korea, which in turn extended their potential blocking leverage through the Group of Ten (G-10) highly protectionist states in agriculture.

Finally, the EU continued to pursue its agenda of bilateral and regional trade deals during the run-up to the Seattle Ministerial. In particular, it was negotiating a bilateral agreement with South Africa and was in the early stages of forming another one with Mexico.[16] These arrangements certainly were not of the magnitude of the PNTR between the United States and China, but they also consumed precious time during the final months and weeks before the Seattle Ministerial. They may also have been intended to play out the same negotiating strategy as had been used successfully by the United States against the EU during the Uruguay Round in the early 1990s. That strategy would create a credible alternative trade policy agenda as a way to succeed even if the WTO talks themselves failed. By enhancing their position relative to the United States in case the WTO effort failed, they aimed to reinforce their bargaining leverage for key issues. By formally linking Europe and Mexico, they might also gradually reduce US leverage as the predominant market for Mexico. In any case, overall the EU was not prepared to establish itself as a structural leader and to join as a co-leader with the United States.

A striking example of the inability of either the United States or the EU to provide structural leadership during this critical time period can be seen in the battle to appoint a new director general in 1999. In a key decision well along in the intensely contested process, US officials supported New Zealand's candidate, Michael Moore, thereby contradicting their initial rhetoric about the need to encourage leadership by prominent developing states. In this way, they helped to polarize the two opposing camps, which in turn reduced the options for compromise and resolution of the crisis. US officials exacerbated this problem by insisting that the new director general support the explicit inclusion of labor and environmental considerations in trade negotiations. "The Clinton administration's apparent concession to the demands of labor and environmental constituencies undermined its strategy of engaging the emerging-market economies in global economic governance and imposed substantial costs on the WTO."[17] This is consistent with both Clinton's controversial speech at Seattle on sanctions and labor rights, and the finding above that his highest priority was reinforcing political support among Democratic Party constituencies.

The EU was at least as ineffective during the WTO leadership crisis. Individual EU members were split between candidates Moore and Supachai of Thailand to the point where the EU could do little more than issue a statement of "institutional support." Lacking any internal consensus, "the semi-integrated state of EU policymaking imposed substantial costs on an important global organization."[18]

The combination of a lack of US and EU preparedness in turn contributed to a disconnection between the two delegations that were expected to contribute the most prominent leadership in Seattle. Furthermore, there was considerable personal ill will between the two negotiators for these trading giants. Barchefsky and Brittan did not communicate directly with each other, and at times seemed to be intent on scoring political points by publicly embarrassing each other.[19] Certainly no one can expect that the principal US and EU negotiators will always be close friends; evidence from previous rounds demonstrates that, in fact, such friendships are rare. At the same time, however, a strong, effective working relationship between the two largest traders is crucial; at a minimum, it is essential that they see each other to be both "fair" and credible.[20] When this relationship breaks down, it is impossible to build the required US–EU consensus in a timely manner and strategically induce additional members into the circle of agreement.

Broadening the circle

In the process of gradually broadening the circle of agreement prior to Seattle, the two other Quad members, Japan and Canada also lacked the will to lead structurally, and indeed the means to do so. Japan's strategy was to lie low in order to avoid a leadership role in a "development" round that would surely highlight new steps to liberalize agriculture. It was precisely this continuing Japanese position, fortified by key traders South Korea and Switzerland, that merged with the EU to balance the US pursuit of deep agricultural liberalization. High-level Japanese officials also were not well positioned to help lead even in entrepreneurial ways because they were preoccupied with continuing internal economic and political turmoil and the 1997–1999 international financial crisis, which sharply slowed the economic growth and development of several countries in East Asia.

Canada's comparatively reduced role during this period was more surprising. Some senior officials have noted Canadian policy makers' declining interest and drive in recent years to provide important entrepreneurial leadership and support for US–EU structural leadership in the WTO as the North American basis of its trade has become increasingly predominant.[21] Indeed, from 1991 to 2000 the share of total Canadian exports destined for the United States increased from 76 to 87 percent![22] Thus, there also appears to have been an inadequate degree of coordination among the United States, the EU, and what traditionally had been the next most powerful traders, Japan and Canada.[23]

Even the World Trade Organization itself, as an institution, was embroiled in conflict and confusion in the months preceding the Seattle meeting. The 1998–1999 battle over selecting the director general to replace Renato Ruggiero (1995–1999) consumed precious time and political capital, and created ill will among not only country representatives but also the senior WTO officials in Geneva. Former senior WTO officials have reported that the new deputy director generals were not on speaking terms with each other during this period. Thus, because it lacked a director general and effective leadership at the top, senior members of the WTO secretariat could not play their traditionally important entrepreneurial role in facilitating development of the negotiating text and consensus building.[24] By the time Michael Moore was finally selected as the new director general, a mere three months remained to prepare for the ministerial.

The situation by 1999 was further complicated because the credibility of Ambassador Ali Mchumo of Tanzania as chair of the WTO General Council was undermined by his role in the battle over selecting the new director general.

Even though the WTO members were almost exactly split between Moore and Supachai, Mchumo proposed that the General Council agree to appoint Moore.

> Even the official minutes of this meeting make clear the dismay of Supachai's supporters at the chair's proposal. Those present at the meeting recalled gasps of surprise, followed by an acrimonious meeting that lasted late into the night and resumed the next day.[25]

Furthermore, Council chair Mchumo floated a draft declaration that added to the general uncertainty, highlighted disagreements between developed and developing countries, and made consensus building virtually impossible.[26]

Thus, WTO officials, like those from the EU, were operating under new leadership and in relatively new and uncharted territory. Senior WTO officials had no clearly defined plan or strategy for Seattle and, importantly, US leaders organizing the meeting did not make careful use of GATT-WTO officials' long experience with negotiating conferences. Furthermore, key developing and least developed states had been mobilized into action against a new round beginning with the Singapore Ministerial in 1996 and the EC's positions in particular on broadening the agenda to include the "new issues." As a result, these members flooded, even overwhelmed, the WTO preparatory process with proposals. Indeed, by the fall of 1999 there were about 100 separate submissions by developing and least developed member states regarding agenda items. The large majority asserted the demand to implement commitments made during the Uruguay Round before any formal commencement of a new round.

By the crucial point about a month before the meeting the negotiating draft remained far too long and disputed. Members insisted on their preferred wording and agenda items so late in the process that there was much more than the normal negotiating and sorting out of the agenda still to be accomplished at the meeting itself. Normally the Council chair and the WTO director general would have helped the United States, EU, and key members in carving out the agenda well in advance. Their entrepreneurial leadership in this situation would have been crucial, but was simply unavailable under all these constraints.

Under these circumstances, it was not surprising that a group of smaller LDCs joined a blocking coalition to press for their demands on implementation to be met before they would agree to launch a new round in Seattle.[27] Their consensus to block the progress on the draft declaration represented a major failure of structural leadership prior to the ministerial by the United States, the EU, and the increasingly fluid group of key trading member states.[28]

In the end, there is a certain irony in the sharply contrasting images of public and private structural leadership by US officials at the Seattle Ministerial. Publicly, President Clinton offered dramatic, detailed, and passionate pleas for the WTO members and Secretariat to "open the meetings, open the records, and let people file their opinions . . . in a free society, people want to be heard. And human dignity, and political reality, demand it today."[29] Inside the meeting rooms, however, United States Trade Representative Barchefsky was seen by some as ad hoc, stubborn, and overly exclusive in her decisions about which ministers were allowed to participate in key decisions and meetings. Certain experienced ministers from smaller states and regions worldwide were angered, most pointedly when some were barred from particular Green Room sessions. It is likely, however, that they were most concerned about their lack of timely access to information they could report to senior officials at home.

Overall, in retrospect the Seattle meeting seemed destined to fail. The process was certainly complicated by the extensive street protests, the USTR's conflicting roles as conference chair and US negotiator, and the US president's controversial interview for the Seattle newspaper. Moreover, the assertiveness and demands of key smaller developing and least developed states posed an important challenge to the leading states, their pyramiding process, and the WTO director general's goal of involving them in the process. Despite these problems, however, it was not inevitable that US–EC and small-group leadership would fail. If US and European political leaders and their top officials had set different priorities and made different decisions, WTO officials and other key ministers might have been even more effective as entrepreneurial leaders to help hammer out a consensus. They might, for example, have agreed to specific commitments on implementation in exchange for the decision to begin a new round at a designated future date. Thus, it was the weak structural leadership capability on the part of the United States and EU separately and nearly non-existent joint leadership capacity that in turn effectively disabled the ability of the most involved states to gradually develop a consensus among the membership at large for launching a new round.

However, it is also important to ask how, in the face of so many difficulties, problems, and failures, the Seattle Ministerial made as much progress as it did toward reaching a final agreement. Some experienced officials emphasized that Director General Moore was effective as an entrepreneurial leader in gathering small groups of ministers for traditional intensive consultations and Green Room sessions. He did facilitate significant progress. There was agreement or near agreement at the end in the key areas of agriculture, implementation, transparency, and the concerns of the LDCs in addition to implementation. Key final compromises were still required in the areas of investment, competition policy, and food safety. In the end, of course, there is no way to know, but in light of the substantial compromises and progress made, it is useful to consider how much more might have been agreed given additional time and small-group meetings.[30]

The "failed" session did have an important impact in the same way as other failed ministerials in GATT's past, such as the infamous 1988 Mid-Term Review of the Uruguay Round in Montreal. As is noted above, key issues were agreed and the remaining disagreements were significantly clarified. Furthermore, the massive demonstrations and negative press created a crisis environment for international trade. Seattle was certainly a focal point in not only trade regime development but also the public deliberation and debate of economic and financial globalization. In part because of the generally negative impressions about the WTO conveyed by the media during the Seattle Ministerial, over the ensuing months the majority of ministers became convinced that it was imperative to overcome the failure. Many delegates expressed the sense that without future progress, the overall trade regime could be in serious trouble. For example, in 2000 one leading reporter argued that:

> the search for consensus is often placed in the hands of multilateral organizations such as the World Trade Organization or the World Bank. These institutions have become even more ineffective because they have been given responsibilities that exceed their authority, capabilities and resources. It is hard to imagine that a single young, under-funded multilateral institution such as the WTO will ever be capable of providing the unifying framework needed to break the stalemate over the rules for international trade.[31]

In sum, Seattle was the "lowest point, but possibly even, in the end, the best for the system."[32] Experienced negotiators soon recognized that once again a key turning point in the process had to be used as the basis for a reversal. Dramatic failure had to be converted into a success in the near future. Certainly the successful launch two years later of the Doha Round suggests the validity of this understanding.

The launch at Doha

The Doha "development" Round negotiations were launched in November 2001, thus overcoming the "failure" of Seattle. Several major factors contributed to this outcome. Most important, the new US presidential administration by mid- and late 2001 had the political initiative and space of its first year, and the experienced Robert Zoellick made serious and effective efforts as USTR to take the leadership role in international trade, in part in order to reverse the failure of Seattle. This contrasts sharply with the final two years of the second Clinton administration in the aftermath of impeachment of the president. President Clinton had already achieved several major trade policy victories, culminating with the China PNTR, and ultimately his administration decided that the political costs of further alienating US labor constituencies were too high in the context of Vice President Gore's presidential campaign.

By itself, however, the political initiative and hard work of George W. Bush's administration might not have been sufficient to launch the new round. After all, there was little or no change in other key factors: President Bush's ideas, declared policies, and early initiatives in trade did not appear to be very different from those of President Clinton; Congress had not yet granted fast-track authority to Bush; and key business groups were still not overly enthusiastic about the benefits of a new trade round. Furthermore, early in the new administration, the new USTR, Robert Zoellick, lacked the close working relationship with, and easy access to, the president that had been important to Mickey Kantor and even Charlene Barchefsky. The other crucial factors were deep change in the international political context – specifically, September 11, which rapidly and fundamentally transformed the nature of both President Bush's foreign policy and US relations with states worldwide; sharp improvement in US–EU relations in trade policy; and greatly enhanced US–EU effectiveness in working with other key WTO members.

US presidential initiative and priority

President Clinton's trade representative in 1999 had as a clear priority the PNTR deal with China. After the 1996 congressional elections, and even more after PNTR with China, she was substantially constrained by the split between the president's trade policy and his main political base. At the outset, President George W. Bush's commitment to trade policy leadership seemed very similar to that of the first Clinton administration. In fact, the Bush administration pursued an ambitious agenda in 2001 of initiatives for the Free Trade Area of the Americas, deeper trade integration with Mexico, the resolution of US–European disputes, and bilateral agreements with Chile and Singapore.

Taking a page from the book on trade policy written under President Reagan and subsequently revised by the Bush and Clinton teams, the new administration intended to move "on multiple fronts" to "create a competition in trade liberalization."[33] Naturally, in light his experience as governor of Texas, George W. Bush pressed first on the Western Hemispheric initiative. At the Summit of the Americas in Quebec in 2001, the president joined thirty-three other heads of state in committing to negotiate a Free Trade Area of the Americas by January 2005.

With respect to the WTO, USTR Zoellick proved to be primarily concerned with regrouping after Seattle and launching a new round at Doha. Congress never granted President Clinton fast-track negotiating power, and USTR Barchefsky devoted much of her efforts to comparatively low-visibility deals that did not require congressional approval. The China PNTR agreement was the exception, and it exacted substantial political costs for the Clinton administration. In the context of a new presidential administration and stronger Republican position in Congress, President Bush's main agenda could be pursued without immediate need for "fast-track" authority. With a strong drive led by new USTR Robert Zoellick, US officials approached the Doha Ministerial with intensive leadership efforts at home and abroad. Beginning in the summer of 2001, Zoellick could devote most of his efforts and time to a successful rescue of the WTO process after the debacle at Seattle.

Even prior to his confirmation as USTR, Zoellick began reaching out to environmental groups and labor unions.[34] An example of this is the commitment to abiding by the rules of the US–Jordan free trade agreement, which was completed under the Clinton administration. The deal brokered between Jordan and the United States is unique in that "it makes tariff cuts conditional on each nation's compliance with its own laws on labor and the environment."[35] In the context of the Bush administration's general skepticism toward such commitments, Zoellick's acceptance of the labor and environment condition-ality demonstrated his commitment to a successful launch in Doha. Still, however, early in the administration the USTR was a relatively low-priority cabinet position lacking the kind of access to the president granted to his closest advisers and friends.

Sea change in US foreign policy and diplomatic strategy

The Doha meeting took place in the immediate aftermath of the September 11, 2001 terrorist attacks in the United States and the war in Afghanistan during September and October. The political climate following the attacks and the subsequent invasion of Afghanistan in October heightened the need of the United States to score a broad diplomatic and international success in the Doha Round, especially as a means to gather support and momentum for the "war on terror." Launching the round was a concrete way of reasserting broad US international leadership. The fact that the Doha meeting coincided with the outset of the "war on terror" clearly affected the negotiating positions of key states such as Pakistan. Its negotiator was reportedly instructed by the prime minister to abandon his adamant opposition and support a new round. Additionally, at Doha, WTO director general Michael Moore spoke about the need for cooperation following the shock of 9-11:

> Underscoring views from Washington and Brussels that the terrorist attacks on the US made strengthening the rules-based trading system all the more important, Mr. Moore said he was encouraged by the "spirit of cooperation and a realization of the importance of the task ahead seen recently."[36]

In the United States and the Congress in particular, September 11 strength-ened the domestic political support for the administration's foreign policy. Although the main thrust of US policy was the war on terrorism, both public opinion and political opponents in the Congress swung to support the president under emergency conditions.[37] The result was that USTR Robert Zoellick could set to work to complete the groundwork for the ministerial meeting knowing that he could count on renewed support at home.

Another factor contributing to the successful launch of Doha was the position taken by the European Union. Finally, the EU adopted a more flexible position on agriculture.[38] Speaking before a press conference on July 30, 2001, the British prime minister, Tony Blair, commented on the launch of a new trade round in Qatar: "Only a global round can provide the context for real liberalization of agriculture markets."[39] By promising to liberalize the agricultural sector, the EU demonstrated a level of structural leadership necessary to appease many of the LDCs and the Cairns Group and, effectively, eliminated a major reason why Doha could have failed.[40] The EU also moved in the direction of liberalization of low-end manufactured goods such as clothing and textiles. The EU protects these industries less than the United States, and was therefore able to "champion the push by developing countries for more market access."[41] EU support of this issue area served mainly to enhance developing countries' interest in negotiating at Doha.[42]

A basic factor in the Doha success was that the EU trade minister, Pascal Lamy, had had two years to prepare, whereas he had been in post only a few weeks prior to Seattle. Equally important, he proved to be highly effective in coordinating and co-leading with US officials, and in fact joint US–EU efforts in multilateral trade policy leadership improved radically as compared to 1999. This development set the stage for much more effective pyramiding by the United States and the EU in engaging newly active WTO members in a more flexible process of agenda setting.

In stark contrast to Seattle, therefore, top EU and US negotiators Pascal Lamy and Robert Zoellick had an unusually intense and effective working relationship. They had worked together beginning in the early 1990s in support of the G-7 summits. Indeed, for the EU the role of trade negotiator takes on a special importance.

Personal chemistry matters in trade policy even more than in other areas of transatlantic relations. Trade is the most important field of foreign policy where the EU consistently acts as one, and the extensive powers of Mr Lamy's office mean that much of Brussels' regular dialogue with Washington is channeled through him.[43] The two negotiators went to Qatar believing it to be imperative to launch a round and to shape the agenda on the basis of US–EU objectives.[44] It was no surprise, then, when "[t]hey hit it off" at Doha.[45] Their ability to work well together was fundamental to EU and US structural leadership of the ministerial. When it came to finalizing detailed agreements, however, the US and EU negotiators had many rounds of tough bargaining ahead. As Lamy said in March 2001, "We became friends under other circumstances. Friends are friends. But business is business."[46]

The launch of the Doha Round engaged the attention of trade ministers worldwide to a greater degree than the preparations for Seattle, particularly because Doha was situated against the backdrop of Seattle's failure. Furthermore, developed countries, led by the United States, devoted considerable attention to the LDCs before and during Doha, which they did not do prior to the Seattle Ministerial. Well before September 11, a new, more inclusive process with greater flexibility, including a series of preparatory meetings and deadlines for producing the "modalities" for negotiation, helped increase the legitimacy of senior WTO officials among the overall membership. These sessions also helped to focus the attention of busy ministers on the WTO process.[47] Because the developed countries, supported by the WTO secretariat, engaged the LDCs in the process at an early stage, the LDCs were able to increase their representation at ministerial meetings.[48] This contributed to the LDC ministers' enhanced sense of importance in the process, backed by the lingering threat that they might continue to block consensus.[49] These meetings also provided timely information for US and EC negotiators on key ministers' positions and inclinations, thus helping guide revisions to pyramiding strategy.

Most importantly, though, the US and EU were willing to compromise with the LDCs,[50] and thus they developed a degree of agreement with the LDCs that was virtually impossible at Seattle.[51] Additionally, the new director general "Supachai Panitchpakdi [of Thailand] was the first secretary general from a developing country, which was an important symbolic step stressing the WTO's global scope."[52] He made several entrepreneurial proposals and suggestions that helped align the views of developed and developing countries. Furthermore, by simply agreeing to locate the meeting in a developing country, Qatar, the developed members were able to deflect criticism from those who say that less developed countries are totally overlooked. The physical location of the meeting also greatly reduced the risk of antiglobalization protests; Qatar is still a long way from allowing a totally free flow of information and large-scale demonstrations of the Seattle sort.[53] At the same time, in comparison with most other states in the region, Qatar's ruler had been making steady, incremental steps toward political reform, and its media were relatively unrestricted. Finally, the Green Room process at Doha excluded some of the traditionally involved European states and actually was more often biased in the number of small countries, especially African developing and least developed states.

The participation of China as a new, "developing" WTO member also appears to have helped to engage the developing countries. Prior to the November meeting, the *Financial Times* noted that "Chinese support is likely to make other developing countries, especially in Asia, less resistant to another round."[54] China's rapid economic expansion and free-market orientation position it as a developing country with strong ties to the developed world; thus, China serves as a bridge between the two camps and can mitigate differing concerns. Equally important, interviews with negotiators for developing states confirmed deep concern about the likely effects of severe competition from China in products such as textiles. For this reason, the governments of LDCs expected to be most affected by Chinese exports were actively negotiating for compensation or the means to protect against an expected sudden loss of export markets. They needed Chinese, Western, and WTO support for measures to ease adjustment in the textiles and clothing sector. These factors contributed to a greater degree of mutual interests between key developed and developing countries, which in turn helped increase developing states' willingness to consider accepting a new round.

Overall, both before and at Doha the negotiating process for advancing the international trade regime was resilient in its ability to bounce back from what could have been a deep paralysis after Seattle. Preparations for the Doha Ministerial were far better than those prior to Seattle, including many more briefings and general meetings.[55] US and EU positions were developed and coordinated in advance, providing the basis for joint structural leadership, and WTO and other key officials coordinated the formulation of a much more developed negotiating draft. Once at Doha, "a sense of urgency kept the momentum going, because leaders felt that another failure could hurt the credibility of the WTO."[56]

Conclusion

In the first set of cases, why did Seattle fail and how was Doha subsequently able to succeed? Many factors contributed to the outcome at Seattle. First, beginning in 1992, President Clinton's ambitions concerning NAFTA and the WTO-based international trade regime required his administration to diverge significantly from the Democratic Party main line, costing him the bulk of his party's support for his trade efforts. Thus, by 1994 his senior political advisers judged that in the aftermath of passing NAFTA and the WTO agreement, future trade initiatives would have to be at least seen as neutral by basic Democratic constituencies. USTR Charlene Barchefsky accomplished much in this environment, but she had to work on less visible and controversial agreements "under the political radar screen" and avoid top political advisers by seeking approval directly from the president.

Next, by Seattle in late 1999, the impeachment scandal had lost Clinton his working relationship with the Republican side of Congress, which was his main base of political support for structural leadership with international trade initiatives. Third, the administration's highest-priority focus of achieving a PNTR compact with China both tied down senior officials' time and brought the ire of US labor unions. Once again, this cost the Clinton administration support with a core Democratic constituency. In the context of Vice President Gore's bid to win the Democratic nomination against Senator Bill Bradley, top White House advisers made it clear inside the administration that any WTO agreement must include a labor rights clause. President Clinton followed with his provocative proposal to link trade sanctions and labor rights in the midst of the Seattle Ministerial.

Fourth, the negotiating agenda for the Seattle Ministerial represented much more the priorities and preferences of EU negotiator Leon Brittan individually and the EU than any broader set of collective interests in trade policy liberalization. Next, Clinton's trade representative, Charlene Barchefsky, had a famously poor relationship with Brittan, the EU's negotiator until just prior to the ministerial; in fact, they would not talk with each other at all. Finally, Michael Moore, the new director general of the WTO, emerging from the bitter battle to fill that position, had been in his job for only two months when the Seattle Ministerial began. His efforts at Seattle were reported to be quite effective, but there just was not adequate time and negotiating space to carve out a negotiating text. These major leadership obstacles in the United States, the EU, US–EU relations, and the WTO secretariat in Geneva, combined with the manifest mistakes and different priorities of Barchefsky, Clinton, and the local police during the ministerial, substantially undermined US–EU structural leadership and the entrepreneurial efforts of Moore and key officials from other states.

To a significant degree, Doha was able to overcome the Seattle failure only because of the sharp shift in US relations with the rest of the world that September 11 engendered. Even before that date, however, much effort was made in the buildup to Doha not to repeat Seattle's mistakes. The most important single factor in this case was strong structural leadership on the part of the Bush administration. This time, the administration had the better part of a year to prepare for the event, and USTR Robert Zoellick drew on his experience to take a strong leadership role to prepare for the new ministerial. Furthermore, just as with past failed GATT ministerials, the sense of deep crisis engulfing the international trade system helped to create the political space and opportunities in the domestic politics of key states, which was necessary to reverse the situation.

The administration's effort would have come to naught, however, if other factors had not lined up in favor of a Doha success. In particular, China's new participation was instrumental in facilitating the engagement of developing and least developed countries in the process. The gentle relations that the United States had with most of the world in the wake of September 11 made for an environment exceedingly open to cooperation, in which opposition to progress of the round seemed in some ways inappropriate. Although the administration still did not have fast-track authority from Congress, the need for it was not as great, because of its success at establishing leadership and its general congressional support.

Another crucial factor was the close working relationship between Robert Zoellick and Pascal Lamy. The cooperative structural leadership of these two individuals was supported by the effective preparations in Geneva and the firm and organized management of the meeting by Qatar's minister. Finally, the mini-ministerial meetings held in Sydney and Montreal proved somewhat useful in engaging a wider, more representative set of trade ministers from least developed member states. When combined with much greater representation of African states and regional groups in Green Room sessions at Doha, the overall effect was to substantially enhance the participation, if not necessarily the direct influence, of least developed countries in the process.

Collapse at Cancún, 2003

The background to Cancún in 2003: higher EU and US foreign policy priorities and failed leadership in trade

There were two main differences in the leadership of WTO negotiations in 2004 as contrasted with 2003. First, and most important, in 2003 US and EU officials were not able to actively press key parties in the pyramiding process and manage the main negotiating coalitions, as they were prior to Doha in 2001 and during the summer of 2004. Why? First, a key difficulty was that the EU's CAP reform occurred too late, and US–EU negotiations over agriculture reached agreement less than one month before Cancún. Additionally, US and EU trade ministers were not in agreement over the role and relative importance of the four Singapore Issues of investment, competition policy, transparency in government procurement, and trade facilitation (for which working groups had been set up during the Singapore Ministerial in 1996). As a result, in 2003 there was not sufficient structural leadership by US and EU officials in particular to create a focal point in the negotiating process. Key negotiating issue areas were too far behind in their schedules, and, not unlike in Seattle, the conference chair's negotiating draft left too many major disagreements to be resolved at the meeting itself.

Second, unlike in 2004, prior to Cancún entrepreneurial and structural leaders failed to produce a basic package of proposed agreements that offered clear benefits to each major party and coalition. The EU and G-10 needed to win something on the Singapore Issues, while the G-90 of developing and least developed states (see p. 144), and to a lesser extent the new "G-20" of leading developing states, would not make the required bargains until the EU and US negotiators offered further compromises in agriculture. Furthermore, the G-20 leaders focused more on group cohesion than on advancing the process, and key Caribbean ministers in the ACP and G-90 established a blocking position rather than concede on the EU's demands on the Singapore Issues.

Finally, the collapse of negotiations at Cancún created the missing focal point. The media, critics, and key government officials all interpreted the failure as a crisis with threatening implications for the global trade system. This contributed substantially to the degree of joint US–EU leadership as well as entrepreneurial leadership emerging by 2004, which culminated with the "July Package" approved on August 1.

Failed US–EU structural leadership in 2003

The establishment of mini-ministerial meetings in Sydney (2002) and Montreal (2003) with about twenty-five key trade ministers represented an attempt to continue the process followed before Doha. By this time, however, the beneficial effects on LDC ministers were dissipating. With an ever-expanding membership, this strategy had proved to be an effective way of keeping trade policy at the WTO a high priority for member states. However, African and other LDC ministers began to doubt whether participation in these meetings actually translated to any influence over the negotiating agenda or draft texts. New key players such as China and increased assertiveness by coalitions such as the African Group, the African, Caribbean and Pacific countries (ACP), and LDCs diversified the playing field of the WTO and opened new opportunities for least developed states to shape the process.[57]

In 2003, US trade officials were ambitiously executing their "competitive liberalization" approach with a series of bilateral and regional trade initiatives in different stages of completion, which they expected to provide leverage over the involved states in WTO negotiations. The more subtle aspect of this is to enhance the leverage of US structural leadership by demonstrating that its position without an international trade agreement would be continually improving relative to other players. During the summer, recently signed bilateral agreements with Singapore and Chile were awaiting congressional approval. FTA negotiations were under way with Australia, Morocco, all five Central American states for the Central American Free Trade Agreement (CAFTA), and five states in the Southern African Customs Union: Botswana, Lesotho, Namibia, South Africa and Swaziland.[58] Finally, on July 1, the United States announced its generalized system of preferences (GSP) approval, to include preferences expanded to Argentina, the Philippines, and Turkey. Preferential access to the US market is an important lever for US structural leadership because certain African and Caribbean states in particular depend on regional and GSP for their exports.

However, other closely related and important issues were at play. Looming large over the entire Doha process was the unresolved issue of access to patented retroviral drugs for HIV/AIDS treatment. US government officials opposed to public licensing for importing patented drugs confronted the Brazilian government, in particular, as the worldwide leader in asserting the right of the state to act in a public health emergency. India was prominently positioned to supply generic HIV/AIDS drugs as part of the increasingly important bilateral economic arrangements with Brazil. Although the issue was defused by a last-minute agreement between the US and Brazilian presidents, it soured the environment for major compromises during the critical months of June and July. The associated WTO agreement on TRIPs was not completed until August 30, only ten days before Cancún.

Also complicating the process of pre-negotiations was the cotton initiative by the four least developed African states, which pressed the United States in particular for major reforms of its agricultural subsidies at the same time as a WTO dispute settlement ruling against its subsidies. The USTR would not directly address the Africans' demands outside of the broader international agricultural negotiations. Despite the logic of his position, he failed to provide moral or structural leadership on the issue to at least help defuse the tension created by very poor African states demanding relief from heavy US subsidization of its producers and exporters. At the same time, however, it is likely that he was constrained by Brazil's case brought on US cotton payments. In June, a WTO panel ruled that subsidies to US cotton farmers in 1999–2002 through marketing loans, export credits, commodity certificates, and direct payments lowered world market prices and harmed Brazil's trade interests. The United States was required to end them by July 1, 2005.

Furthermore, other senior US officials were preoccupied with more crucial questions, particularly the Iraq invasion of March 2003 and the ensuing war and occupation. Even after President Bush declared major combat operations ended on May 1, US foreign policy leaders were heavily engaged with Iraq and the opposition of French and German leaders, among others. At the G-8 summit in France during early June, the leaders generally supported the Doha Round and objectives, but could not make the key commitments required to accelerate the process. This was in part because the EU's CAP reform was still under negotiation, and there was no common US–EU position on agriculture. Furthermore, both Bush and British prime minister Blair were enmeshed in the Iraq issue.

About a week later, on June 10, twenty-seven developing states presented a position paper in Geneva demanding the resolution of their main issues, including agreement in Cancún on the modalities for agriculture and non-agricultural market access. Their position was generally opposed to the WTO-facilitated decision to have Ambassador Carlos Pérez del Castillo of Uruguay, as chair of the General Council, begin consultations with members on the Singapore Issues. However, this position was clearly more moderate than that of many LDCs, as represented by the G-90, which combines the ACP, LDC, and African Union groups for the purpose of negotiating with the largest trading states. This group of twenty-seven developing states evolved directly into the important new G-20. In fact, it included all the most important developing states in the G-20, except Egypt, Nigeria, and South Africa.

European leaders were preoccupied during the spring and summer of 2003 trying to finalize both the major EU expansion with ten new states and the design of and agreement on the EU's new constitution. Closely related, the EU's CAP reform was required by January or very early in 2003 to provide time for US and EU negotiations and formulation of joint leadership strategy and positions. Instead, a limited reform package was not even drafted until mid-June. Then, on June 26, as the EU announced its decision to reform the CAP once again, the USTR and US Secretary of Agriculture responded promptly to increase the external pressure on them to make serious compromises in the Doha Round:

> The United States believes that the WTO agricultural negotiations must be ambitious and provide real reform and improved market access for U.S. farmers and ranchers. That's why we've proposed to eliminate export subsidies, slash global agricultural tariffs, and cut $100 billion in annual trade-distorting domestic farm support in a fashion that harmonizes the limits at much lower levels. We've joined the voices of reform in the developing world in calling on others, particularly those with the largest subsidies, such as the European Union and Japan, to embrace reform.[59]

The EU did not formalize CAP reform with regulations from the Council until after Cancún. Indeed, the second set of regulations was only completed in late April 2004. In sharp contrast, this crucial step had been completed about eight months prior to the Seattle meeting.

The US–EU August 13 draft agreement on agriculture was produced in response to a joint request by the ministers at a preparatory meeting in Montreal of July 28–30. These ministers sought to avoid repeating the Uruguay Round US–EC deadlock over agriculture, but instead of advancing the process, the draft galvanized criticism from the Cairns Group, the G-20, and the LDC and G-90 groups. Many LDCs reacted strongly against lack of special and differential treatment provisions. Brazil and other G-20 states objected to a clause specifying that competitive agricultural exporting states would not be treated the same as LDCs or major food-importing members. Key Brazilian officials, in particular, appear to have been offended by this clause. Furthermore, developing and LDC state officials criticized the United States for less ambitious reductions in domestic support programs and border protection, despite the new offers in reducing export subsidies.

With CAP reform still not even official and the US–EU agriculture agreement completed only by mid-August, there was effectively no time prior to Cancún to win over key parties such as Brazil and India, and coalitions such as Cairns, the Africans, ACP, and G-90. US and EU negotiators were not effective in dealing individually and in small groups with the key G-20 states, particularly Brazil, Argentina, India, and South Africa, in order to head off the group's formal formation and agenda. Most important, the United States and Brazil were not in basic agreement about either the FTAA or the WTO Doha Round, and thus US structural leadership initiatives for bilateral and regional agreements offered no leverage over Brazil. In fact, Brazilian officials were skeptical toward, if not directly opposed to, the FTAA as perceived by US officials. The Brazilians were engaging in their own "competitive liberalization" strategy with India and other G-20 states, in part as a way to balance US–EU structural leadership and pyramiding prior to and during Cancún.

Thus, as leaders in their own regional free trade agreements (FTAs), the principal states in the G-20 required much more attention and negotiation than were provided by US and EU negotiators. Their negotiators were not deterred in their actions by clear US threats to resort to multiple bilateral and regional FTAs if the WTO process failed. US and EU FTA activity was probably even counterproductive with regard to deepening cooperation among these key states. Additionally, Brazilian officials would certainly have raised their expectations for US and EU agricultural liberalization when informed in June and August by the WTO of their success in cases brought against US subsidization of cotton and EU sugar subsidies, respectively.[60] For all of these reasons, it could be argued that rather than a comprehensive agreement at Cancún that did not go very far beyond the draft US–EU agreement in agriculture, senior officials of at least Brazil and India preferred no agreement.

The other linchpin to US–EU structural leadership in 2003 was a common, or at least very effectively coordinated, position on the package and relative importance of Singapore issues in the Doha Round. From its earliest roots, the Singapore Issues were fundamentally the EU's agenda, and with the approach of Cancún their officials seemed unwilling to offer any indications of possible compromise. While careful not to contradict or criticize the EC position publicly, senior US officials, for example at the TNC meeting in Geneva on June 10, clearly argued that each of the four issues should be negotiated on its own merits in a different format. They did agree with the EU position that modalities were to be agreed for each. At the same time, it was clear that US officials were more willing to compromise for the sake of an overall trade agreement. They were generally understood by other ministers to be more flexible on the first two Singapore Issues, investment and competition policy, as required to gain the agreement of many smaller trading states, and the G-90 in particular.

Increasingly, it became clear that US negotiators would provide structural leadership for trade facilitation, the fourth and least controversial element of the four, and somewhat less so for transparency in government procurement, the next least difficult item. In this way, the US position was responsive to clear signals before Cancún that key developing states and many LDCs would refuse to agree to negotiate the Singapore Issues without more substantial US–EU reductions in their domestic agricultural support programs.

In contrast, the EU held out on the Singapore Issues, most likely in order to avoid making compromises both before and during the Cancún meeting. EU trade negotiator Pascal Lamy believed that developing countries, if not LDCs, should understand that agreements on investment and competition make sense because they are important to their economic growth and development. Why block agreements that will facilitate foreign direct investment and competitive economies? The smaller the economy, the less leverage with large companies and the more to be gained from common investment rules. At the same time, structural US–EU leadership required some signals for likely, or at least possible, compromises on this basic disagreement. Without this, it appeared that the EU preferred no agreement to one without all four Singapore Issues. Finally, it can be argued that as a result of the EU's position, General Council chair Castillo dedicated a disproportionate amount of time and effort until mid-August trying to negotiate modalities for the Singapore Issues.

These issues acquired a symbolic importance by the Seattle Ministerial in 1999 as the blocking point for least developed and developing members that objected to major delays in the implementation of certain Uruguay Round agreements, including the core issue of agricultural reform. Since at least 2001, the Singapore Issues had also been opposed by states concerned about the implications for their domestic regulatory regimes regarding investment and government procurement. Least developed states are concerned about the competitiveness of local companies once foreign corporations establish themselves in their economies under the trade regime investment and competition frameworks. After resisting considerable pressure by certain OECD states to agree to the Multilateral Agreement on Investment (MAI), many least developed and developing states are suspicious of the breadth in types of investment covered and rights established for foreign companies. Furthermore, key INGOs such as Oxfam pressed hard on the MAI issue, encouraging LDCs not to agree. The leading international organization in the development area, the United Nations Development Programme (UNDP), circulated a new book in 2003 on trade and human development which argued that "an investment agreement under the current world trade regime will likely considerably limit developing countries' policy autonomy."[61]

It was difficult to generate even the traditional level of pressure for compromise at a mid-term review in the period leading to Cancún. Major segments of the negotiating work were substantially behind, and the WTO director general tried to capitalize on this to generate momentum for tough bargaining, but if anything the distance between key parties was perceived as too great, realistically, to be resolved at a ministerial. Rather, as with the preparations for Seattle, many ministers likely believed that the chances for a meaningful mid-term agreement were not very good. Whereas prior to the "July Package" as adopted August 1, 2004, there was excitement and an anticipation of possible breakthrough, there was simply no critical turning point or trade policy crisis to create domestic political space before the Cancún meeting in 2003.

Leadership and bargaining at Cancún, September 2003

In addition to the differences between key ministers prior to the meetings, the process at Cancún was not adequate to induce the required bargaining and compromises. For reasons explained below, the real bargaining began too late and too much time was dedicated to only the Singapore Issues. Overlapping with the first factor above, because the United States and EU were so late in their own negotiations that they were surprised by the extent of G-20 cohesion and ability to slow the pyramiding process. The worse the prospects for agreement looked, the less the ministers of key Caribbean, ACP, and G-90 states perceived they would lose with a no-agreement outcome. Also, many of the most prominent IGO and NGO leaders were advising LDC and developing state officials that the deal on the table was not worth their serious compromises.

At Cancún it was not only the EU that needed to compromise on the Singapore Issues, and in fact its lateness in doing so likely reinforced the G-10 (most protectionist states in agriculture) countries' insistence that they would reduce their barriers only in exchange for agreements to open markets in non-agricultural products and to include at least one of the Singapore Issues: trade facilitation. Some small Caribbean states in particular clearly preferred no agreement to the main proposals on the table, whereas the EU minister did, in fact, need to win some significant concession in terms of the Singapore Issues. Furthermore, ministers from developing states such as India and Mauritius insisted on maintaining high barriers to LDC products while USTR Zoellick demanded that all states, even LDCs, commit to a minimum common denominator: bind, or set ceilings on, tariffs and negotiate trade facilitation. Neither US nor EU negotiators were prepared to work through these confrontations.

Despite these several difficulties, it is possible that extraordinary structural leadership by the US and EU negotiators and entrepreneurial leadership by the conference chair, the WTO director general, and other ministers could have resolved the disagreements. Certainly there were divergent preferences among key states, and even between the United States and the EU, but there was also substantial agreement in key areas of most issues. The meeting failed because those possible zones of agreement were not fully or effectively pursued and exploited by top negotiators.

The first basic reason in this regard was a failure of EU structural leadership and lack of US–EU negotiating strategy on the Singapore Issues. EU negotiator Lamy waited until the Saturday of a ministerial that began on a Thursday to indicate that he would be willing to exclude the most controversial Singapore Issues in order to reach an overall agreement. This, in turn, triggered a hard-line response by the G-10 of hardcore agricultural protectionist states such as South Korea. They asserted that without significant inclusion of Singapore Issues there could be no major agricultural reform.

A second reason was that despite the last-minute resolution of the HIV/AIDS drugs issue by Presidents Bush and Cardoso (of Brazil), USTR Zoellick (in close coordination with Minister Lamy) did not visibly commit to positive compromises, effectively and reasonably manage the African cotton initiative, provide positive inducements to key LDC ministers, and actively manage the evolving G-20 coalition. On the Singapore Issues, US negotiators seemed reluctant to undermine the EU position, and they offered no early or likely specific compromises to help gain consensus from the most opposed LDCs. In responding to the cotton initiative led by the four very poor African states, Zoellick was perceived more as irritable, even arrogant, rather than the polished diplomat well experienced in African trade politics. It was understood that his position on cotton was constrained by his need to negotiate an overall agricultural agreement, which was in turn the most sensitive issue in domestic politics. However, his attitude toward the four small states needed at least to acknowledge the untenable situation caused by substantial US subsidies to cotton producers and manufacturers. This failure, in turn, soured the environment required for winning over other LDCs and ACP states to the idea that there could be an agreement which would benefit them more than the no-agreement alternative. Specifically, the US–EU emphasis on phasing out agricultural export subsidies did not offer concrete gains in agriculture to many LDCs, which expected deep reductions in domestic support programs and import barriers.

Also critical, US officials failed to take adequate account of the G-20 and particularly its leaders. Certainly the history of such broad-based developing state and LDC negotiating coalitions suggested weakness under the pressure of an actual meeting. Still, as is explained above, this time there were strong indicators in July and August of unusual seriousness of purpose and determination on the part of G-20 leaders. In light of the USTR's apparent surprise about the G-20's coherence and staying power, he was either ill advised by senior staff or mistaken in his own judgments, or possibly both.

The third key factor was the G-20's heavy focus on holding the group together and establishing itself as a power to be reckoned with. Their leaders appeared to be dedicating an undue amount of time and effort at holding press conferences and meetings regarding the coalition itself rather than addressing the most important negotiating issues. More specifically, throughout much of the process the G-20 appeared intransigent, with a blocking or heavily "claiming" strategy. Led by Brazil, Argentina, India, South Africa, and others, including China, the G-20 aimed to prevent the US–EU pyramiding process from building the consensus necessary to forge an interim agreement. Because of the EU-US failures, for example focusing mainly on a divide and conquer strategy, and their own, the G-20 ended up reinforcing the blocking position of a few ACP states that sought to paralyze the entire process. As the EU and US focused their efforts on breaking up the G-20, El Salvador exited at Cancún, and Peru and Colombia followed, each in the context of a choice posed by US officials: exit the G-20 or forgo a bilateral FTA with the United States.[62] But in this situation their actions only caused the ministers of the more powerful G-20 states, and even many small ones, to dig in their heels.

The final cluster of factors involves the entrepreneurial leadership of the meeting by WTO officials and conference chair Luis Ernesto Derbez of Mexico. Derbez in particular was criticized by some ministers for dedicating the entire Green Room process, right into the Saturday morning, to the Singapore Issues. Given the opportunity, WTO director general Supachai might have addressed agriculture earlier, but in any case even on the Saturday morning during the last substantive Green Room session, only the Singapore Issues were on the table. Lamy reportedly expected the Green Room process to engage agriculture much sooner. Furthermore, for the issues at stake in the Green Room, the unprecedented number of African and ACP ministers involved were not able or willing to win over their colleagues from the other African, ACP, and LDC states.

Finally, as chair of the ministerial, Derbez was also criticized for ending the meeting prematurely. The abrupt ending certainly caught some ministers and many close observers by surprise. Surely it was frustrating and aggravating for those negotiators still expecting to engage in the usual process of eleventh-hour brinksmanship, often including an extension of the negotiation by a day or more, to create heavy pressure to compromise or fail. This author does not give much credibility to this claim, however, because there simply had not been adequate progress on the main issues and overall negotiating package to justify an extension of the process. It is certainly possible that Derbez could have more effectively managed the balance in time dedicated to agriculture and the Singapore Issues, but it is simply not possible to know how much difference that would have made.

The "July Package": renewed leadership and gradual agreement in 2004

The failure of Cancún itself created precisely the crisis mentality and publicity required to capture the attention and focus of senior leaders and attentive political constituencies in states worldwide in 2004. As critics of the global trade regime heralded the importance of the collapse, the trade and foreign economic policy leaders in key capitals worked to develop ideas and compromises in the Doha Round process. Additionally, the sense of urgency was raised and maintained by reiterating the fact that both the USTR and the EC trade commissioner would be replaced later in the year, and the US administration might turn over after the November elections. The visible movement was not immediate, as, for example, the USTR would not join the EU negotiator and the WTO director general to meet with G-20 officials in South America in early 2004, but Zoellick gradually realized that he would have to deal with the G-20. Despite the intense political pressures of a presidential election year, he provided clear structural leadership by sending a letter to trade ministers worldwide in January 2004 inviting them to make the most of the coming months and arguing that the Doha process could reach agreement. In early May, EU ministers Pascal Lamy and Franz Fischler, in turn, sent a letter to their trade partners offering a significant compromise in terms of special treatment for the weakest and most vulnerable trading states.

Just as the US invasion of Iraq dominated the foreign policy agenda during the spring and summer of 2003, by 2004 it was clear that the continuing insurgency and nation building in Iraq would be by far the most salient foreign policy issue in the presidential campaign. However, with Senator Kerry constantly criticizing the administration for its loss of traditional US allies over Iraq, by 2004 the president's political advisers and campaign leaders likely decided that media coverage of presidential and US leadership and coalition building in trade would provide a helpful balance to Kerry's arguments. For example, in July, just two weeks before the WTO agreement was to be completed, President Bush signed the AGOA Acceleration Act of 2004 (AGOA III), which extended the special trade benefits in the African Growth and Opportunity Act from 2008 to 2015.

With the EU's CAP reform formalized in April, the path was finally cleared for careful coordination between US and EU officials. In agriculture, US and EU officials were agreed, at least at a general level, on phasing out export subsidies, substantially reforming domestic subsidies, and lowering tariffs. By June, if not earlier, they reached a key agreement to jointly push for consensus on a blended formula for tariff reductions, the most controversial of the three agricultural issue areas, which included both the "banded" and the "Swiss" approaches. Still, EU and US preferences diverged over the subsidies issue, where EU officials mainly sought reform while US negotiators also aimed for reductions.

Errors were recognized and corrected in the EU's strategy for the Singapore Issues, and the US strategy was largely adopted. Gradually the EU agreed to drop the demand for inclusion of competition and investment policy in the Doha agenda in exchange for agreement by other parties to continue negotiations in Geneva outside the round itself. This allowed the US and EU officials to jointly promote formal inclusion of the less controversial issue, trade facilitation, and possibly also government procurement, but with the understanding that substantial compromises would be required in agriculture in order to gain the agreement of LDCs in particular. Additionally, US and EU officials understood that significant progress in reducing trade barriers to non-agricultural products (non-agricultural market access, NAMA) would be required to win the agreement of G-10 states such as Japan and South Korea in reducing agricultural subsidies and import barriers. Furthermore, progress in NAMA tariff reductions was important to gaining the agreement of key political constituencies in the US and EU states for a final Doha Round package.

Beginning in April, WTO deputy director general Rufus Yerxa provided important entrepreneurial leadership on the issue of trade facilitation. He initiated several informal meetings with key ministers from developing states, leading to a heads of delegation meeting on 29 April where it appeared that a consensus could be developed to include trade facilitation in the July package. Through the early to middle months of 2004, other key leaders and coalitions worked to produce positive bargaining positions.

At a crucial meeting in Paris on May 14, at the same time as the OECD summit, twenty-eight ministers were able to make a breakthrough by emphasizing the feasibility of exchanging substantial compromises in the main agricultural issues for a strong agreement in market opening for non-agricultural products. This meeting, representing significant entrepreneurial leadership by senior Mexican officials, created a key focal point in the negotiations in that the parties began to sense that an overall framework agreement could be reached in the ten weeks remaining before the end of July deadline. WTO director-general Supachai observed, "We are beginning to see a shape for the final outcome of our July package." Brazilian foreign minister Celso Amorim concluded, "I sense a positive movement of all major actors and it makes me optimistic."[63] The media reports and many experts tend to identify later meetings, especially by mid-July, as the focal or breakthrough point, but these sessions in May represent the true turning point.

In the aftermath of this key meeting, Kenya's minister, with the implicit if not explicit approval of US officials, provided entrepreneurial leadership in offering to win the agreement of other African and related states for the market opening in exchange for a major bargain in agriculture. Most important, after small-group bargaining sessions held in the following weeks, the LDC and developing state officials were able to gain the agreement of their coalitions and regions, and the G-10 states and EU and US negotiators could compromise in agriculture in return for market opening for other products and substantive negotiation of trade facilitation.

At the beginning of June, the entrepreneurial minister from New Zealand, Tim Groser, who chaired the agricultural negotiations (the WTO Committee on Agriculture), announced that there was adequate consensus on the domestic support issue to draft a text that would reflect agreement at about the 80 percent level. The largest remaining challenge then was how to build agreement on an approach to market access (tariff reductions), the most difficult issue of all. Resolving this issue would require bridging the gap between the US–EU position of a blended formula and strong G-20 opposition. Just days later, June

8–10, the Group of Eight (G-8) held their annual summit at Sea Island, Georgia. Security issues were paramount, but the leaders were able to agree to "move expeditiously" to establish a framework agreement on the key Doha Round issues by the end of July. Equally important, they publicly confirmed the basic formula established for a deal on trade and development: reducing agriculture subsidies and market barriers (including cotton), increasing market openings for trade in goods, increasing opportunities in the services, and enhancing economic development.

In a stroke of US–EU structural leadership supported by entrepreneurial efforts of other key ministers, a small, informal negotiating group was formed in the May–June period by the US, EU, Brazilian, Indian, and Australian ministers. Its composition reflected the structural leadership position in agriculture established by the G-20 and Brazil and India in particular, as well as the Cairns Group, where Australia was prominent. Essentially, US and EC officials decided that direct participation by these three key states would be required in order to later win the agreement of the additional ministers required for a minimum winning coalition. The G-5 or FIPs (Five Important Persons) process proved critical to carving out the specifics of a bargain that could be sold to the other G-20 and Cairns members. This consensus, in turn, was gradually broadened to include the G-10 members on the one side and the ACP, African, G-33, and G-90 groups on the other.[64] The five ministers worked intensively to eventually achieve agreement on what became the July package, leaving mainly the question of whether the crucial LDC ministers not directly represented could be won over.

Immediately after the G-8 summit, the FIPs group met informally in São Paulo, Brazil, during the UNCTAD (United Nations Conference on Trade and Development) XI ministerial conference. The FIPs meetings and other events associated with this UNCTAD session in mid-June also proved decisive. Brazil and others strongly opposed the US and EU blended approach to cutting agricultural tariffs as "unbalanced" and unacceptable for developing states. Therefore, just before the meeting, the G-20 released their own approach to market access: a set of principles that avoided the specific disputes and attempted to create space for a compromise between LDC demands to emphasize special and differential treatment and the US requirement for the LDCs to bind tariffs. In parallel, in the UNCTAD meeting the Brazilian president, Lula da Silva, offered an important compromise by proposing that eighty-eight least developed and developing states should be eligible for inclusion in a revised general system of trade preferences. At the same time, the EU drew both support for and skepticism toward a high-visibility offer to give the G-90 (minus South Africa) the round for "free." In a clear gesture of structural leadership, both US and EU negotiators indicated their willingness to consider a different approach to work through the fundamental blocking point: market access. Thus, the progress in Brazil led to another FIPs meeting a week later in order to negotiate a new, more specific approach to market access.

Because the FIPs process essentially represented a five-way sharing of structural leadership in the agriculture issue area, the other key negotiating coalitions were clearly anxious about the outcomes. Public protests at the lack of direct representation in the FIPs were issued on the one side by the G-10, protectionist importing states led by Switzerland and Japan, as well as on the other side by the African, ACP, and LDC groups. The G-90 states used their ministerial meeting in Mauritius on July 13 both to coordinate their final positions and to call on the G-20 and FIPs to fully incorporate their proposals. The objections to the FIPs process by least developed states were mirrored by various NGO protests against the "undemocratic" process, and warnings of dire results if the needs of poor farmers were not addressed. Indeed, leading INGOs and their coalitions sent letters of concern to the G-20 ministers individually and to key NGOs in each of their home countries.

On 16 July, WTO director-general Supachai and General Council chair Shotaro Oshima circulated the draft framework text on the Doha Round trade negotiations. This set in motion the last-ditch effort to build a minimum winning consensus group around a relatively general agricultural text (Annex A to General Council Decision) by the end of July. In the end, the final package approved on August 1, 2004 in Geneva by the WTO General Council included in agriculture only a set of statements more like principles than precise commitments. Instead of a specific tariff reduction formula, it agreed on reductions proportional to the extent of the tariff. Similarly, it called for reducing only the most trade-distorting subsidies, surely a concession to the EU. The G-10 won agreement that there would be weaker restrictions on "sensitive products," developing states would have special and differential treatment, and LDCs would be exempt from commitments. They also agreed to a priority deal in cotton, large tariff reductions on industrial products, and more aggressive negotiation of services.

The lack of specific wording on special products or duty- and quota-free treatment for imports from LDCs drew public criticism from various LDC states. With some justification, they argued that Annex A was much more precise on issues important to developed countries. One prominent coalition of five INGOs in the areas of development and the environment advocated the rejection of the draft agreement. Still, because the package as a whole was critical to resolving each issue, neither the US nor EU negotiators could agree to specific wording in the issues of most importance to the G-20 and LDCs until the overall draft text was much more concrete.

The July package included new commitments not only across all three main areas of agriculture but also for non-agriculture market access, the two Singapore Issues of less controversy – trade facilitation and government procurement – and other areas. Overall, it established adequate progress to trigger the scheduling of a deadline for more advanced agreements by July 2005, which would lead to a "final" ministerial meeting in Hong Kong to complete the Doha Round in December. If successful eventually, the round would most significantly finally draw LDCs in particular, but also many developing states, much more substantially into the trade regime. By finally regulating the three main areas of agricultural policy as related to trade, and by establishing a fuller, more precise approach to special and differential treatment, the international trade system finally would be established as central to economic development, despite the certainty of continuing controversy about its real contribution to social economic advancement in a broader sense in LDCs. The further reduction of tariffs on industrial products would reassert and deepen the trade regime's role in this important area. Furthermore, its rules would again be refined and made more precise in issue areas such as rules, and substantially extended in scope to the new areas of trade facilitation and government procurement. WTO authority in dispute settlement would likely be affirmed and extended somewhat by adding certain specific elements to the process.

Once again, the United States and EU made significant gains in jointly leading the organization to establish a foothold in important new areas, despite their need to compromise away the depth in these reforms. This time, however, from the beginning there was a novel reversal of traditional positions, with the EC negotiator advocating early for both a new round and an extensive set of new bargaining issue areas. In the end, it turned out that this attempt at leadership was neither sufficiently collectively focused nor carefully coordinated with US leaders. US officials had to gradually persuade EC ministers to moderate their demands and expectations, especially for the new issue areas of investment and competition policy.

Importantly, the Brazilian and Indian ministers established themselves as co-leaders in the most contentious issue area, agriculture, because they were able to gradually press the US and EC for substantial agricultural reforms they would not offer on their own. In this way, once again the ground was prepared for deeper agreements in a future round, but for the first time there was also a precedent set for shared structural leadership beyond the United States and the EU at the very heart of the international trade negotiating process.

Part III

Conclusion

6 Why international institutions fail and succeed

The global trade regime is the result of an unusually long and rich history of international negotiations. This negotiating process is based on well-established traditions, expectations, and rules, which offer vital insights for international cooperation across other key issue areas. Fundamental differences in the resources and leverage brought to these negotiations are most effectively studied through structural leadership. In this context, patterns of co-leadership, pyramiding, strategic sequencing, and coalition-building processes of critical importance to international bargaining are extremely well illustrated in the international trade context. Bargaining innovation, problem solving, and maneuvering toward agreements are captured with the concept of entrepreneurial leadership, which is also well developed in multilateral trade negotiations. Entrepreneurial leadership in trade is especially rich with insights about the formulation and management of focal points and reversals in bargaining outcomes.

Intellectual leadership and innovation, particularly external ideas mediated by inside participants and insights from government experts in the most involved agencies and departments, are also central to regime development. Academics, experts on government advisory panels and committees, and activists from nongovernmental organizations have also contributed important ideas about both negotiating process and issue area content. Ideas from both inside and outside the most involved governments play crucial roles, for example, as entirely new issue areas are incorporated into this broad-based regime, and as INGOs and other public international organizations increasingly influence the proposals and positions of smaller states in particular.

Although this book finds that critical episodes of political leadership in trade are not as disjointed and infrequent as they appear to be in most other issue areas, domestic political economic interests, particularly in the largest trading states, have been consistent and crucial constraints on the pace and substance of international trade negotiations. Even in the 1940s and 1950s, therefore, the puzzle is to explain how and why powerful domestic political economic interests are balanced or compromised by policy makers in order to pursue broader foreign economic policy goals. Often the answer has been that a US president's belief system strongly inclines him toward trade liberalization and he presents trade policy as a central element of American diplomatic and security interests. In other words, the president restrains the security complex or endows it with officials who understand trade policy to be part of, or at least fully consistent with, national and international security policy. Equally important, however, is that international political leadership by officials from other states has become increasingly essential to successful initiatives and agreements.

Having a single, clear explanation of key factors driving trade regime development is most important for two reasons. First, the regime itself is central to the international economic exchanges and connections of states, markets, and companies worldwide. Second, as the most longstanding and developed example of negotiations within an international regime, it is rich with fundamental insights into the evolution of other regimes. In this regard, avoiding certain errors or weaknesses in the trade bargaining process is just as relevant as emulating its strengths and accomplishments. As both the independence and the centralization of the WTO's roles continue to grow incrementally, it is also crucial to investigate more thoroughly the effects and implications of its authority. At the same time, it is crucial to examine its credibility and legitimacy with the most involved actors, both governmental and private.

The most accurate and analytically useful way to characterize the causes of trade regime development at key points in time is the political leadership of negotiations, especially in its structural and entrepreneurial forms. At the same time, domestic political constraints have been pervasive in the major trading states, including the United States and France most prominently, thus requiring that trade policy leaders constantly manage protectionist or nationalist interests and coalitions. When the incentives or goals of leaders and protectionists converge, for example in advance of national elections, it is nearly impossible to advance trade liberalization. Elements of each of the other most relevant theories outlined in Chapter 1 are useful and important, but even in combination these approaches do not suffice to explain the outcomes of trade negotiations. Despite widespread use of the term "hegemony," there is little evidence that US officials dictated or dominated the rules and procedures of international trade:

> American leaders, whether in government or the private sector, recognized the very limited extent to which they could control major developments in the world economy. Still, there is no question that the leadership of the United States in Bretton Woods and later multilateral enterprises, such as the Marshall Plan and GATT, did help to dismantle trade and investment barriers and to stabilize the world's currencies. These steps, in turn, facilitated world trade and recovery.[1]

What these authors, Pollard and Wells, describe in their work is not domination but rather a step-by-step process of international political leadership. This was to a substantial degree the case even in the period after World War II, when US relative economic standing was at its peak.

Trends in structural leadership

US officials advanced early trade regime development through structural leadership, despite its clearly episodic nature, which was supported by important elements of entrepreneurial leadership by British and other European officials and thinkers. Structural leadership has most prominently included pressing the most ambitious procedural and substantive proposals, forging co-leadership as required, winning over additional parties and managing opposing coalitions, and mobilizing and maintaining domestic support. At key points in time, US officials also capitalized on the new ideas and approaches generated both inside and outside of government agencies. The fundamental political economic framework of "embedded liberalism" represented the blending through compromises of US ideas and leverage for promoting the liberal multilateral trade system with British and European ideas and insistence on protecting the welfare state.

One clear pattern established in Chapters 3–5 is that US officials have usually advocated the most ambitious international trade negotiations in three different ways. First, they have led in terms of timing by being the first to argue for starting a new round or closing an existing one. Second, they have usually been early advocates for including new issue areas in the negotiations. The inclusion of substantial agricultural policy reform is a special case in this regard, as US officials have sought to introduce policy reforms onto the negotiation agenda almost continuously from the 1960s to the present. Finally, they have generally proposed the deepest reductions in barriers or most profound policy reform and liberalization. In certain cases, it can be argued that they did this in part in order to circumvent or "jump over" powerful domestic opposition, or in order to exert maximum pressure on European states for compromises as they established their common proposals. At the same time, ambitious US initiatives in each of these three forms and continuing rhetorical support for them provide important evidence of international political leadership. Equally important, in most cases these proposals included degrees of reform that clearly exceeded the positions or demands of the most involved domestic groups. An interesting exception is that proposals to strengthen the GATT or (proposed) WTO as an organization have not been as strongly promoted or accepted by US officials as, for example, Canadian negotiators in the case of the WTO.

Except for the pivotal case of agricultural reform and the Common Agricultural Policy in particular, EC and European leaders usually also joined their US and British counterparts in the cause of international trade policy reform. Due to the European political commitments and perceived costs of agricultural reform, their negotiators needed assurance of adequate expected benefits in other areas, especially industrial tariff reductions, to justify the overall package. Thus, most often with some delay, US and European officials could mobilize the other key negotiators and advocate agreements. However, the serious boundary restriction on European leadership in its inability to agree on any substantial agricultural reform had the overall effect of excluding many other members from perceiving sufficient benefits to join the regime until the 1980s.

Particularly under the overall lead of Presidents Roosevelt, Truman, and Kennedy, key cabinet officials and negotiators, with support from British negotiators, provided the initiatives and incentives required to establish the GATT and double its membership from the original twenty-three members. Their vision for US foreign policy integrated trade with security policy, and liberal economic policy was a core idea for them. Their use of symbols and rhetoric about US international economic policy and leadership was highly visible and effective. Presidents Roosevelt and Kennedy, in particular, and their most involved cabinet officers were sufficiently engaged and committed to contain domestic protectionism and catalyze negotiating progress. They mobilized and built support among key domestic political actors, provided vital foreign assistance, and learned from and compromised with British officials, who then helped to win the agreement of other key European states. The reality that US officials could not dictate, or even dominate, the ITO negotiations in Havana turned out to be a key reason for the International Trade Organization's demise under President Truman. The ITO's breadth of coverage and depth of authority, as well as other concessions to the Europeans, eroded domestic support, which helped persuade President Truman not to swing his full weight behind it.

In early GATT negotiations, lack of or insufficient US structural leadership led to failure to agree. Surprisingly, however, failures at key junctures sometimes provided precisely the opportunity needed by structural and entrepreneurial leaders to reinvigorate their bases of domestic and international political support. They characterized the failure as presenting a crisis situation, which raised the stakes for building future leadership and subsequent success. Thus, the failure represented by the weak outcomes in the Dillon Round was central to the Kennedy administration's drive to reestablish the legitimacy of the trade regime and US leadership in international economic policy. In part, senior US officials intended US leadership to manage and contain increased European regionalism and assertiveness, and even more so after President de Gaulle vetoed British entry into the EEC in January 1963. Liberal economic ideas were more prominent in the United States by the 1960s, and President Kennedy emphasized the linkage of peace, prosperity, and an open international economic system, thus once again clearly linking security and economy. He also worked directly and consistently to establish the domestic political basis for US leadership of the negotiations. "When the trade bill was presented to Congress, Kennedy went all out to secure passage."[2] Despite the US inability to lead at key points in the Dillon Round, under President Kennedy US proposals were used to press for the most ambitious goals in terms of when to launch rounds and how far to liberalize.

From the outset, President Johnson was less personally committed than his predecessor to the GATT process and to the explicit linkage of trade and international security. He was clearly less skilled in, and focused on, presidential speeches and rhetoric on international economic policy. Johnson was increasingly engulfed in both creating the Great Society at home and escalating the war in Vietnam. In response to President de Gaulle's vision for a more independent Europe between the superpowers, Johnson administration officials emphasized reinforcing the US international competitive position with Europe while also cementing and extending the EEC. Republican critics in Congress singled out the trade area with intense criticism of the administration for giving away too much to other countries. The pressure of Republican attacks domestically and the EEC's internal decision-making difficulties both complicated the negotiation process. During the mid-1960s, the French and Germans clashed over the issue of British entry into the EEC, and there was no coherent European strategy or policy for trade liberalization. The requisite consensus building with other GATT members simply could not be accomplished without a much more committed US role and unified European position. The process languished in the mid-1960s, and the domestic basis for US structural leadership was eroding.

A crucial finding from this period is the extent to which US compromises in trade goals intended to advance security and political objectives in Europe (and the Cold War) reinforced the political position and leverage of US protectionist interests. Their strengthened position, in turn, encouraged and provided leverage to the protectionist inclinations of European groups and states, thus causing a dynamic of reinforced US and European protectionism as European interests were favored over GATT and US global political economic purposes. The irony of this outcome was that an important US impetus for initiatives through GATT was reinforcing the US global role through enhancing the international trade regime, particularly when the EEC was expanding its membership or substantive cooperation. As the EEC developed, US officials consistently sought to reinforce the international regime. This had the effect of making the crucial moments or episodes of US structural leadership even less likely or shorter in duration than they would have been, for example by enhancing the protectionist impulses associated with national elections or the opposing political party controlling the US House or Senate. It also reinforced the protectionist positions in agriculture of other states such as Japan and reduced the negotiating space for expanding the trade system into agriculture and making it truly relevant to its developing member states.

Thus, by the Kennedy Round of 1963–1967, the top US trade officials were simultaneously constrained by competing foreign policy priorities, congressional pressures, and other related protectionist interests. The foreign policy priority given to European unity in particular reduced the ability of US negotiators to press the Europeans for compromises in pursuit of ambitious US proposals. Working within these constraints, US officials had to persuade their British, French, and German counterparts to go along before bringing the decision to carefully defined small groups of ministers, but once in place, US–European support would win the day. When US officials failed to lead or their European counterparts failed to follow, as in agriculture and major non-tariff barrier removal, then the launch of a new negotiation or completion of a key agreement was not possible.

In this bargaining context, turning points were critical devices, as were issue linkage and package deals. Entrepreneurial leadership by negotiators and structural leadership by US and European thinkers and officials were crucial in framing the issues, linkages, and packages. Introducing the linear, rather than only bilateral, tariff reduction approach was essential to the process. Intellectual leadership in this case came first from European sources. In the case of a system of special preferences for developing states, Australian and UNCTAD officials provided intellectual leadership, which was in turn supported by the entrepreneurial leadership of Director General Eric Wyndham White in direct opposition to US preferences. Each of these cases demonstrated, however, the limits of intellectual innovation without US structural leadership to incorporate and promote the ideas. Ideas related to negotiating process or content could be introduced by the negotiators of another key state, but if they were not adopted by US officials as well, then they were not integrated into the bargaining process. This highlighted the importance of entrepreneurial leadership, but also its limits in that it was generally subordinate to US structural leadership. On the other hand, US structural levers such as the agricultural waiver from GATT in 1955 also had important reverberation and self-limiting effects in the future. By later "reverberating" to reinforce protectionist agricultural interests in other key states, including European ones and Japan, they restrained later US structural leadership capabilities in expanding trade regime coverage to and substantially liberalizing agriculture.

In sum, prior to the 1970s episodes of US structural leadership, including determined and persistent initiatives by US trade and related officials backed directly and consistently by the president, along with the guidance of British negotiators, could generally win over key allies one by one. Senior US officials could gradually mobilize and build the necessary consensus with the British, then the other mainly Western and industrialized trading states, which in turn gained the approval of the entire membership. Consensus was built in a "pyramidal" fashion whereby additional major parties were gradually persuaded, often by approaching each state bilaterally at first. As agreement was won, those officials assisted with the process of adding the next key state to the consensus group. At some focal points in bargaining, an especially effective GATT director general also proved to be a key source of entrepreneurial leadership. Director General Wyndham White provided important entrepreneurial leadership, and in particular institutionalized what would later be called the Green Room process of small-group consensus testing and building.

As compared to Presidents Roosevelt, Truman, Kennedy, and even Johnson, Presidents Eisenhower and Nixon and their administrations asserted significantly less structural leadership of international trade, for three main reasons. First, they had higher priorities than trade policy, and their administrations were much less clear about trade policy liberalization as a core concept. Although Eisenhower certainly recognized the vital relationship between economics and security, his and Nixon's priorities highlighted Cold War and related international strategic policies. Competing foreign policy priorities after 1947 were also central for Truman. The trade system muddled along without a major round between 1947 and 1960 because neither Truman nor Eisenhower opted to make it a top-priority policy area. Unlike the Democratic presidents, in general the Republicans did not provide skilled rhetoric in the cause of US international economic leadership.

Second, Eisenhower and Nixon considered their policies toward Europe and the international economy to be heavily constrained by budgetary constraints and economic recession or inflation. They were forging foreign economic strategy that would reduce rather than expand their resource requirements. Nixon confronted the critical and symbolic shift in the US trade balance to a deficit position and sharply increased inflation domestically, which helped lead to an overvalued dollar, thus further complicating the trade deficit. Finally, and closely related, US policy initiatives in international trade negotiations were also limited by domestic political constraints in the form of protectionist pressure from Congress and congressional demands for a rebalancing of the costs of international leadership, industry sectors aligned against liberalization, and a mass public not engaged on the issue. Domestic protectionist forces and Eisenhower's own inclinations consistently constrained his trade policy initiatives in the 1950s. Furthermore, Republicans in Congress tended to be skeptical about trade liberalization until about 1973, when they effectively switched positions with the Democrats, who thereafter became more consistently protectionist in their positions. Nixon could only count on support from Republicans in this regard by late in his tenure as president. Like Eisenhower, in his early years Nixon's main support in Congress came from the Democrats.

By 1973, the Nixon administration, in part driven by the perceived need to contain the influence of an enlarging European Community, took the initiative in negotiating the launch of the Tokyo Round. Still, the launch was based on a much less substantive agreement than those initiating the Kennedy and Uruguay

Rounds, and US structural leadership was short-lived.[3] Furthermore, US officials confronted not only powerful blocking capabilities of the EC but also strong opposition from Japan and key developing states such as India and Brazil. In order to launch the Tokyo Round in 1973, US negotiators worked bilaterally with the EC over the CAP and agricultural liberalization for an extended and unprecedented period of time, then with Japan in the same area.

An important distinction from many previous studies is to distinguish between blocking, particularly delaying, leverage, and structural leadership. Prior to the mid-1970s, the Europeans (other than the British) could delay actions, effectively exclude agriculture from the agenda, and provide intellectual leadership in the specific case of proposing across-the-board tariff cuts to replace the item-by-item approach leading to the Dillon Round. Even so, for several reasons they could not provide structural leadership, as illustrated by the failed French attempt in 1963 to initiate France's own new negotiating approach.

However, the EC grew very substantially in size and stature with the entry of Britain, Denmark, and Ireland in January 1973, from the original six to a bloc of nine as the Tokyo Round was about to be launched. This foreshadowed an important transition in the fundamental causes of trade regime development.[4] Along with other changes, once the British began negotiating on behalf of their own and European interests rather than those of the Anglo-American axis, the dynamics of trade policy leadership demanded not only European acquiescence but also the active support of the EC. US structural leadership remained necessary but was no longer sufficient on its own, and entrepreneurial leadership from other states became more central to the negotiating process.

One key reason for the centrality of European powers' support was the increasing need to forge consensus among not only Japan and Canada but also the gradually larger and more diverse inner group of roughly the fifteen most actively involved GATT ministers. At times, key additional members were more readily persuaded to join a negotiation or agreement by individual or combined European trading powers than by US officials alone. Beginning in the mid-1970s, the leadership capabilities, bargaining leverage, and sheer market power represented by the US and leading European states in cooperation were both necessary and sufficient to convince the ten to fifteen other most involved ministers, who in turn helped to persuade enough additional ministers to eventually forge a consensus among the overall GATT membership. After pyramiding with the several largest trading states, the process focused on the few most engaged and influential developing states. However, this requirement for joint US–EC leadership meant that negotiations would be more complex and difficult, and ever more time-consuming.

Essentially, by the mid-1970s US structural leadership had to be reinvented. It was no longer adequate to drive the negotiating process, even when supported and assisted by entrepreneurial efforts of European officials and the GATT director general. New ideas and intellectual leadership were required to overcome emerging forms of protectionism and make the regime relevant to the majority of its members. With the British negotiating for the Community rather than facilitating US–European compromises, European leverage was significantly enhanced for the long term. US leaders also had to refashion their leadership approach to be effective with a more assertive Congress in foreign policy and a perception on the part of foreign leaders of diminished US global influence in the aftermath of Vietnam and the international economic turmoil of the 1970s.[5]

Joint structural leadership in international trade

The crucial transition occurred in the mid- to late 1970s as officials of the major European states and the EC had to be persuaded to join the United States in episodes of leadership of the trade regime. European officials generally did not share US global interests, but they joined basic American commitments to the ideas and practical economic advantages offered by the international trade regime. They also had key connections to other states, both large and smaller, and the increasing leverage of granting or expanding privileged access to their markets for developing and least developed states. In this way, they were important in facilitating pyramiding with the other major trading states and key developing states.

US–EC co-leadership also responded to the US demands for sharing leadership responsibilities and trade officials' perceptions of a need for more consistent structural leadership as the trade regime became more complex and diverse in issues and members. As US presidential administrations increasingly assertively pursued a rebalancing of responsibilities, other major states with similar principles were pressured to increase their leadership for regime development.[6] At the same time, US policy makers were less inclined to sacrifice their trade liberalization goals for the greater good of European unity. Furthermore, when US administrations were less enthusiastic about institutional initiatives or preoccupied with elections, the EC, supported by Canada, other large traders, and most involved ministers, could help sustain the process and regime.[7]

In parallel, by the 1980s British and German agricultural interests and policies gradually shifted away from the strict agricultural protectionism inherent in the CAP. By the late 1980s, the combination of reduced economic interests in agricultural protection and increasing European inclinations to lead in trade, as well as pretensions to lead in international development, moved the EC more in line with US trade liberalization policies. With the end of the Cold War, developing states liberalized unilaterally and joined the GATT-WTO in increasing numbers. Key ideas associated with the trade regime were much more widely debated and implemented to one degree or another in states worldwide. Furthermore, some of the more economically advanced developing states, for example those of East Asia and Latin America, embraced much more liberal trade practices as they joined the OECD or forged trade agreements with OECD states. As a result, the opportunities to pyramid developing states on key issues increased and they played a more central role across a broader range of trade negotiation issue areas.

From closing the Tokyo Round in 1979 through completion of the Uruguay Round in 1993–1994, US structural leadership was clearly the most vital driving force. Co-leadership by EC and European officials also proved crucial to pyramiding, managing potential blocking coalitions, and creating focal points in the negotiations. Still, European leadership generally followed that of US officials, and the sticking point of agriculture and difficulties of internal EC decision making on common positions often reduced the scope or intensity of joint US–EC structural leadership. It proved extremely difficult to extend GATT coverage into agriculture, as required to make the regime relevant to most members, when the EC either could not agree on CAP reform or would not negotiate real reductions in barriers or subsidies. Indeed, the complexity of joint leadership and US–EC bargaining deepened as European companies built on negotiating gains from the 1970s to assert agricultural exporting power and gain major market shares from US exporters. Their success triggered increased resistance by US agricultural interests to liberalization and demands for major reform of the CAP. Furthermore, on key occasions joint US–EC deals in agriculture and broader structural leadership were abruptly undermined by the direct intervention and blocking power of one official – the French president, who had earlier served as minister of agriculture!

The dynamics of structural leadership over this period changed in three important ways. First, between the closing of the Tokyo Round and the mid- to later stages of the Uruguay Round, the Cold War ended and the EU moved to finally establish a truly unified, common market. As a result, by the early 1990s US policy makers were no longer concerned about the effects of international trade liberalization on European unity. In fact, the EU gradually grew to be a much greater presence in overall economic capacity and global trade. This meant that the US, EU, and European officials had to manage global trade relations in the context of two ever more competitive and more equal economies. In certain ways, their ideas about, and approaches to, international economy became even more compatible, but joint leadership was complicated by domestic interests catalyzed by heightened levels of international economic, financial, and business competition.[8] Sharp and continuing US–European cleavages over political military issues could also prove important in even further limiting the opportunities for joint structural leadership.

Second, bargaining coalitions, including most prominently the Cairns Group of agricultural exporting states, assumed substantially increased importance in the negotiation process. They did so mainly through either their blocking leverage or their entrepreneurial leadership. The Cairns Group proved pivotal in balancing the most protectionist middle powers in agriculture, including the Group of 10, and pressuring EC and European negotiators to make significant compromises. An informal group of five Latin American states rejected any overall agreement at the Montreal Ministerial in 1988 in the absence of substantial compromises on agriculture.

Smaller states learned that under certain circumstances they could also create focal points in the bargaining process. Indeed, building from their negative experience in the Tokyo Round, leading developing states experimented more often with blocking leverage when they preferred no agreement to US–EC or developed state proposals. Over four years, US officials worked intensively to "educate" and persuade states to launch the Uruguay Round, in part based on the necessity to introduce service sectors into the regime and keep it up with the realities of rapidly evolving domestic economies and international trade. Still, it required every imaginable lever of US structural leadership and innovative entrepreneurial leadership by the conference chair and other highly skilled negotiators to gradually persuade and cajole agreement at Punta del Este in 1986.

This study tracks in particular the evolution of structural leadership through developing state coalitions after the WTO was established in 1995. The development of certain structural leadership capabilities by the Brazilian and Indian ministers, among others, built upon the G-20 bargaining group at Cancún, appears to parallel the path of the increasing European role in the 1960s and 1970s. By 2003, both US and EU officials called for more sharing of leadership responsibilities, recognized the increased relative role of G-20 members in global trade, and understood the need for enhancing structural leadership as the trade regime became considerably more complex and diverse in issues and members. Furthermore, US–EU balancing in agriculture has reinforced not only the leverage of domestic protectionist interests in the United States, key European states, Japan, and South Korea but also the potential structural role of key developing states and coalitions. US–EU balancing has led each party to seek out allies against each other, and encouraged developing states to take advantage of the increased bargaining space for them individually and through coalitions with either side and against both. As the US–EU states constrain each other, they also open opportunities for structural leverage and entrepreneurial leadership by key developing states and groups such as the new G-20.

Instead of only blocking unacceptable agreements, from the period leading to Seattle in 1999, key developing state leaders from Brazil, India, South Africa, Mexico, Argentina, and several other states have also asserted a positive negotiating agenda on behalf of coalitions. Particularly prominent in bargaining from Seattle to present are the LDC, African, and ACP groups, and most recently the G-20 from the summer prior to Cancún in December 2003.

In response, entrepreneurial leaders such as the WTO director general or the ministers chairing the General Council, the Trade Negotiating Committee, or major WTO negotiating groups have initiated innovations in the basic negotiating procedures and processes. Developing state ministers have participated more often and in larger numbers in key Green Room sessions. So-called mini-ministerial meetings have been held to engage more developing state ministers and improve the information flow among ministers and senior WTO officials.[9] Developing and least developed state ministers were especially prominent in Green Room bargaining in Doha in 2001, Cancún in 2003, and leading to the August 2004 agreement. Coalitions led by these states have been crucial to the outcomes of Cancún and the agreement of summer 2004. Most important, the August 1, 2004 agreement was substantially forged through the intensive bargaining of a G-5 with ministers of the US, EU, Australia, India, and Brazil, which explicitly incorporated the structural leverage of Brazilian and Indian ministers established by the G-20 at Cancún and thereafter. Finally, small-group consensus building and even episodes of joint structural leadership by the US, EU, Brazilian, and Indian ministers have been crucial to the bargaining process through 2005 in preparation for, and during, the Hong Kong Ministerial meeting in December 2005.

Third, with the increased complexity of bargaining and the growth of regions and regionalism in international politics and economy, US officials turned increasingly to bilateral and regional trade agreements. Most prominently, the completion of NAFTA and emergence of major APEC negotiations both directly affected international trade bargaining. As European, and particularly French, officials hardened their agricultural positions, US negotiators established credible commitments to Western Hemispheric and Asian-Pacific trade arrangements, mainly on their own merits but also as strategic levers to help extract EC compromises. Continuing with the Bush administration from 2001, the US strategy, then termed "competitive liberalization," was pursued ambitiously.

Most recently, as a result of the various failures of US–EU structural leadership prior to Cancún, these key states were unable to prevent the formation of the G-20. As a result, at Cancún US negotiators attempted to execute a second-best strategy in this regard: undermine and defeat the G-20 by manipulating their structural leverage from the emerging regional agreement with Central America (CAFTA), the special preferences for African states based on the AGOA of 2000, and bilateral agreements, both past and emerging. By dividing, co-opting, and arm-twisting G-20 members along these lines, they aimed to break down the coalition's structural leverage. The effort worked in breaking out the very few small Central American and African states most involved in these agreements with the United States, but not for the principal G-20 states and their direct support on most issues from the LDC, African, and ACP groups.

This extensive and intensive process of US leadership in forging bilateral and regional arrangements has established important precedents for the system more generally. Since the mid-1990s, European officials have followed a very similar strategy, resulting in bilateral and regional EU trade arrangements with more than 100 states. US officials and certain experts object to the EU practice of excluding certain issue areas, and agriculture in particular, from these agreements, but the overall trend is well established.

Indeed, most recently leading developing states and coalitions are attempting to employ a parallel strategy. They are building on political or cultural and economic connections to forge bilateral (for example Brazil–India) and regional trade arrangements and global bargaining leverage. Least developed states are maneuvering to maintain existing preferential access to US and/or EC markets, while also formulating interconnected negotiating coalitions with large developing states to press for the elimination of OECD states' protectionism against their products. The final report in 2005 of a "Consultative Board" of eight leading experts established by the WTO director general expresses deep concern about the overall outcome of this trend – "The erosion of non-discrimination."

> Certainly, much trade between the major economies is still conducted on an MFN basis. However, what has been termed the "spaghetti bowl" of customs unions, common markets, regional and bilateral free trade areas, preferences and an endless assortment of miscellaneous trade deals has almost reached the point where MFN treatment is exceptional treatment.[10]

Each of these basic changes in the dynamics of structural leadership, along with the sharply increased role of transparency as a fundamental principle of trade liberalization and WTO operations, has made structural leadership more complex and difficult. Process opportunism, or lining up influential allies and deterring and managing opposing coalitions, is ever more challenging. Structural leaders still increase the chances for agreement by quietly gaining support for cooperation before formal talks commence. Agreements are still reached among a core group of key players, but the size of the core group has expanded and each of its members must be able to persuade and win the acquiescence of an increasing number of other states. These leaders still seek to increase the size of the consensus group to the point where the status quo ante is removed as an option and the opportunity costs are high for remaining neutral. At the same time, the opportunity for the strategic use of secrecy, partial communication, and imperfect information to establish alliances among actively negotiating states before proposals are made public has become more limited.

Entrepreneurial leadership

Entrepreneurial leadership is historically and increasingly important in GATT-WTO negotiations. One crucial element of this form of political leadership is cross-issue linkages and packaging, which have steadily assumed greater importance, not only because of path dependency or longstanding bargaining practice and traditions but also in response to the new complexity and complications of trade bargaining. Both because there was no conceivable way to accurately calculate the overall gains and losses of a Uruguay Round agreement with so many different bundles of issues, and because there were clear gains for most states in at least a few areas, its complexity was also its salvation. Such linkages and packaging have grown to be expected, even essential, elements of standard international trade bargaining practice, and the most recent Doha Round will only be agreed once these linkages and packaging are fully worked out. Beginning in the 1960s, negotiating practice institutionalized the expectation that every state, but especially the major ones, must have at least one area where it could expect important gains, and the larger the number of bargaining areas, the greater the expected likelihood of such gains.

The role of entrepreneurial leadership only becomes more central as more members have established a tradition or history of developing and encouraging especially adept, expert negotiators. Highly effective trade negotiators and leaders have emerged from Canada, Switzerland, Norway, Australia, New Zealand, several other European states, India, Brazil, Argentina, Mexico, Chile, South Africa, Hong Kong, Singapore, Malaysia, Pakistan, Thailand, and several other Latin American and East Asian states, among others. A number of developing states in particular are represented by skilled negotiators, and this has increased the pool of highly competent officials to chair WTO groups and committees, and to fill upper-level positions in the WTO, up to and including the director general and deputy director general positions. Ambassador Jaya Krishna Cuttaree of Mauritius, for example, was an entrepreneurial leader in coordinating the negotiating positions of the African, LDC, and ACP groups prior to the Cancún meeting, and he was one of the final four WTO director general candidates in the 2004–2005 selection process.

Uruguay is one of the most obvious examples, with negotiators such as Julio LaCarte, Enrique Iglesias, and Carlos Pérez del Castillo, who for decades have led some of the most important GATT and WTO committees and groups. LaCarte is widely recognized as one of the most effective negotiators in the post-World War II history of international trade. Castillo has chaired the General Council, the Dispute Settlement Body, the Council for Trade-Related Aspects of Intellectual Property Rights (TRIPS), and the Council for Trade in Goods. Indeed, after a highly distinguished career in trade policy and negotiations, Iglesias became president of the Inter-American Development Bank, and Castillo was one of the three leading candidates to become the new WTO director general in 2004–2005.[11]

At the same time, most of the more than two dozen directors who manage the major WTO departments and divisions come from developed states, as do most of the panel members for the Dispute Settlement Body and judges for the Appellate Body. Thus, entrepreneurial leadership in the WTO must be examined in terms of dozens of negotiators at any one time, mainly those from member states but also the WTO itself. Most often it will originate with officials from developed, OECD states, but increasingly since the 1990s also from developing state negotiators. Structural leadership is still generally confined to the US and EU officials, a few of the most effective negotiating coalitions, and, increasingly, Brazil and India. Still, at certain times particular ministers and coalitions have provided important procedural and substantive initiatives, especially the Cairns Group and the recently formed G-20. Finally, small states such as Jamaica and Kenya are developing a tradition of entrepreneurial trade negotiators along similar lines, but also based on their ability to represent and institutionalize coherent regional trade groups for global bargaining.

Intellectual leadership

From GATT's origin, the role of ideas and concepts has been crucial. Most important, however, are those enshrined as the fundamental principles of multilateral trade bargaining and institutions. Sets of rules and procedures have also been central, but US and other leading officials have permitted deviations from strict rule adherence so long as other members have demonstrated a durable belief in tariff reduction and institutional liberalization. In other words, basic principles are more important than constant adherence to rules. The trade regime has succeeded, where others have failed or stalled, because it long restricted membership to those states that accepted basic free trade principles. The trade regime could allow temporary flexibility among contracting parties precisely because of their durable commitment to liberalization.

In part owing to the durability of these principles, as well as the long-established patterns and processes of trade negotiations, intellectual leadership is most directly traceable to actors inside the trade system. Ideas often appear to originate from the officials of highly active states such as Canada, including those in supporting roles at home in the trade agency or bureaucracy. At the same time, the ideas forged or elaborated by influential scholars of GATT such as John Jackson, Robert Hudec, or Gilbert Winham have certainly found their way into the bargaining process through trade ministers and negotiators. Canada's proposal in 1990, for example, to have the Uruguay Round include a new, more substantial international organization for trade included key elements as proposed in Jackson's scholarly work.

Many of the ideas and concepts that find their way into trade negotiations involve procedural innovations or new issue areas that broaden the scope of the organization. A crucial procedural example was the European proposal for a new approach to tariff reductions in the Dillon Round, which was adopted and proposed thereafter by US officials. One prominent new issue area is the service sectors, included in the Uruguay Round. The many failed attempts to expand into agriculture are another key example of where new ideas were especially important. Of course, the Uruguay Round involved several other important new areas, such as intellectual property rights and trade-related investment which are also highly controversial in many developing and least developed member states.

Possibly building on the practices of US officials in the past, EU minister Leon Brittan drew the ideas and concepts related to competition policy and investment related to trade from scholarly, think tank, and governmental bureaucratic sources. He proceeded to travel worldwide in order to educate, persuade, and win over ministers one by one on these issues from 1996 into 1999. Indeed, EU principal structural leadership on the Singapore Issues, as supported by officials from Japan and other states such as South Korea, provided the main driving force during this period. This was especially the case for the most controversial initiatives: investment rules and competition policy. The overall concept of the Singapore Issues as a package failed to win over even US officials. Still, over the course of time competition and investment rules may gradually find their way into the formal trade regime.

Brittan's Singapore Issues initiative is a key example of an attempt at structural leadership based heavily on a set of new ideas and issue areas that failed to a substantial degree because of its inadequate representation of collective interests. His agenda was overly narrow and aligned too closely with the main EU substantive motivations for a new round. It neglected to emphasize the vital, continuing negotiations in agricultural liberalization in particular, but also the concerns of officials from developing and least developed states about inadequate implementation of the commitments made under the final Uruguay Round agreement. Without addressing the "implementation" issue or integrating a deeper level of agricultural policy liberalization, Brittan was neglecting the central expectations and needs of his "followers." Indeed, even under the much more effective leadership of the EU's new trade minister, Pascal Lamy, just prior to the Seattle Ministerial in 1999, this problem remained. As late as the Cancún Ministerial in 2003, Lamy was unable to modify the same basic set of demands on the Singapore Issues. Essentially, Brittan lost track of, or strayed too far from, the "heart, minds, and souls" of his fellow trade ministers and their heads of state. Earlier and much deeper negotiation and coordination of his efforts with US officials might have converted his effective structural leadership in terms of effort and process into one of substantive leadership as well.

A much more pervasive and successful example of intellectual leadership is that related to the concept of "transparency." Emerging especially in the 1990s from Western scholarly publications and think tank reports, opponents of and skeptics toward globalization in its several forms, practices of key INGOs such as Transparency International, and government officials from the United States, New Zealand, Australia, the EU, and elsewhere, the concept of openness in governance can also be traced back to the US presidential administration of Jimmy Carter. The idea that public-sector operations should be visible to, if not directly accessible to, citizens has become a prevailing understanding and expectation in Western governments. Public international organizations and associated international regimes have followed by adopting "transparency" as an operating principle in most respects, but the demands of a diverse base of member states and the difficulties of radically changing organizational behavior have slowed its implementation in practice. Still, WTO members have both adopted the basic concept as a new principle for the trade system and moved relatively efficiently to carry it out in most of its functions. Most visibly, transparency is the core purpose of the WTO's Trade Policy Review process, which makes the specifics of trade regulation and related broader economic policies of each member state readily available to all others. Gradually, as a result of pressure from INGOs and key states such as the United States and New Zealand, the WTO Dispute Settlement system is also enhancing the opportunities for third parties and members generally to observe proceedings and gain prompt access to most documents.

Of course, the idea of transparency with respect to any public organization is ultimately a means to achieve accountability and credibility or legitimacy. In this regard, public international organizations are not fundamentally different from domestic public bureaucracies. Performance or effectiveness in accomplishing the main goals likely remains the most important form of accountability, particularly when the tasks at hand are relatively technical in nature.[12] Nevertheless, senior WTO officials could more meaningfully and systematically forge more direct connections with publics, elected officials, and INGOs worldwide. And leading trade ministers could be more explicit and publicly conversant about their immediate responsibility to a directly elected president or a prime minister.

The main difficulty with transparency as a means to accountability is that certain core WTO functions such as dispute settlement and rounds of negotiations can be more difficult if not impossible to accomplish in a fully transparent context. By their very nature, for example, the more visible the early consultations and bargaining over disputes and formal requests to the WTO, the less likely they are to be resolved without proceeding into the formal, highly legalistic, and time-consuming panel process. Similarly, some negotiating issues can be resolved more efficiently and effectively outside the direct view of officials from other public international organizations, INGOs, and domestic interest groups. In these cases, assuming that the negotiators themselves are competent and well informed, visibility and transparency may be best achieved by rapid release of draft texts and frequent press and NGO briefings.

Ironically, the "idea" of the current Doha Round as the "development" round appears to be attributable to former EU minister Brittan in a remark made in the 1990s. Once so labeled, of course, the essential purpose of the round has become what proved impossible for the GATT: to make the trade regime a central, positive element of economic development. To a degree, this is being accomplished during the round by institutionalizing certain "development"-oriented ideas: the creation of a specific substantive WTO work program for LDCs, the extension of the transition period for LDC members until 2016 for intellectual property and pharmaceutical products, and the adoption of more lenient or flexible accession guidelines for LDCs joining the WTO. If and when trade liberalization becomes highly relevant to development, the WTO's reputation and "accountability" will be fundamentally enhanced for many member states and non-state actors.

Overall, there have been at least three major changes in the nature of intellectual leadership over this period of more than fifty years. These changes are clearly significant in light of the long-term and relatively institutionalized bargaining procedures of GATT-WTO rounds, and the path dependence, or difficulty in changing members' expectations and practices. First, the nature of the ideas introduced has grown very substantially in breadth. From relatively simple ideas about the techniques of bargaining in GATT in the 1950s, more recently there have been introduced ideas about (1) new issue areas to be encompassed in the regime; (2) major expansions or changes in the prior issue areas, such as dispute settlement; (3) cross-cutting or linking with different international treaty systems, but especially labor and human rights, the environment, and development; and (4) new principles, including additional expectations or standards to be met in establishing accountability and legitimacy for public international organizations. Ideas integrating trade and labor or worker rights, and environmental issues have been resisted by WTO members and the WTO's strong, relatively technical culture of trade liberalization, whereas those integrating trade and development have been embraced and incorporated.

Second, these expansions have extended the space for new states and non-state actors to provide intellectual leadership of trade negotiations. Entrepreneurial leaders from states outside the United States, the EU and the OECD are more often able to play a key role in introducing or reinforcing ideas in the bargaining process. In parallel, non-state actors in addition to corporate associations have begun to play important supplementary intellectual leadership roles. This development has occurred later than with the World Bank and IMF, but it is possible that the more incremental process in trade will produce a more important and enduring role for INGOs and international organizations central to economic development.

Third, structural leadership still involves competition to control the negotiating agenda, including a gatekeeper role for the entry of new or revised ideas, such as including a social or labor rights clause in trade agreements. At the same time, the heightened role of transparency, new players, and a complex and wide range of negotiating issues (and cross-cutting linkages) make the process substantially more open to ideas from new sources. This has included, for example, more informed decisions by developing states to either avoid or make use of the formalized dispute settlement process in part due to effective support from a modest non-profit-making body, the Advisory Centre on WTO Law or (ACWL) in Geneva. This technical, legal "ideas" center, as well as European and US legal firms seeking new business, has provided a foundation for developing state structural leadership. Brazil and India, in particular, have emerged in the Doha Round negotiations, along with their coalition, the G-20 more broadly, as structural leaders. This is due in part to their past intellectual leadership, but also the new, more open environment for intellectual leadership by INGOs and IGOs, which reinforces the potential for developing state structural leverage.

WTO reform and leadership of bargaining in public international organizations

The long history of the GATT-WTO negotiating process reveals an important pattern in the evolution of roles of individuals and the states they represent. As key individuals and their trade ministries establish a pattern of experience in entrepreneurial leadership, they gradually become positioned to play a structural leadership role. Indeed, leaders from states such as India have evolved through a long process of transformation from pursuing a largely blocking role, at first individually and later by leading coalitions, to one of structural co-leadership in agenda setting and framing with Brazilian and other officials. By applying the joint market power of states such as China, India, and Brazil, and also pressing the development agenda of LDC and developing states (especially those with many millions of very poor citizens), Indian trade negotiators have leveraged themselves into a central bargaining role.

In essence, they have joined Brazilian officials in strategically outmaneuvering US and EU pyramiding. Their role at Cancún was mainly a blocking one, in part because they were consumed by the tasks of holding the G-20 together, but also because they were publicly committing themselves and demonstrating their staying power. Their maneuvering was complicated by the "rejectionist" position of a few small Caribbean and other ACP states, which clearly preferred the no-agreement outcome. Furthermore, at Cancún Brazilian and Indian officials preferred to pursue positions in the zone of possible agreement and were committed to advancing the overall process to conclude the Doha Round. At the same time, their coalition was attempting to represent other coalitions and states that might have preferred no agreement. On the basis of decades of accumulated experience, the backing of LDC, African, and ACP coalitions, and their own development agenda, they effectively stalled and paralyzed the US and EC ministers' ability to win over additional parties. Almost every one of the large developing state ministers whom the United States and the EC needed to win over were committed to the G-20 position, and neither the WTO director general (from Thailand) nor the conference chair (from Mexico) was well positioned to direct all his entrepreneurial skills and connections against the G-20. At the same time, in the aftermath of Cancún, Brazilian and Indian officials proved themselves committed to achieving an overall Doha Round agreement.

Furthermore, not only long entrepreneurial experience and reputation but also intellectual leadership plays a role in building a foundation for future structural leadership. In the 1940s, US ideas about liberalism and international markets merged with British and continental European ideas to frame the GATT and its founding principles. Episodic US structural leadership from the 1940s through the 1970s was built in part upon a rich and broad base of ideas and concepts emanating from academic, intellectual, and public policy centers, as well as government officials in the United States. Both in terms of selecting which issue areas to emphasize for each round of negotiations and deciding how to frame and advocate their negotiating agenda, US negotiators were advantaged by access to and understanding of new ideas related to trade. Public-sector advisory boards and congressional leaders, also drawing on the ideas of corporate leaders, drew on this rich base of ideas and concepts to present their preferences for negotiating issues and positions. Probably the central idea in the initiation of the Uruguay Round, why and how to extend GATT coverage to the service sectors, originated from US business managers and was adapted and advanced by US negotiators.

Similarly, as European officials gradually evolved in their positions from often rejecting or blocking US initiatives, and particularly after the British joined the EC in 1973, they were advantaged and supported with intellectual leadership in trade from a broad base of university, public-sector, and public–private bodies. Additionally, the combined influence of "Thatcherism" in Britain from 1979 (and the rule of the Conservatives until 1997), German chancellors Schmidt's (1974–1982) and Kohl's ideas (1982–1998), and the administration of President Reagan in the United States from 1981 through 1988 greatly encouraged intellectual leadership related to "neoliberalism" well beyond the life of these governments. President Reagan's strong, persistent, rhetorical leadership for free trade was strictly limited to non-communist states, but it also marked a crucial shift in the position of Republican administrations to supporting worldwide trade policy liberalization.

European ideas or initiatives also emerged earlier in reaction to Nixon's protectionist policies to advance his domestic priorities and Carter's "tri-lateralist" approach to engaging with and leading the Europeans. As intellectual leadership from US sources in the 1980s increasingly focused on "strategic trade theory" and its implications, ideas from Britain, Germany, and even Japan emphasized the centrality of GATT's basic principles and practices. In other words, there is a reverberation effect of not only ideas but also intellectual leadership by incorporating the ideas into bargaining strategies. US officials appear to have initiated the idea of "competitive liberalization," which was shaped into a strategy for manipulating bilateral and regional trade partners and agreements for leverage in GATT-WTO negotiations. European and EU officials, in turn, adapted this concept, applying it to balance US leverage. More recently, negotiators for the largest developing states are reinventing their own version, as they build South–South bilateral, regional, and region-to-region agreements, for example with the EU to enhance bargaining leverage against the United States.

In turn, a key outcome of the reverberation effect is to enhance the potential leverage and bargaining opportunities of developing states, which can exploit US–EU differences and reduced structural co-leadership ability. Brazil has not only won two pivotal WTO dispute settlement cases against US and EU agricultural support systems but also blocked the US ability to forge the FTAA, which in turn reduces its global structural leverage. This positions Brazil as a structural leader with the United States both in the FTAA context and in completing the Doha Round. India holds a similar position but for different reasons, in part its ability to represent the interests of poor people reliant on cheap food imports, or "food security."

The base of ideas underlying trade and development issues has been substantially enriched from the 1990s by technological globalization and the increasingly active roles of public international organizations and NGOs in the area of trade and economic development. States such as India, Brazil, and Argentina have their own significant base of domestic sources for ideas and concepts, but many other developing and least developed state trade officials have gained access to new intellectual concepts and approaches through the internet, new initiatives or studies by UNCTAD, the World Bank, the UNDP, and the efforts of many domestic and internationally networked NGOs. Essentially, intellectual leaders have emerged both from larger and more experienced developing states and from international organizations and NGOs that seek out the most involved officials of developing and least developed states. Furthermore, the timely access to basic factual and analytical information has been greatly improved by WTO improvements in its website, other IGOs such as the South Centre, and key NGOs such as the ACWL in Geneva.

The most involved INGOs vary widely in nature, for example from those focusing more on information, such as the International Centre for Trade and Sustainable Development and the Third World Network, to those conducting extensive analysis and advocacy such as Oxfam. The most influential ideas and proposals in this regard are those advocated by key international organizations and NGOs working in close coordination or strategic alliances. Particularly since the Singapore Ministerial in 1996, the South Centre in Geneva has worked closely with developing state officials to formulate position papers and negotiating strategies.[13] At the Cancún Ministerial, several leading NGOs with a trade and development focus, supported by key officials of UNCTAD and the UNDP and their recent reports, asserted their role as intellectual leaders for certain LDCs.

In sum, reforming the WTO is a process worthy of more than relatively simple recommendations for new management or decision-making bodies, or other organizational changes. Reform of WTO processes and institutions is most productively conducted through innovations and changes that for example facilitate and accelerate the learning, experience, and coalition building of key officials from developing and least developed states. It is experience in entrepreneurial leadership roles in the Green Room, chairing negotiating coalitions, WTO groups and committees, the General Council, or even a ministerial meeting, which efficiently and effectively positions both officials and their states for broader leadership of multilateral trade bargaining.

For many years, this experience was dominated by the smaller European states such as Switzerland and Norway, but beginning especially during the Tokyo Round in the 1970s, it has increasingly included a significant number of developing states. This trend was well established during the Uruguay Round, but only regularized and institutionalized after the Seattle Ministerial. Uruguayan negotiators provide an excellent example of how this process works in practice, but they are not alone. Negotiators from other states, for example in Latin America and East Asia, have also proved to be highly adept at entrepreneurial leadership, taken on ever more important roles, and gradually helped to establish a tradition of trade policy leadership from their state. In turn, spreading and deepening this type of experience also accelerates the process of WTO incorporation of more LDC and developing state ministers into its director-level positions and processes. In the latest round of competition for a new director general, three of the final four candidates represented developing states (Brazil, Uruguay, and Mauritius), despite the fact that the EU's Pascal Lamy won the job.

Is the glass half full or half empty? WTO skeptics will argue the latter and optimists the former. In fact, however, there is a sizable pool of developing state, and to a lesser extent least developed state, officials who are fully qualified to serve as deputy director generals and even director general of the WTO. Supachai of Thailand has broken the ice as director general from 2001 to 2005, but of course it will take the service of additional highly qualified officials such as Chile's Alejandro Jara (deputy director general to Pascal Lamy) to establish consistent high-level leadership by negotiators from developing and least developed states. In this way, not only will the priorities and resources of the WTO be focused on development issues and implementation for the Doha Round but this practice will be institutionalized for the long term.

In sum, this study establishes that the role of international political leadership can be identified and evaluated as a causal factor that leads to specific negotiating outcomes, despite the steady, often overwhelming constraints of domestic interests and politics. This is accomplished by establishing the requirements and dimensions of political leadership, both in general and specifically in terms of institutionalized international negotiations. After integrating insights from several other important arenas of theory most relevant to international trade negotiations, the result is a framework that can also be applied to analyze negotiations in other important international issues areas.

The conclusions emphasize, first, that structural leadership can in fact be provided by two states in close coordination, or even by a small group of three or four states. Furthermore, the small group can include experienced officials from large developing states that have established a long tradition of active participation in the institutionalized negotiations. At certain specific times, structural leadership is also produced by individuals representing key coalitions and middle-size states.

Next, it highlights entrepreneurial leadership by individuals from a wide range of national backgrounds, including numerous developing and some least developed states. Senior WTO officials have also been important providers of entrepreneurial leadership, despite the fact that GATT-WTO members have long restricted the autonomy and power of even the director general and his deputies. For these reasons, the single most effective and promising approach to WTO reform is enhancing the paths and possibilities for developing and least developed state ministers (and negotiators) to gain experience at entrepreneurial or even intellectual leadership which will position them for structural leadership opportunities. Most such opportunities will be through participation in small-group decision making and leadership of a major negotiating coalition or main WTO committee, but substantially increasing numbers also must be in senior WTO staff positions, i.e. directors and their senior staff and advisers.

Enhancing the effectiveness and accountability of public international organizations

This study has focused on one of the WTO's two main roles. It has assessed the GATT-WTO as a forum for negotiating agreements on the rules, norms, and procedures of a global trade regime. Since 1995, the WTO has also served as the legally binding dispute resolution system. In this book, this latter role is taken as an output or product of trade negotiations. Dispute resolution raises other key issues, such as those related to enforcement and compliance, which are appropriately the focus of other studies.

In its capacity as a negotiating forum, the GATT-WTO offers one of the few best available examples of how states bargain in institutionalized settings. In particular, the GATT-WTO-based international trade regime provides a crucial window on how states develop confidence and trust in public international organizations and international regimes. An increasingly global set of member states has been able to reach agreement on what appears to be the most authoritative and relevant international dispute settlement system in existence, as well as an ever more comprehensive global trade regime. Crucial episodes of international political leadership have helped to guide negotiations through a long series of failures and successes over six decades.

At the same time, it may well be that the senior WTO staff, e.g. deputy director generals and directors, need more independent operational capabilities in certain areas, for example in monitoring, reporting, and encouraging compliance with the wide range of GATT-WTO treaties. Furthermore, it could prove important and useful to members to enhance the centralization of specific functions in the WTO, including the maintenance and reporting based on its master database of all members' national-level trade rules and legislation. More specifically, members should be able to readily confirm when and how other members have, or have not, corrected problems, violations, and questionable practices noted in the regular Trade Policy Reviews conducted by WTO staff. This rather informal and insufficiently funded function could be greatly improved and operated more like those of the International Monetary Fund (IMF) with regard to its surveillance role and the International Atomic Energy Agency in terms of safeguards agreements.

This work offers insights for many younger or less developed public international organizations and associated international regimes as well as for certain older ones, in any issue area of international relations. The WTO's hallmark as a negotiating forum is decentralization and high levels of engagement and activity by individual member states in the daily routine of the organization. It represents a decentralized, member-driven approach to international organization, with clearly less independence in terms of decision-making and roles for its senior staff (except in dispute settlement capacity) than the World Bank or IMF. Its relatively modest staff and budget are supplemented by the active support and engagement of officials from the many member state missions in Geneva.

This deep engagement by member state officials in Geneva accomplishes three basic purposes. First, it reduces the size of the staff and budget required in the WTO in order to carry out its mission. Second, it trains and educates officials in negotiating in institutionalized settings, as well as in the content of trade law and policy. Finally, it establishes a degree of confidence and trust in the organization on the part of these officials and the many who have served in Geneva in the past. Their confidence is built in part on their own experience in providing ideas, guidance, and resources for negotiations.

In the end, their engagement assures the continuation of a decentralized negotiating process. In turn, the nature of these negotiations demands leadership in its structural, entrepreneurial, and intellectual forms. To the extent that members provide the officials who help guide the negotiations, and that the outcomes of negotiations are considered important to members, the process will be deemed useful and effective. As an increasing number of members have officials serving in leadership positions, the content of negotiations will be guided toward issue areas of importance to them. It is precisely the continually broadening base of member state experience in leadership roles that are entrepreneurial and structural in nature which will reform the WTO in both its process and its content. Therefore, the most senior US, EU, Indian, and Brazilian officials, among others, also must provide leadership with regard to increasing the base of effective participation. One fundamental element of international political leadership is ensuring that international organizations operate first on the basis on merit, wherein the most capable, innovative, and experienced ministers and negotiators win the highest positions, regardless of their nationality. In this way, as negotiations become ever more complex, they are also more inclusive and representative.

Notes

1 Why study international political leadership and the global trade regime?

1 Past success has also drawn an increasing array of critics of GATT-WTO operations and the international trade regime, who have pressed for a wide range of changes.

2 On this point, see R. Blackhurst, "The Capacity of the WTO to Fulfill Its Mandate," in A. Krueger, ed., *The WTO as an International Organization*, Chicago: University of Chicago Press, 1998, pp. 31–58.

3 For an example of why it is important to distinguish the independence of international organizations in terms of different dimensions (decision-making procedures, supranational bureaucracy, and dispute settlement mechanisms) see Y. Haftel and A. Thompson, "The Independence of International Organizations," *Journal of Conflict Resolution*, vol. 50, no. 2, April 2006, pp. 253–275. They also find that independence is explained in part by age; that is, institutions are persistent, as explained also by path dependency and expected by historical institutionalism. The WTO has been criticized for its lack of transparency and pluralistic procedures. On the challenge of legitimacy confronting public international organizations, see Robert O. Keohane and Joseph S. Nye, "Redefining Accountability for Global Governance" in M. Kahler and D. Lake, eds., *Governance in a Global Economy*, Princeton, NJ: Princeton University Press, 2004. They note that despite a lack of transparency, such organizations may be seen as legitimate if they develop effective policy in a clearly technical area, p. 405. The attacks on the WTO are most often related to its success as an organization devoted to economic globalization. In comparison, the World Bank and IMF are also criticized for their failed policies and efforts at development.

4 See, for example, John Odell's characterization of the WTO as "a weak, strong organization" in "Problems in Negotiating Consensus in the World Trade Organization," American Political Science Association annual convention, San Francisco, August 2001, pp. 2–5. Indeed, a key puzzle for students of public international organizations is how and why members have endowed it with such unprecedented independence in certain areas while sharply limiting its centralization in terms of information collection and reporting on member states.

5 The WTO was also expected to facilitate working-group-level negotiations on key issues in the absence of an ongoing round of negotiations.

6 S. Huntington, "The Lonely Superpower," *Foreign Affairs*, 1999, vol. 78, no. 2, p. 42.

7 See A. George and A. Bennett, *Case Studies and Theory Development in the Social Sciences*, Cambridge, MA: MIT Press, 2005; A. George and T. McKeown, "Case Studies and Theories of Organizational Decision Making," *Advances in Information Processing in Organizations*, 1985, 2, 21–58. Also useful are C. Jonsson and J. Tallberg, "Institutional Theory in International Relations," in G. Peters *et al.*, eds., *Institutional Theory in Political Science*, forthcoming; and P. Pierson, *Politics in Time: History, Institutions, and Social Analysis*, Princeton, NJ: Princeton University Press, 2004.

8 For simplicity of presentation, the GATT-WTO, as a negotiating forum that gradually evolved into a public international organization, will generally be used interchangeably with the global trade regime or system. Technically, three different international institutional forms should be distinguished: organizations, regimes (sets of norms, rules, and procedures that govern behavior in an issue area such as trade), and orders (a broad or overall structure of relations among states such as a liberal economic order). This simplification works unusually well in trade precisely because the regime is essentially the principles, rules, and procedures developed over the many years of member state efforts through the GATT-WTO.

9 See, for example, the introduction and conclusion in Paul F. Knitter and Chandra Muzaffar, eds., *Subverting Greed: Religious Perspectives on the Global Economy*, Maryknoll, NY: Orbis Books, 2002.

10 This final case study benefits from comparative insights and updates based on the author's experience directly observing the entire ministerial meeting of 2003 in Cancún, Mexico.

11 In all possible cases, those interviewed included former officials or those holding new positions, because they are generally more able and willing to speak frankly about their prior experience.

2 Political leadership in international institutionalized bargaining

1 Joseph S. Nye, "The Changing Nature of World Power," *Political Science Quarterly*, summer 1990, vol. 105, no. 2, p. 187.

2 See, for example, J. G. Ikenberry, *After Victory: Institutions, Strategic Restraint, and the Rebuilding of Order after Major Wars*, Princeton, NJ: Princeton University Press, 2001.

3 The classic statement of hegemonic stability theory is Charles Kindleberger, *The World in Depression, 1929–39*, Berkeley: University of California Press, 1973. See also Stephen Krasner, "State Power and the Structure of International Trade," *World Politics*, 1976, vol. 28, pp. 317–347, and David Lake, *Power, Protection, and Free Trade*, Ithaca, NY: Cornell University Press, 1988. For a skeptical appraisal, see Duncan Snidal, "The Limits of Hegemonic Stability," *International Organization*, 1985, vol. 39, no. 4, pp. 579–614. Snidal argues that the line between benign and coercive hegemony is at least fuzzy, and probably false.

4 Decline also reduces the hegemon's ability to regulate the rules of the regime. Rule-making authority is a product of "oligopolistic power," or "the power to demand." As long as peripheral states depend on one dominating market, the hegemon may dictate institutional norms by threatening closure. Vinod K. Aggarwal, *Liberal Protectionism: The International Politics of Organized Textile Trade*, Berkeley, CA: University of California Press, 1985, p. 186.

5 In *After Hegemony: Cooperation and Discord in the World Political Economy*, Princeton, NJ: Princeton University Press, 1984, Robert O. Keohane emphasizes

that "[d]ecisions to exercise leadership are necessary to 'activate' the posited relationship between power capabilities and outcomes," p. 35; and pp. 136–141.

6 Of the twenty-six articles contained in the ITO Charter, twenty-three were essentially verbatim reproductions of American submissions. US officials also largely composed the remaining articles, and ITO signatories added them to the charter with only minor modifications. Donald G. Beane, *The United States and GATT: A Relational Study*, Amsterdam: Pergamon, 2000, p. 3 and p. 10.

7 J. Odell and B. Eichengreen, "The United States, the ITO, and the WTO: Exit Options, Agent Slack, and Presidential Leadership," in Anne O. Krueger, ed., *The WTO as an International Organization*, Chicago: University of Chicago Press, 1998, p. 189.

8 One excellent example is the "rational design" project represented in *International Organization*, 2001, vol. 55.

9 I. M. Destler, "A Government Divided: The Economic Complex and the Security Complex," in D. A. Deese, ed., *The New Politics of American Foreign Policy*, New York: St. Martin's Press, 1994.

10 E. C. Luck, "Gaps, Commitments, and the Compliance Challenge," in E. C. Luck and M. W. Doyle, eds., *International Law and Organization: Closing the Compliance Gap*, New York: Rowman and Littlefield, 2004, p. 310.

11 J. Goldstein and L. Martin, "Legalization, Trade Liberalization, and Domestic Politics," *International Organization*, vol. 54, pp. 612–613.

12 See Lloyd Gruber, *Ruling the World: Power Politics and the Rise of Supranational Institutions*, Princeton, NJ: Princeton University Press, 2000.

13 Yoram Z. Haftel and Alexander Thompson, "The Independence of International Organizations," *Journal of Conflict Resolution*, April 2006, vol. 50, no. 2, pp. 253–275 at p. 270.

14 Andrew Moravcsik, "The European constitutional compromise and the neo-functionalist legacy," *Journal of European Public Policy*, April 2005, vol. 12, no. 2, pp. 349–386; and *The Choice for Europe*, Ithaca, NY: Cornell University Press, 1998.

15 See, for example, Michael Barnett and Martha Finnemore, "The Power, Politics, and Pathologies of International Organizations," *International Organization*, autumn 1999, vol. 53, no. 4, pp. 699–732.

16 J. Goldstein, "Creating the GATT Rules," in J. G. Ruggie, ed., *Multilateralism Matters*, New York: Columbia University Press, 1993, and Patrick Low, *Trading Free: The GATT and US Trade Policy*, New York: Twentieth Century Fund Press, 1993.

17 G. Garrett, "The Causes of Globalization," *Comparative Political Studies*, August/September 2000, 33, no. 6/7, p. 977. Still, this effect can be expected to be partially offset for countries at higher levels of development because they tend to be less protectionist, probably because their residents tend to benefit from openness. The argument certainly can be applied to the EU, which is conducting an ever larger share of its trade within the common market. Patrick Low, Director of Economic Research and Development at the WTO, argues that states with the most advanced and open sectors, such as the EU in financial services, will advocate trade liberalization in those sectors (interview of January 2003, Geneva, Switzerland).

18 James MacGregor Burns, *Leadership*, Hagerstown, NY: Harper Colophon Books, 1978, p. 343.

19 Steven F. Hayward, *Greatness: Reagan, Churchill, and the Making of Extraordinary Leaders*, New York: Three Rivers Press, 2005, pp. 167–168.

20 Bernard Brodie, *War and Politics*, New York: Macmillan, 1973, p. 374.
21 Burns, *Leadership*, p. 461.
22 Ibid., 134.
23 J. W. Doig and E. C. Hargrove, eds., *Leadership and Innovation: A Biographical Perspective on Entrepreneurs in Government*, Baltimore: Johns Hopkins Press, 1987, p. 14.
24 R. O. Keohane, *After Hegemony: Cooperation and Discord in the World Political Economy*, Princeton, NJ: Princeton University Press, 1984, p. 35.
25 In this regard, see the important work by Jean Blondel, *Political Leadership: Towards a General Analysis*, Beverly Hills, CA: Sage, 1987; W. Lammers and M. Genovese, *The Presidency and Domestic Policy: Comparing Leadership Styles*, Washington, DC: CQ Press, 2000; E. C. Hargrove, *Presidential Leadership: Personality and Political Style*, New York: Macmillan, 1966; and A. Rudalevige, *Managing the President's Program: Presidential Leadership and Legislative Policy Formulation*, Princeton, NJ: Princeton University Press, 2002.
26 Oran R. Young, "Political Leadership and Regime Formation: On the Development of Institutions in International Society," *International Organization*, summer 1991, vo. 45, no. 3, p. 306.
27 Ibid., p. 307.
28 See, for example, ibid., p. 299, and J. G. Ruggie, "International Regimes, Trans-actions, and Change: Embedded Liberalism in the Postwar Economic Order," in S. D. Krasner, ed., *International Regimes*, Ithaca, NY: Cornell University Press, 1983, pp. 195–231. On the crucial role of the Reciprocal Trade Agreements Act of 1934, see S. Haggard, "The Institutional Foundations of Hegemony: Explaining the Reciprocal Trade Agreements Act of 1934," and J. Goldstein, "Ideas, Institutions, and American Trade Policy," both in *International Organization*, winter 1988, vol. 42, no. 1, pp. 91–119 and 179–217.
29 See R. J. House, P. J. Hanges, M. Javidan, P. W. Dorfman, and V. Gupta, eds., *Culture, Leadership, and Organizations: The GLOBE Study of 62 Societies*, Thousand Oaks, CA: Sage, 2004.
30 Power asymmetries, however, do not necessarily directly determine the distribution of benefits from agreements. This is in part because the benefits and costs of GATT-WTO agreements are very difficult, if not impossible, to calculate. The number of parties and bundles of issues being negotiated have both increased sharply over time.
31 D. Lax and J. Sebenius in "Thinking Coalitionally: Party Arithmetic, Process Opportunism, and Strategic Sequencing," in H. Peyton Young, ed., *Negotiation Analysis*, Ann Arbor, MI: University of Michigan Press, 1991, pp. 153–193, coined the terms "value-claiming" and "value-creating," but they are ambiguous about the effects of each strategy on the probability and terms of cooperation. The authors suggest that integrative strategies improve the chances of agreement because "[t]he point of negotiation is for each negotiator to do better by jointly decided action than he could do otherwise." Improving mutual gains is a logical means to this end. Yet the authors recognize that absolute and relative gains matter: the "negotiator's dilemma" is the inherent tension between creating value and claiming it. Creating value may not produce agreement if negotiators still cannot agree on how to distribute gains. Lax and Sebenius, "The Manager as Negotiator," p. 42. In *Traders in a Brave New World*, Chicago: University of Chicago Press, 1995, p. 21, E. Preeg argues that "[s]uch leadership needs to be based on national self-interest or an altruistic calling, and since World War II a dominant U.S trade-leadership role has been based on both."

32 John S. Odell, *Negotiating the World Economy*, Ithaca, NY: Cornell University Press, 2000. Odell argues that the extent to which states pursue distributive or integrative strategies is determined by the context of negotiations, including the availability of exit options and objective market conditions. Offering practical bargaining advice, Roger Fisher and William Ury insist, "In a complex situation, creative inventing is an absolute necessity. In any negotiation it may open doors and produce a range of potential agreements satisfactory to each side." Roger Fisher and William Ury with Bruce Patton, eds., *Getting to Yes: Negotiating Agreement without Giving In*, London: Hutchinson, 1982, p. 83.

33 The concept of reciprocal concessions or gains, or "reciprocity," has been fundamental to US foreign policy from its very earliest roots in the eighteenth century, and the founding principles of GATT very much reflect the notion of bargaining around reciprocal concessions. Leadership herein emphasizes the broader, longer-term form of reciprocity, in that a leader is willing to invest time, skills, connections, domestic policy agenda, and resources to advance the international trade regime. It is important to recognize, however, that the more a leader's interests align with the regime itself, the less cost is involved in enhancing it. Similarly, the more overlap between a leader's interests and those of other key states, the less costly it is to accept new member states or to forge winning coalitions among members. Finally, it is not argued herein that the United States is consistently acting in this leadership capacity. To the contrary, the argument is that US leadership tends to be sporadic and to occur in fits and starts. Thus, when it is most present, the GATT or WTO negotiating process is predicted to be most likely to reach agreement, and visa versa.

34 In "Dominance and Leadership in the International Economy: Exploitation, Public Goods, and Free Rides," *International Studies Quarterly*, June 1981, vol. 25, no. 2, p. 252, Charles Kindleberger clearly leaves open the possibility of two or more countries providing leadership, although he briefly argues that it had not occurred from the 1930s through the 1970s.

35 Ibid., p. 297.

36 A very useful case study of a coalition as "leader" is Richard A. Higgott and Andrew Fenton Cooper, "Middle Power Leadership and Coalition Building: Australia, the Cairns Group, and the Uruguay Round of Trade Negotiations," *International Organization*, autumn 1990, vol. 44, no. 4, pp. 589–632.

37 The argument originates with T. Schelling, *The Strategy of Conflict*, Cambridge, MA: Harvard University Press, 1960, and C. P. Kindleberger, "Dominance and Leadership in the International Economy: Exploitation, Public Goods, and Free Rides," *International Studies Quarterly*, 1981, vol. 25, pp. 242–254. See D. Lake, "Leadership, Hegemony, and the International Economy: Naked Emperor or Tattered Monarch with Potential?" *International Studies Quarterly*, December 1993, vol. 37, no. 4, pp. 459–489; D. Snidal, "The Limits of Hegemonic Stability," *International Organization*, 1985, vol. 39, pp. 579–614; R. Pahre, *Leading Questions: How Hegemony Affects the International Political Economy*, Ann Arbor: University of Michigan Press, 1999.

38 Gilbert Winham observed the "pyramidal pattern" in practice following the Kennedy Round where agreements were initiated by the major powers at the top and then multilateralized by gradually introducing other parties. *International Trade and the Tokyo Round*, Princeton, NJ: Princeton University Press, 1986, pp. 175 and 376.

39 See Daniel Kahneman and Amos Tversky, "Prospect Theory: An Analysis of Decision under Risk," *Econometrica*, 1979, vol. 47, no. 2, pp. 263–291. For a

concise overview, see Jack S. Levy, "An Introduction to Prospect Theory," *Political Psychology*, 1992, vol. 13, pp. 171–186.

40 On focal points, see James D. Fearon, "Bargaining, Enforcement, and International Cooperation," *International Organization*, spring 1998, vol. 52, no. 2, pp. 269–305, 286; Schelling, *Strategy of Conflict*.

41 Quoted in Odell, *Negotiating the World Economy*, 13.

42 Lax and Sebenius, "Thinking Coalitionally," p. 166. The bargaining range is the space between each side's reservation value. The reservation value is the limit at which agreement is preferable to the status quo. Negotiation often includes efforts, through coercion or linkage, to change an adversary's perceived reservation value.

43 John Odell, "The Seattle Impasse," in Daniel L. M. Kennedy and James D. Southwick, eds., *The Political Economy of International Trade Law: Essays in Honor of Robert E. Hudec*, Cambridge: Cambridge University Press, 2002. See also Alan Oxley, *The Challenge of Free Trade*, London: Harvester Wheatsheaf, 1990, pp. 132–144; Patrick Low, *Trading Free: The GATT and U.S. Trade Policy*, New York: Twentieth Century Fund Press, 1993, pp. 211–212; Hugo Paemen and Alexandra Bensch, *From the GATT to the WTO: The European Community in the Uruguay Round*, Leuven, Belgium: Leuven University Press, 1995, pp. 44–45.

44 Lax and Sebenius, "Thinking Coalitionally," p. 186.

45 The effects are not always negative for structural leadership. US presidential elections are often set as an end point for agreement, and they can provide a powerful source of pressure to reach agreement before a new administration takes over. Still, it is assumed that for the most part domestic political economy is a constraining rather than a facilitating domain.

46 On audience costs and signaling, see James D. Fearon, "Domestic Audiences and the Escalation of International Disputes," *American Political Science Review*, 1994, vol. 88, pp. 577–592; Kenneth A. Schultz, "Domestic Opposition and Signaling in International Crises," *American Political Science Review* December 1998, vol. 92, no. 4; and Schultz, "Do Democratic Institutions Constrain or Inform? Contrasting Two Institutional Perspectives on Democracy and War," *International Organization*, spring 1999, vol. 53, no. 2, pp. 233–266. Fearon and Schultz discuss these concepts in the context of security affairs, but the same logic applies here.

47 Kenneth Oye identifies three types of linkage. Exchange linkage involves taking compensation for acting against one's best interest. Extortion, "a weapon of political coercion," damages both parties if the linker acts on threats. Finally, explanation linkage facilitates cooperation by highlighting existing cross-issue trade-offs. Kenneth A. Oye, *Economic Discrimination and Political Exchange: World Political Economy in the 1930s and 1980s*, Princeton, NJ: Princeton University Press, 1992, pp. 38–44.

48 On the role of linkages, see Christina Davis, *Food Fights over Free Trade: How International Institutions Promote Agricultural Trade Liberalization*, Princeton, NJ: Princeton University Press, 2003. Legalization, including delegating authority to supranational bodies, tends to activate disparate protectionists. Christina Davis also argues that under certain circumstances legalization positively affects liberalization, since the use of GATT-WTO trade law legitimizes free trade principles. Her evidence indicates a more consistent relationship between linkage and trade cooperation. Christina Davis, "Linkage and Legalism in Institutions: Evidence from Agricultural Trade Negotiations," Paper presented at the

International Studies Association Annual Convention, New Orleans, March 24–27, 2002.

49 Young, "Political Leadership," p. 293.

50 Jarrod Wiener, *Making Rules in the Uruguay Round: A Study of International Leadership*, Brookfield, VT: Dartmouth, 1995, p. 223.

51 In Dahl's standard formulation, power is the ability to compel a political actor to do something he would not otherwise do. Robert A. Dahl, "On the Concept of Power," *Behavioral Science*, 1957, vol. 2, pp. 201–215.

52 Wiener, *Making Rules*, p. 223.

53 Robert O. Keohane, "Governance in a Partially Globalized World," in David Held and Anthony McGrew, eds., *Governing Globalization: Power, Authority, and Global Governance*," Cambridge: Polity Press, 2002, p. 341.

54 An important application of this in the GATT-WTO context is the ambassador to the GATT-WTO from a small state who heads a key committee or negotiating issue area in which his or her state does not hold a major stake. This individual represents a member state, but, more important, his or her state is not one of the "principals in the bargaining process." Young, "Politcal Leadership," p. 288.

55 They are also useful in terms of enhancing compliance with existing regimes, as outlined by Keohane, *After Hegemony*, pp. 103–106, in that a violation in one area of rules may have costly results in other areas of importance to a state. Interestingly, however, the new WTO regime departs from Keohane's advice not to rely heavily on retaliation for compliance, in that the dispute system is founded on WTO-sanctioned retaliation against a non-complying member state. From one perspective the system seems to work reasonably well for the largest trading states, but not so well for small member states with little effective ability to retaliate. On the other hand, small states are gaining the leverage to press for changes in some areas of large-state trading practices. In any case, small states value the way in which the trade regime constrains the behavior of larger member states.

56 Lloyd Gruber in *Ruling the World* offers an important analysis of how powerful states can control the agenda by removing the status quo ante from the choice sets of other actors, particularly to dominate small states by making it infeasible for them to remain outside newly bargained arrangements such as international trade and monetary regimes. His argument is certainly relevant to the options confronting many of the developing states late in the Uruguay Round, as opposed to the Tokyo Round, where all but four developing-state members opted out of the new arrangements. Still, it would be difficult to sustain the argument that small states generally were forced to join the GATT or WTO because they must opt to engage in an intensive negotiation, usually over several years, involving multiple decision points and domestic regulatory reforms along the path to final membership. Probably more important to this discussion is the "proposition that the trend toward trade liberalization around the world in recent decades is explicable in terms of the increased opportunity costs of closure." Garrett, "Causes of Globalization," p. 963.

57 See, for example, D. Druckman, "Determinants of Compromising Behavior in Negotiation: A Meta-analysis," *Journal of Conflict Resolution*, 1994, vol. 38, pp. 504–556 at p. 527.

58 For useful findings contrasting the international security and trade regimes in terms of external and internal precipitants of turning points, see Druckman, ibid., p. 520.

59 "Redefining Accountability for Global Governance," in Miles Kahler and David

Lake, eds., *Governance in a Global Economy*, Princeton, NJ: Princeton University Press, 2004, p. 411.

60 Young, "Political Leadership," p. 281.

61 This draws on the Rational Design Project, which focuses primarily on the "dependent variables of institutional design," *International Organization*, 2001, vol. 55, no. 4, p. 1063. My principal orientation is that "states use international institutions to further their own goals, and they design institutions accordingly"; thus, institutions are "rational, negotiated responses to the problems international actors face," pp. 762 and 769. In this regard, Geoffrey Garrett's argument in "The Causes of Globalization," *Comparative Political Studies*, 2000, vol. 33, p. 945, about international institutions and trade integration is instructive. "It seems more reasonable to contend that preference convergence among governments was a precondition for the effectiveness of these institutional solutions. Thus, we should focus on explaining why this convergence in preferences occurred."

3 The founding: World War II to the turbulent 1970s

1 Franklin D. Roosevelt, "Annual Message of the President to the Congress," January 1941, at http://www.ourdocuments.gov/doc.php?doc=70&page=trans criptin.

2 Samuel I. Rosenman, ed., *Public Papers and Addresses of Franklin D. Roosevelt, 1938–1950,* vol. 10, New York: Random House, p. 314.

3 Lend-Lease Agreement between the United States and the United Kingdom, February 1942, http://www.yale.edu/lawweb/avalon/20th.htm

4 http://www.brettonwoodsproject.org/item.shtml?x=320747 "The creation of the World Bank and the IMF came at the end of the Second World War. They were based on the ideas of a trio of key experts – US Treasury Secretary Henry Morganthau, his chief economic advisor Harry Dexter White, and British economist John Maynard Keynes. They wanted to establish a postwar economic order based on notions of consensual decision-making and cooperation in the realm of trade and economic relations. It was felt by leaders of the Allied countries, particularly the US and Britain, that a multilateral framework was needed to overcome the destabilising effects of the previous global economic depression and trade battles."

5 As explained by J. Goldstein, "Creating the GATT Rules," in J. G. Ruggie ed., *Multilateralism Matters*, New York: Columbia University Press, 1993, pp. 201–232, the protectionist US domestic politics of agriculture greatly complicated later US attempts to pursue agricultural liberalization through the GATT.

6 A.W. DePorte, *Europe between the Superpowers: The Enduring Balance*, New Haven, CT: Yale University Press, 1986, p. 133.

7 Ibid., p. 134.

8 See H. Feis, "The Geneva Proposals for an International Trade Charter," *International Organization*, February 1948, vol. 2, no. 1, pp. 39–52 for a summary of the ITO Charter as it stood following the Geneva negotiations. "The text is a triumph of definition of conflicting desires and ideas rather than a conclusive common accord." Although writing prior to the Havana conference, Feis foresees that "unless the current crisis is met and overcome, the Charter may never be brought into effect," p. 50.

9 Part II of the GATT corresponds to Chapter V of the Havana Charter. Because the

GATT was restricted to tariff-cutting measures, it fell under presidential prerogative given by the Reciprocal Trade Agreements Act of 1934 and did not require congressional ratification.

10 S. Aaronson, *For the People, but Not by the People*, Baltimore: Johns Hopkins University, 1993, p. 19.

11 Aaronson highlights that "[t]rade was not a politically salient issue. In general, Americans became concerned about trade policies only when they feared economic distress," Ibid., p. 8, and that "[p]olls reported that the American people were relatively uninterested in foreign trade or in establishing such an organization," p. 2.

12 "There was no shared notion of the national interest in trade in the postwar period. Nor was there a consensus among the branches of government or special interests as to how best to stimulate America's trade." Ibid., p. 19.

13 http://www.yale.edu/lawweb/avalon/20th.htm

14 National Security Council 1953.

15 Cited in Burton I. Kaufman, *Trade and Aid: Eisenhower's Foreign Economic Policy 1953–1961*, London: Johns Hopkins University Press, 1982, p. 40.

16 See Judith Goldstein, "The Impact of Ideas on Trade Policy: A Comparative Study of the Origins of American Agriculture and Manufacturing Policies," *International Organization*, Winter 1989, pp. 31–71; and "Creating GATT Rules: Ideas, Institutions and American Politics," in J. Ruggie, ed., *Multilateralism Matters*, New York: Columbia University Press, 1993.

17 The proposed Organization for Trade Cooperation was to be granted certain new enforcement and dispute settlement capabilities.

18 See John M. Rothgeb, Jr., *U.S. Trade Policy: Balancing Economic Dreams with Political Realities*, Washington, DC: CQ Press, 2001, pp. 104ff.

19 Ibid.

20 The US waiver from GATT in 1955 for quotas on certain agriculture imports provided the Europeans with a clear precedent in US policy for arguing against the inclusion of agriculture in the GATT.

21 I. M. Destler, "A Government Divided: The Security Complex and the Economic Complex," in D. A. Deese, ed., *The New Politics of American Foreign Policy*, New York: St. Martin's Press, 1994, p. 138. The US "security complex," which deals with traditional diplomatic and military issues, gives priority to national security goals and relationships. The "economic complex" addresses trade, monetary, and financial issues, and emphasizes domestic impacts. In most cases where there have been clashes in priorities between economic policy and national security, the latter has prevailed. Two professional groupings have evolved "that speak different languages, focus on different variables, and have difficulty communicating with one another" (p. 141). Across several administrations, particularly throughout the 1970s and 1980s, this division led to major decisions being taken in one sphere without sensitivity to the other.

22 Ibid.

23 Ibid., p. 142, citing William Hyland, "America's New Course," *Foreign Affairs*, spring 1990, vo. 69, pp. 7–8. The two complexes in US foreign policy making corresponded to the "two post-war settlements" described by G. John Ikenberry as the "containment order" and the "Western order," or the liberal international institutions and arrangements linking the Western industrial states and Japan. "The Myth of Post-Cold War Chaos," *Foreign Affairs*, May/June 1996, vo. 75, no. 3, pp. 79–91, and *After Victory*, Princeton, NJ: Princeton University Press, 2001, p. 170.

24 J. S. Nye, "United States Policy toward Regional Organization," *International Organization*, vol. 23, 1969, p. 738.
25 Kaufman, *Trade and Aid*, p. 182.
26 In the 1950s, the United States also sought to gain greater access to Japanese markets and to control the effects of market disruption from Japanese exports. Thus, the United States pursued a continuing partnership with Japan, while also attempting to weaken its ability to act as a "spoiler" within the GATT system.
27 S. Dryden, *Trade Warriors: USTR and the American Crusade for Free Trade*, New York: Oxford University Press, 1995, p. 41.
28 Press release, White House, March 7, 1962.
29 See Goldstein, "The Impact of Ideas," 1989.
30 T. W. Zeiler, *American Trade and Power in the 1960s*, New York: Columbia University Press, 1992, p. 62.
31 In the Agreement with Respect to Corn, Sorghum, Ordinary Wheat, Rice and Poultry, and the Agreement with Respect to Quality Wheat, the Six agreed to "undertake not to modify their national import systems in such a way as to make them more restrictive" to non-member imports. *General Agreement on Tariffs and Trade*, TIAS, 1700, 61 Stat., pts. 5 and 6.
32 *General Agreement on Tariffs and Trade*, TIAS 3930; 8 UST 1790.
33 G. Curzon, *Multilateral Commercial Diplomacy*, London: Michael Joseph, 1965, p. 100.
34 From the outset of the round, negotiators realized that the bilateral negotiating process was ineffective in prompting the level of concessions needed to maintain the round's momentum. Interview with Ake Linden, Geneva, Switzerland, 21 November 2002.
35 A. E. Eckes, *Opening America's Market: US Foreign Policy since 1776*, Chapel Hill: University of North Carolina Press, 1995, p. 183.
36 Eric Wyndham White, Press release number 993, GATT, June 30, 1967.
37 See D. Lee, "Middle Powers in the Global Economy: British Influence during the Opening Phase of the Kennedy Trade Round Negotiations, 1962–4" *Review of International Studies*, 1998, vol. 24, p. 515. For analysis of Britain's influence in the Kennedy Trade Round (KTR), an aspect of this round which tends to be overlooked given the importance of US–EC dialogues. "Britain was a middle power with few material power capabilities, but the non-material resources of state-actors were utilized to exert influence on a great power, influence which determined the outcome of the opening phase of the KTR."
38 Eric Wyndham White, op. cit.
39 As the EU gained internal strength and consensus, it was more consistently able to use its blocking leverage to erode the structural leadership of US officials. During the Kennedy Round, the EU emerged with an opportunistic, value-claiming attitude – seeking to extract gains from the United States and exploit American vulnerability. Interview with Daniel Hartridge, Washington, DC, November 22, 2002.
40 Lee, "Middle Powers," 1998, p. 517.
41 "Components of a strategy for the Kennedy Round." Report, White House, Confidential, issue date: December 10, 1963, date declassified: December 1, 1987, unsanitized, complete, CD-ROM 19988090102937, LBJ Library.
42 J. W. Evans, *The Kennedy Round in American Trade Policy: The Twilight of the GATT?*, Cambridge, MA: Harvard University Press, 1971, p. 19.
43 "The Kennedy Round," Working Paper, Report, White House, Secret, issue date: January 1, 1968, date declassified: June 7, 1982, unsanitized, complete, CD-ROM 1984010101475, LBJ Library, 22.

44 The key British role is documented fully in Lee, "Middle Powers."

45 Interview with Dick Rivers Washington, DC, September 30, 2002.

46 Memorandum from the President's Deputy's Special Assistant for National Security Affairs (Bator) to President Johnson, May 15, 1967, Bator Papers, Box 29, LBJ Library.

47 Interview with D. Rivers, op. cit.

48 S. D. Krasner, "US Commercial and Monetary Policy: Unraveling the Paradox of External Strength and Internal Weakness," *International Organization*, autumn, 1977, vol. 31, no. 4, p. 637.

49 Gary Clyde Hufbauer and Joanna Shelton Erb, *Subsidies in International Trade*, Washington, DC: Institute for International Economics, 1984, p. 4.

50 Interview with A. Linden, op. cit.

51 John F. Kennedy, Special Message to the Congress on Foreign Trade Policy, January 25, 1962, *Public Papers of the Presidents*, Washington, DC: Government Printing Office, 1962, pp. 68–77.

52 John F. Kennedy, Annual Message to Congress on the State of the Union, *Public Papers of the President of the United States: Lyndon Baines Johnson, 1968–1969*, vol. 1, Washington, DC: Government Printing Office, 1970, entry 14, pp. 25–33.

53 Interview with A. Linden, op. cit.

54 John F. Kennedy, Special Message to the Congress, op. cit.

55 "The Kennedy Round," Working Paper, Report, White House, Secret, issue date: January 1, 1968, date declassified, June 7, 1982, unsanitized, complete, CD-ROM 1984010101475, LBJ Library, 11.

56 John F. Kennedy, Special Message to the Congress, op. cit.

57 John F. Kennedy, Annual Message to Congress on the State of the Union, op. cit.

58 F. Costigliola, *France and the United States: The Cold Alliance since World War II*, New York: Columbia University Press, 1987, p. 137.

59 Evans, *The Kennedy Round*, p. 139.

60 "A View of US–UK Policy Relations," Airgram, Department of State, Secret, issue date: May 23, 1966, date declassified: [no declassification date], CD-ROM 1978070100311, LBJ Library.

61 Thomas W. Zeiler, "Managing Protectionism: American Trade Policy in the Early Cold War," *Diplomatic History*, 1998, vol. 22, p. 353.

62 Memorandum from the President's Deputy's Special Assistant for National Security Affairs (Bator) to President Johnson, May 15, 1967, Bator Papers, Box 29, LBJ Library.

63 Lee, "Middle Powers," p. 32.

64 Eckes, *Opening America's Market*, p. 79.

65 E. Preeg, *Traders in a Brave New World*, Chicago: University of Chicago Press, 1995, p. 3.

66 In issue areas where the EEC could negotiate as a bloc, it naturally gained greater negotiating authority, and here it was able to affect positive agenda-setting change. In the Kennedy Round, however, the EEC was not often able to gain the internal consensus needed to change the substance of the round significantly. In the chemical sector, however, the ASP package – created at the insistence of the EEC – attests to the positive agenda-setting power of the EEC. The EEC leverage would grow in later rounds, but would remain limited. The internal divisions between EEC members would continue to undermine the bloc's potential power as a leader within the GATT and later the WTO organization. Interview with A. Linden, op. cit.

67 John F. Kennedy, Annual Message to Congress on the State of the Union, op. cit.

68 Preeg, *Traders in a Brave New World*, p. 123.
69 *The Kennedy Round of Trade Negotiations*, presented to Parliament by the President of the Board of Trade, GATT Library, Geneva, July 1967, London: Her Majesty's Stationery Office, 1967, p. 6.
70 "The Kennedy Round Crisis," Working Paper, Report, White House, Secret, issue date: June 1, 1967, date declassified: October 13, 1982, unsanitized, complete, CD-ROM1984010101458, LBJ Library, 5.
71 Interview with D. Rivers, op. cit.
72 "Visit of German Chancellor Erhard. Washington, D.C. Background Paper: The EEC and the Kennedy Round." Department of State, Confidential, issue date: September 19, 1966, date declassified: August 9, 1994, unsanitized, complete, CD-ROM 1995110103183, LBJ Library.
73 "Agreement Relating Principally to Chemicals, Supplementary to the Geneva Protocol to the General Agreement on Tariffs and Trade." BISD [Basic Instruments and Selected Documents], 15th Supplement, 1968.
74 "The Kennedy Round Crisis – 1967: Chronology and Annotated Index of Documents," Report, White House, Secret, issue date: June 1, 1967, date declassified: October 13, 1982, unsanitized, complete, CD-ROM 1984010101457, LBJ Library.
75 Ibid.
76 *The Kennedy Round of Trade Negotiations*, op. cit., p. 6.
77 "The Kennedy Round," Working Paper, Report, White House, Confidential, issue date: January 1, 1969, date declassified: June 7, 1982, unsanitized, complete, CD-ROM 1984010101475, LBJ Library, 20.
78 Lee, D., "Middle Powers," p. 116.
79 "The Kennedy Round," Working Paper, Report, White House, Confidential, issue date: January 1, 1969, date declassified: June 7, 1982, unsanitized, complete, CD-ROM 1984010101475, LBJ Library, 43.
80 Eric Wyndham White, op. cit.
81 The use of the linear cut method was instrumental in expanding the scope of the round. It help to insulate member states' decisions from domestic industrial pressures. This, in turn, allowed for greater liberalization and facilitated domestic ratification of agreements. Interview with A. Linden, op. cit.
82 Krasner, "US Commercial and Monetary Policy," p. 635.
83 John F. Kennedy, Special Message to the Congress, op. cit.
84 Lee, "Middle Powers," p. 78.
85 Cited in Dryden, *Trade Warriors*, p. 95.
86 Telegram 3374, 24 April 1967, Roth to Bator, Roth Papers, Box 3, Tab 84, LBJ Library.
87 Eric Wyndham White, op. cit.
88 Interview with Daniel Hartridge, Geneva, Switzerland, November 22, 2002.
89 Interview with John Croome, Geneva, Switzerland, November 22, 2002.
90 Daniel Hartridge emphasized that since the Kennedy Round, Japan had been reluctant to assert power within the organization. In future rounds, the Japanese would continue to take a back seat, preferring to exercise power sporadically when in need of concessions or when defending domestic markets. Although a major trade partner, Japan would fail to step forward to direct the negotiations in a formative way. Interview with Daniel Hartridge, op. cit.
91 Memorandum, Department of State, Confidential, issue date: Jauary 15, 1965, date declassified: March 8, 1993, unsanitized, complete, CD ROMD Id: 1994090102495, LBJ Library.
92 *The Kennedy Round of Trade Negotiations*, op. cit., p. 6.

93 Interview with A. Linden, op. cit.; and interview with Julio Lacarte, Chestnut Hill, MA, October 9, 2003.

94 On the causes and consequences of congressional partisanship and assertiveness, see D. Rohde, "Partisan Leadership and Congressional Assertiveness in Foreign and Defense Policy," in Deese, ed., *The New Politics*, pp. 76–77, 98–99.

95 World Trade Organization, CD ROM, *GATT Basic Instruments and Selected Documents*, 1998, GATT 4.

96 D. P. Calleo, *The Imperious Economy*, Cambridge, MA.: Harvard University Press, 1982, pp. 68 and 418; Destler, "A Government Divided," p. 140.

97 D. Karol, "Divided Government and US Trade Policy: Much Ado about Nothing?" *International Organization*, autumn 2000, vol. 54, no. 4, pp. 825–844.

98 World Trade Organization, CD ROM, *GATT Basic Instruments and Selected Documents*, 1998, GATT 6.

99 D. M. McRae and J. C. Thomas, "The GATT and Multilateral Treaty Making: The Tokyo Round," *American Journal of International Law*, 1983, vol. 51, p. 53.

100 World Trade Organization, CD ROM, *GATT Basic Instruments and Selected Documents*, 1998, GATT 6.

101 See the thorough investigation of this period by S. A. Aaronson, "For the People, but Not By the People: A History of the International Trade Organization," Ph.D. diss., Johns Hopkins University, Baltimore, 1993. She argues that "[i]n this setting, the ITO seemed to lack urgency," p. 6.

102 Essentially, opponents complained that the ITO Charter was at once too liberal and not liberal enough. International trade politics sometimes makes for bizarre bedfellows. J. Odell and B. Eichengreen, "The United States, the ITO, and the WTO: Exit Options, Agent Slack, and Presidential Leadership," in A. O. Krueger, ed., *The WTO as an International Organization*, Chicago: University of Chicago Press, 1998, pp. 181–209. See also H. V. Milner, *Interests, Institutions, and Information: Domestic Politics and International Relations*, Princeton, NJ: Princeton University Press, 1997, pp. 137–147.

103 See Destler, "A Government Divided."

4 The General Agreement on Tariffs and Trade, 1975–1995: from endangered species to unprecedented authority

1 See I. M. Destler, "A Government Divided: The Security Complex and the Economic Complex," in D. A. Deese, ed., *The New Politics of American Foreign Policy*, New York: St. Martin's Press, 1994.

2 A. E. Eckes, *Opening America's Market: US Foreign Policy since 1776*, Chapel Hill: University of North Carolina Press, 1995, pp. 254 and 262.

3 Ibid., p. 265.

4 See D. P. Calleo, *The Imperious Economy*, Cambridge, MA: Harvard University Press, 1982; R. O. Keohane, *After Hegemony: Cooperation and Discord in the International Political Economy*, Princeton, NJ: Princeton University Press, 1984; and D. A. Deese and J. S. Nye, eds., *Energy and Security*, New York: Harper & Row, 1981.

5 S. Dryden, *Trade Warriors: USTR and the American Crusade for Free Trade*, New York: Oxford University Press, 1995, p. 191.

6 Ibid.

7 Eckes, *Opening America's Market*, p. 161.

8 World Trade Organization, CD-ROM, *GATT Basic Instruments and Selected Documents*, 1998, GATT 4.

9 Interview with Richard Rivers, Washington, DC, September 30, 2002. "Fast-track" authority was an innovation allowing the president to notify Congress 90 days before signing trade agreements and begin consultations with the involved congressional committees. Once sent to Congress for formal review, agreements could only be accepted or rejected in their entirety, without amendments.

10 Director General Olivier Long, World Trade Organization, CD-ROM, *GATT Basic Instruments and Selected Documents*, 1998, GATT 11.

11 S. Krasner, "The Tokyo Round: Particularist Interests and Prospects for Stability in the Global Trading System," *International Studies Quarterly*, 1979, vol. 23, p. 525.

12 Olivier Long, Final Report on the Tokyo Round, World Trade Organization, CD-ROM, *GATT Basic Instruments and Selected Documents*, 1998, GATT 10.

13 Interview with Robert Strauss, May 13, 2003, Washington, DC, and a discussion with W. Richard Cooper, May 14, 2003, Cambridge, MA.

14 Dryden, *Trade Warriors*, p. 214.

15 Interview with R. Strauss, op. cit. See also Dryden, *Trade Warriors*, p. 221.

16 Dryden, *Trade Warriors*, p. 221.

17 Ibid., p. 222, and interview with R. Strauss, op. cit.

18 Interview with R. Rivers, op. cit.; Dryden, *Trade Warriors*, p. 225.

19 Dryden, *Trade Warriors*, p. 226; Interview with R. Rivers, op. cit.

20 H. Fukui, "The GATT Tokyo Round: The Bureaucratic Politics of Multilateral Diplomacy," in M. Blaker, ed., *The Politics of Trade: US and Japanese Policymaking for the GATT Negotiations*, New York: Columbia University East Asian Institute, p. 137.

21 Dryden, S., *Trade Warriors*, p. 235.

22 Ibid., p. 237.

23 Interview with R. Strauss, op. cit.

24 S. Bruce Wilson, Office of the STR, as quoted in Eckes, *Opening America's Market*, p. 161.

25 J. H. Jackson, *The World Trade Organization: Constitution and Jurisprudence*, London: Royal Institute of International Affairs, 1998, pp. 67–69. Ironically the dispute settlement process was used mostly against the United States after the Tokyo Round.

26 P. Low, *Trading Free: The GATT and US Trade Policy*. New York: Twentieth Century Fund Press, 1993, p. 187. Twentieth Century Fund Press, p. 187.

27 The author is grateful in the following account to the comments of an anonymous reviewer who was directly involved in these negotiations.

28 J. Goldstein and L. L. Martin, "Legalization, Trade Liberalization, and Domestic Politics: A Cautionary Note," *International Organization*, 2000, vol. 54, p. 613.

29 R. Vernon and D. L. Spar, *Beyond Globalism: Remaking American Foreign Economic Policy*, New York: Free Press, 1989, p. 497.

30 Low, *Trading Free*, p. 245.

31 Alonzo McDonald, STR, as quoted in Eckes, *Opening America's Market*, p. 136.

32 Eckes, *Opening America's Market*, p. 132.

33 "Japan preferred to play its lone hand and to accept those aspects of the world trade regime that were either convenient or basically innocuous from Japan's standpoint." Lawrence Fox, US Department of Commerce, as cited in Eckes, *Opening America's Market*, p. 141.

34 On issue linkage and agriculture, see C. Davis, "Linkage and Legalism in Institutions: Evidence from Agricultural Trade Negotiations," Paper presented at the International Studies Association Annual Convention, New Orleans, March

24–27, 2002, and "International Institutions and Issue Linkage: Building Support for Agricultural Trade Liberalization," *American Political Science Review*, February 2004, vol. 98, no. 1, pp. 153–169.

35 Alonzo McDonald, STR, as quoted in Eckes, *Opening America's Market*, p. 139; and Davis, "Linkage and Legalism."

36 Alonzo McDonald, STR, as quoted in Eckes, *Opening America's Market*, p. 132.

37 Interview with John Weekes, November 21, 2002, Geneva, Switzerland.

38 C. G. Thies, "A Historical Institutionalist Approach to the Uruguay Round Agricultural Negotiations," *Comparative Political Studies*, 2001, vo. 34, p. 402.

39 Interview with Dorothy Dwoskin, October 2, 2002, Washington, DC.

40 Interview with Frieda Russler, November 22, 2002, Geneva, Switzerland.

41 H. Paemen and A. Bensch, *From the GATT to the WTO: The European Community in the Uruguay Round*, Leuven, Belgium: Leuven University Press, 1995, p. 91.

42 Interview by telephone with Senator Bill Brock, April 12, 2003.

43 Interviews by telephone with Warren Lavorel, December 3, 2002, and Geza Feketekuty, May 12, 2003.

44 Interview with Bruce Wilson, November 22, 2002, Geneva, Switzerland.

45 Paemen and Bensch, *From the GATT to the WTO*, p. 32.

46 J. Croome, *Reshaping the World Trading System: A History of the Uruguay Round*, Geneva: World Trade Organization, 1995, p. 11.

47 Interviews with W. Lavorel and G. Feketekuty, op. cit.

48 Interview with W. Lavorel, op. cit.

49 Croome, *Reshaping the World Trading System*, p. 13.

50 Interview with W. Lavorel, op. cit.

51 Paemen and Bensch, *From the GATT to the WTO*, pp. 84–85.

52 Ibid.

53 Interview with Bill Brock, op. cit.

54 Interview with Andy Stoler, November 19, 2002, Geneva, Switzerland.

55 Paemen and Bensch, *From the GATT to the WTO*, pp. 93–97.

56 J. Wiener, *Making Rules in the Uruguay Round: A Study of International Leadership*, Brookfield, VT: Dartmouth, 1995, p. 103.

57 Interview with David Walters, May 7, 2003, Washington, DC.

58 Interview with Clayton Yeutter, October 2, 2002, Washington, DC.

59 Croome, p. 14.

60 Interviews with B. Brock and D. Hartridge, op. cit.

61 Interview with D. Hartridge, op. cit.

62 Interview with C. Yeutter, op. cit.

63 Interview with B. Brock, op. cit.

64 Interview with G. Feketekuty, op. cit.

65 Ibid.

66 Wiener, *Making Rules*, p. 112.

67 Croome, *Reshaping the World Trading System*, pp. 16–17.

68 Ibid.

69 Wiener, *Making Rules*, pp. 115 and 122.

70 This is called a vote for joint action under Article XXV.

71 Wiener, *Making Rules*, p. 130.

72 Ibid., p. 108.

73 Dryden, *Trade Warriors*, p. 340.

74 Interview with D. Dwoskin, op. cit.

75 The fifteen negotiating groups are as follows: tariffs, non-tariff measures, natural resource-based products, textiles and clothing, agriculture, tropical products,

GATT articles, MFN agreements and arrangements, safeguards, subsidies and countervailing measures, trade-related intellectual property (TRIPs), trade-related investment measures (TRIMs), dispute settlement, functioning of the GATT system (FOGS), and services.

76 Interview with Claude Barfield, May 5, 2003, Washington, DC.
77 Interview with B. Wilson, op. cit.
78 Interview with C. Yeutter, op. cit.
79 Interview with B. Wilson, op. cit.
80 Interview with Robert Fischer, 2 October 2002, Washington, DC.
81 Interview with C. Yeutter, op. cit.
82 Ibid.
83 Croome, *Reshaping the World Trading System*, p. 128.
84 Interview with Charlene Barshefsky, October 3, 2002, Washington, DC.
85 Interview with Peter Allgeier, October 1, 2002, Washington, DC.
86 Interview with C. Yeutter, op. cit.
87 Interview with C. Barshefsky, op. cit.
88 Interview with Julio Lacarte, October 9, 2003, Chestnut Hill, MA.
89 Interview with G. Feketekuty, op. cit.
90 The EC members reached a milestone agreement in 1986–1987 to finally establish a fully functioning common market not later than January 1993.
91 Croome, *Reshaping the World Trading System*, p. 111.
92 General Agreement on Tariffs and Trade (GATT) 6, Geneva: World Trade Organization, CD-ROM, *GATT Basic Instruments and Selected Documents*, 1998. The Cairns Group (or agricultural-product-exporting states) was formed at the initiative of trade officials from Australia in 1986 and developed further under leadership by officials from Uruguay in order to advance agricultural trade policy liberalization.
93 Wiener, *Making Rules*, p. 145.
94 By 1993–1994, China, Taiwan, Thailand, and Malaysia were also among the largest trading states.
95 Croome, *Reshaping the World Trading System*, pp. 169–172.
96 C. Davis, "A Conflict of Institutions: The WTO and EU Agricultural Policy," Paper presented at the annual meeting of the New England Political Science Association, Portland, ME, May 3, 2002, p. 17.
97 Paemen and Bensch, *From the GATT to the WTO*, pp. 134–138.
98 E. H. Preeg, *Traders in a Brave New World*, Chicago: University of Chicago Press, 1995, pp. 86–87.
99 C. Yeutter, "Bringing Agriculture into the Multilateral Trading System," J. Bhagwati and M. Hirsch, eds., in *The Uruguay Round and Beyond: Essays in Honor of Arthur Dunkel*, Ann Arbor: University of Michigan Press, 1999, p. 69.
100 J. Whalley with C. Hamilton and R. Hill, *Canadian Trade Policies and the World Economy*, Toronto: University of Toronto Press, 1985, p. 164.
101 R. Ricupero, "Integration of Developing Countries into the Multilateral Trading System," in Bhagwati and Hirsch, eds., *The Uruguay Round and Beyond*, p. 22.
102 Ibid., p. 22.
103 Paemen and Bensch, *From the GATT to the WTO*, pp. 134–138.
104 Ibid.
105 Ricupero, "Integration of Developing Countries," pp. 21–22.
106 C. Raghavan, "Uruguay Round: At Brussels the Stage Ran Away from Its Managers," *South–North Development Monitor*, December 12, 1990, http://www.sunsonline.org/trade/process/during/uruguay/ tnc/12120090.htm 1990.

107 Wiener, *Making Rules*, p. 11.
108 Ibid., p. 189.
109 J. Whalley and C. Hamilton, *The Trading System after the Uruguay Round*, Washington, DC: Institute for International Economics, 1996, p. 171.
110 Wiener, *Making Rules*, p. 190.
111 Ibid.
112 Interview with Rufus Yerxa, November 22, 2002, Geneva, Switzerland.
113 Low, *Trading Free*, p. 220.
114 Wiener, *Making Rules*, pp. 186–189.
115 Interview with John Croome, November 22, 2002, Geneva, Switzerland.
116 Davis, "A Conflict of Institutions," p. 18.
117 Croome, *Reshaping the World Trading System*, p. 194.
118 Low, *Trading Free*, p. 221.
119 Ricupero, "Integration of Developing Countries," pp. 21–22.
120 Wiener, *Making Rules*, p. 190. It should be added, however, that US strategy for agriculture in the Tokyo Round shifts in emphasis to establishing agreement to introduce a new issue area once it becomes clear that substantive reforms cannot be achieved at that time.
121 Interview with A. Stoler, op. cit.
122 Wiener, *Making Rules*, p. 190.
123 Interview with Carla Hills, May 9, 2003, Washington, DC.
124 Interview by telephone with Abdel-Hamid Mamdouh, March 27, 2003, Geneva, Switzerland.
125 Yeutter, "Bringing Agriculture into the Multilateral Trading System," 1999, p. 71.
126 Croome, *Reshaping the World Trading System*, p. 284.
127 Wiener, *Making Rules*, p. 195.
128 Davis, "A Conflict of Institutions," p. 19.
129 Ibid.
130 Ibid., pp. 18–19.
131 See Croome, *Reshaping the World Trading System*, p. 288.
132 Interview with Peter Thompson, November 22, 2002, Geneva, Switzerland.
133 Wiener, *Making Rules*, p. 197.
134 Ibid., p. 198.
135 Davis, "A Conflict of Institutions," p. 19.
136 Owing to social unrest, French officials' endorsement of reforms was cautious, and they insisted that the EC could not modify the European position during negotiations because any changes would have to be reconfirmed by EC members, Wiener, *Making Rules*, p. 199.
137 Weiner, *Making Rules*, p. 194.
138 Ibid., p. 195.
139 Croome, *Reshaping the World Trading System*, p. 294.
140 Paemen and Bensch, *From the GATT to the WTO*, p. 202.
141 Ibid., p. 210.
142 The Maastricht Treaty was signed by member states in February 1992.
143 Paemen and Bensch, *From the GATT to the WTO*, p. 213.
144 Ibid.
145 Ibid., p. 214.
146 Croome, *Reshaping the World Trading System*, p. 339.
147 Wiener, *Making Rules*, p. 215.
148 Croome, *Reshaping the World Trading System*, p. 340.
149 Davis, "A Conflict of Institutions," pp. 21–22.

150 Croome, *Reshaping the World Trading System*, p. 341.
151 Interview with W. Lavorel, op. cit.
152 Ibid. Despite Lavorel's intention to conclude the process, US officials were forced to back off as a result of last-minute attempts by US textile negotiators to improve their gains. See also Paemen and Bensch, *From the GATT to the WTO*, p. 223.
153 Croome, *Reshaping the World Trading System*, p. 344.
154 Paemen and Bensch, *From the GATT to the WTO*, p. 224.
155 Croome, *Reshaping the World Trading System*, p. 345.
156 Paemen and Bensch, *From the GATT to the WTO*, p. 225.
157 Interview with Mickey Kantor, May 8, 2003, Washington, DC.
158 Ibid.
159 Interview with P. Thompson, op. cit.
160 Croome, op. cit., pp. 346–347.
161 Paemen and Bensch, op. cit., p. 230.
162 Croome, op. cit., p. 347.
163 Ibid.
164 Interview with R. Fischer, op. cit.
165 Paemen and Bensch, *From the GATT to the WTO*, p. 241; and Low, *Trading Low*, p. 224.
166 Interview with R. Fischer, op. cit. See also Low, *Trading Free*, p. 31.
167 Gilbert R. Winham, *The Evolution of International Trade Agreements*, Toronto: University of Toronto Press, 1992, p. 118.
168 Interview with M. Kantor, op. cit.
169 Interview with Steve Jacobs, May 8, 2003, Washington, DC.
170 Paemen and Bensch, *From the GATT to the WTO*, p. 242.
171 Ibid.
172 Ibid., pp. 245–246.
173 Interview with Enrique Iglesias, May 9, 2003, Inter-American Development Bank, Washington, DC.
174 Paemen and Bensch, *From the GATT to the WTO*, p. 247.
175 Ibid., pp. 380–381.
176 John H. Jackson, *The World Trading System: Law and Policy of International Economic Relations*, 2nd ed., Cambridge, MA: MIT Press, 1997, p. 76.

5 Foundations for the future: can the WTO become relevant to development and its least developed members?

1 William J. Clinton, Statement given at the WTO Ministerial, Geneva, Switzerland, May 18, 1998, www.presidency.ucsb.edu/ws/index.php?month=05&year=1998.
2 Interviews with senior WTO officials, January 28, 2003, Geneva, Switzerland.
3 S. Aaronson, *Taking Trade to the Streets: The Lost History of Public Efforts to Shape Globalization*, Ann Arbor: University of Michigan Press, 2001, pp. 2–3.
4 Interviews with Jeff Lang, May 13, 2003, Washington, DC, and Edward Gresser, March 18, 2003, Chestnut Hill, MA; and with other former US officials.
5 See, for example, William J. Clinton, "A New Covenant for American Security," Speech given at Georgetown University, Washington, DC, December 12, 1991, www.ndol.org/ndol_ci.cfm?kaid=128&subid=174&contentid=250537. In addition, Clinton emphasized on December 1, 1999, that he would sign the ILO Convention to Eliminate the Worst Forms of Child Labor, and that he believed "the WTO should collaborate more closely with the ILO . . . to ban child

labor." "Remarks by the President to the Luncheon in Honor of the Ministers Attending the Meetings of the World Trade Organization," Seattle, WA, www.presidency.ucsb.edu/ws/index.php?month.

6 It is certainly possible, if not likely, that his top political advisers preferred that the president did not have fast-track authority because of concerns that if the USTR negotiated controversial new trade agreements they would further alienate key democratic political constituencies.

7 His speech during the second day of the meeting called for the WTO both to create a working group on trade and labor and to work more closely with the ILO "to ban child labor." W. J. Clinton, statement given at the WTO Ministerial, op. cit.

8 Michael Paulson, transcript of interview with President Bill Clinton, November 30, 1999, http://seattlepi.nwsource.com/national/trans01.shtml, and "Clinton Says He Will Support Trade Sanctions for Worker Abuse," *Seattle Post-Intelligencer*, December 1, 1999, p. A1.

9 W. J. Clinton and A. Gore, "Expanding Trade and Ensuring a Healthy Environment," November 16, 1999, http://clinton4.nara.gov/WH/New/WTO-Conf-1999/ factsheets/fs-005.html.

10 The Canadian Minister for International Trade stated directly that Canada was not proposing to begin a new round. See Leon Brittan, "The Outcome of Singapore," Statement given by the Vice President of the EU Commission, IP/96/1172, December 13, 1996.

11 Interview with David Shark, January 30, 2003, Geneva, Switzerland.

12 Interview with Clayton Yeutter, October 3, 2002, Washington, DC.

13 Santer, Jacques, Statement given at the WTO Ministerial, Geneva, Switzerland, May 19, 1998, http://www.wto.org/english/thewto_e/minist_e/min98_e/mc98_e/default19_e.htm.

14 Clinton, Statement given at the WTO Ministerial, op. cit.

15 Interview with Charlene Barchefsky, October 3, 2002, Washington, DC.

16 R. Bernal, "Sleepless in Seattle: The WTO Ministerial of November 1999," http://www.southcentre.org/info/southbulletin01/bulletin01-05.htm.

17 M. Kahler, *Leadership Selection in the Major Multilaterals*, Washington, DC: Institute for International Economics, 2001, pp. 73–74.

18 Ibid., p. 70.

19 Interview with Keith Rockwell, November 19, 2002, Geneva, Switzerland.

20 Interview with Rita Hayes, November 21, 2002, Geneva, Switzerland.

21 Interview with Bruce Gosper, Australian trade negotiator, May 31, 2002, Canberra, Australia.

22 See Table 45 in US Foreign Trade Highlights at http://www.ita.doc.gov. Furthermore, to the extent one believes that trade balances matter, Canada had a relatively large (the third largest after Japan and China) and rapidly growing trade surplus with the United States (the rate of increase for 1996–2002 was essentially the same as that for China).

23 Interview with Carla Hills, May 9, 2003, Washington, DC.

24 Interviews by telephone with Warren Lavorel, December 3, 2002.

25 Kahler, *Leadership Selection*, p. 69.

26 J. Odell, "Problems in Negotiating Consensus in the World Trade Organization," Paper presented at the annual convention of the American Political Science Association, San Francisco, August 30 – September 2, 2001.

27 Interview with C. Yeutter, op. cit.

28 Interview with Peter Allgeier, October 1, 2002, Washington, DC.

29 Clinton, "Remarks by the President," 1999.
30 Interview with K. Rockwell, op. cit.
31 M. Naim, "An Exercise in Futility: International Summits Fail to Provide the Leadership Needed to Solve the World's Problems," *Financial Times*, August 6, 2001, p. 17.
32 Interview with Andy Stoler, November 19, 2002, Geneva, Switzerland.
33 Identification of Trade Expansion Priorities Pursuant to Executive Order 13116 2001, 7.
34 E. Alden, "Companies Seek to Resolve Trade Issues; International Accords Drive to Bridge Political Divide over Provisions to Protect Labour Rights and the Environment," *Financial Times*, January 30, 2001, p. 4.
35 R. Collier, "Free-Trade Battles Re-emerge with Bush; Accord with Jordan Likely to Lead Agenda," *San Francisco Chronicle*, January 20, 2001, p. A3.
36 G. Jonquieres and F. Williams, "WTO Optimistic over Agreement on Talks," *Financial Times*, September 28, 2001, p. 2.
37 Following the successful launch of the Doha Round, the House of Representatives voted on December 6, 2001, to authorize trade policy authority for the president. The legislation passed by one vote, 215 to 214. In addition to the success at Doha, the administration benefited from congressional support for the war in Afghanistan. According to the *New York Times*, the administration used the war to leverage support from representatives who are usually loath to support multilateral trade. On December 7, 2001, Joseph Kahn reports, "The administration put especially heavy pressure on several North Carolina and South Carolina Republicans. Representatives from those states often vote no on trade agreements because of strong textile interest at home. But their districts are also full of conservatives eager to support the president during a war." "House Supports Trade Authority Sought by Bush," *New York Times*, December 7, 2001, p. A1. This negotiating leverage allowed the president and his trade representative, Robert Zoellick, to pursue a deeper and more dynamic policy of trade liberalization than was available to President Clinton and his USTR, Charlene Barchefsky. After September 11 there was partisan consensus between the executive and legislative branches; interview with Jean Lanjouw, September 30, 2002, Washington, DC.
38 Interview with David Hartridge, November 22, 2002, Geneva, Switzerland.
39 A. Parker and R. Shrimsley, "Blair Warns Europe on Reform: Prime Minister Says Prosperity Is at Risk unless EU Leaders Deliver Changes," *Financial Times*, July 31, 2001, p. 1.
40 Blair's statement, while demonstrating British and, potentially, EU support for agricultural reform, did not, however, eliminate the problem created by years of EU obstinacy in the realm of agriculture. Several deadlines regarding agricultural agreements were missed, Stuart Harbinson's agricultural modalities were hardly agreed upon, and the EU did not fully commit to agricultural reform at Cancún.
41 J. Kahn, "A Trade Agenda Tests Murphy's Law; US Sees Talks as a Test of Leadership, but the Road to Qatar Was Rocky," *New York Times*, November 9, 2001, p. C1.
42 The United States was committed to launching the round for other reasons. US, EU, and other negotiators employ a strategy of issue linkage, whereby concessions made by members in one area will be compensated for by others' reductions in another area. While this can facilitate the depth of the round, it also creates a domestic political problem in terms of implementation. "Powerful business groups, such as the [US] Chamber of Commerce, which represents thousands of smaller

and middle-size companies, remain opposed to any linkage, as do certain industries such as textile and apparel makers"; Alden, "Companies Seek to Resolve Trade Issues."

43 E. Alden and G. de Jonquieres, "Old Friends Struggle to Overcome Rough Start on Trade: Robert Zoellick and Pascal Lamy Have Solved One Bitter US–EU Dispute, but Many Differences Remain," *Financial Times*, April 27, 2001, p. 14.

44 Interview with K. Rockwell, op. cit.

45 Based on an interview with P. Allgeier, op. cit.

46 E. Alden and P. Norman, "'Elephants of World Trade' Set for Talks: EU's Lamy Begins Fact-Finding Mission as US Is Focusing on Americas," *Financial Times*, March 8, 2001, p. 37.

47 Interview with Didier Chambovec, January 29, 2003, Geneva, Switzerland.

48 Interview with P. Allgeier, op. cit.

49 Interview with C. Barchefsky, op. cit.

50 Interview with Jeff Schott, Institute for International Economics, Washington, DC, October 1, 2002.

51 In fact, the international trade regime has never seen North–South issues reach such a positive conclusion (interview with Paulo Batto, January 29, 2003, Geneva, Switzerland). This is especially true given the initial unwillingness of many LDCs to launch a new round. Following the conclusion of the Uruguay Round in 1994, several developing countries, primarily led by India and Pakistan, expressed their frustration with the degree to which their concerns had been overlooked. With a pre-round attitude of "we'll lose more than we'll gain," it is somewhat surprising that these countries allowed Doha to be a relative success (Elizabeth Olson, "Seattle Failure Weighs on Future of New Trade Talks," *New York Times*, June 26, 2001, p. W1). This seems to demonstrate an understanding by the LDCs, however, that they were taken more seriously during the Doha Ministerial.

52 Reinhard Rode, "Optimism for the WTO Doha Round: The Bickering Atlantic Bigemony and New Pro Free Trade Coalitions," Paper presented at the Central and East European International Studies Association, Budapest, Hungary, June 26–28, 2003, p. 5.

53 It was a close call as to whether the meeting would be relocated or postponed, owing to physical security concerns about a large gathering of senior officials in the Middle East at this time.

54 Paul Blustein, "China Agrees on Terms to Join WTO," *Washington Post*, June 10, 2001, p. A19.

55 Interview with Carmen Laz-Guarda, December 31, 2002, Geneva, Switzerland.

56 Interview with P. Allgeier, op. cit.

57 Interviews with senior WTO officials, November 1–3, 2002, Geneva, Switzerland.

58 The USTR met on July 2 with the Caribbean states' trade ministers, and the vice ministers of states negotiating the FTA met on July 7–11, in part to prepare for a ministerial meeting in Miami on November 21–23.

59 Statement of Robert B. Zoellick, USTR, and Ann M. Veneman, Secretary of Agriculture on EU CAP, Policy Press Releases/2003/June/06/26/03|EU Agriculture – CAP, http://ustr.gov/Document_Library/Press_Releases/2003/June/Zoellick-Veneman_Statement_on_EU_CAP_Policy.html.

60 Only two days before the ministerial began (September 8), the WTO issued its general public announcement of the cotton decision and confirmed the final panel report on the EC sugar case to Brazil and the EC. Most officials knew about the US cotton decision in June, owing to a leak.

61 UNDP, *Making Global Trade Work for People*, Sterling, VA: Earthscan Publications, 2003, p. 251.
62 Senator Grassley, chair of the Senate Finance Committee, had warned countries, following Cancún, that he would not support any bilateral trade agreements with G-20 member states. Those among the earlier group in June which did not join the G-20 were Botswana, the Dominican Republic, Gabon, Honduras, Malaysia, Morocco, Nicaragua, Uruguay, and Zimbabwe. Except for Malaysia and Uruguay, all of these small states opted for the bilateral negotiations and expectations of special access to US markets.
63 International Center for Trade and Sustainable Development, *Bridges*, May 19, 2004.
64 Indonesia leads the G-33–40 states in an Alliance for Special Products and a Special Safeguard Mechanism designed to win agreement on protection for vulnerable sectors and small farmers against highly subsidized agricultural imports.

6 Why international institutions fail and succeed

1 R. A. Pollard and S. F. Wells, "1945–1960: The Era of American Economic Hegemony," in W. H. Becker and S. F. Wells, eds., *Economics and World Power: An Assessment of American Diplomacy since 1789*, New York: Columbia University Press, 1984, p. 381.
2 J. M. Rothgeb, Jr., *U.S. Trade Policy: Balancing Economic Dreams with Political Realities*, Washington, DC: CQ Press, 2001, p. 118.
3 This study confirms the argument of Richard H. Steinberg on the relatively weak substance of the agreement launching the Tokyo Round, and therefore the lower level of difficulty in negotiations. It parts company, however, with his overall argument that GATT rounds have all been launched on the basis of law-based, as opposed to power-based, negotiating procedures resulting in equitable outcomes. See "In the Shadow of Law or Power? Consensus-Based Bargaining and Outcomes in the GATT-WTO," *International Organization*, spring 2002, vol. 56, no. 2, pp. 339–374. It probably is the case that launching most rounds is easier than closing most. However, there is both wide variation in this regard among launchings and substantial overlap between launching and closing.
4 As is explained in Chapter 4, this transition also occurred in the context of fundamental shifts in the US Congress, American foreign policy, and international politics during the early to mid-1970s.
5 See David W. Rhode, "Partisan Leadership and Congressional Assertiveness in Foreign and Defense Policy," in David A. Deese, ed., *The New Politics of American Foreign Policy*, New York: Harper & Row, 1994.
6 From this perspective, US leaders sought a return on their investments. J. N. Bhagwati, *Protectionism*, Cambridge, MA: Massachusetts Institute of Technology Press, 1998, pp. 40–41.
7 The United States and West European powers operated under GATT auspices in the immediate postwar period, utilizing bilateral negotiations to lower tariffs on an item-by-item basis. Once each side agreed to tariff reduction agreements, the cuts were automatically extended to all members because of the most favored nation principle.
8 Anti-globalization protests and movements also complicated their ability to co-lead at key points in time, particularly when they mobilized domestic interests or congressional leaders. The same process is triggered when the United States or the

EU loses more than one politically salient WTO dispute settlement case in any particular time period.

9 The earlier sessions appear to have been more effective and useful than those held after 2003, possibly because of diminishing expectations and trust in their value by key ministers from developing and LDC states.

10 P. Sutherland *et al.*, *The Future of the WTO: Addressing Institutional Challenges in the New Millennium*, Report by the Consultative Board to Director General Supachai Panitchpakdi, Geneva: WTO, 2004, ch. 2, p. 19.

11 More recently, however, particularly from 1999, certain LDCs have also been represented by influential negotiators. In 2004, for example, Ambassador Amina Mohamed of Kenya chaired the Dispute Settlement Body and Ambassador Trevor Clarke of Barbados headed the Committee on Trade and Development. Similarly, the ambassadors for the four African cotton-exporting states that fought for recognition and concessions at Cancún have gained considerable experience in entrepreneurial leadership and blocking strategies and maneuvers.

12 See the discussion by R. O. Keohane and J. S. Nye in M. Kahler and D. Lake, eds., *Governance in a Global Economy*, Princeton, NJ: Princeton University Press, 2004, pp. 404–406.

13 For more technical, legal purposes associated especially with the WTO Dispute Settlement system, the non-profit Advisory Centre on WTO Law (ACWL) in Geneva is providing considerable legal advice to developing states and LDCs, and supporting WTO case development. Despite its modest staff and resources, it has become a crucial foundation for formal, if episodic, use of the WTO system by these members.

Bibliography

Aaronson, Susan Ariel, "For the People, but Not By the People: A History of the International Trade Organization," Ph.D. diss., Department of Political Science, Johns Hopkins University, 1993.

——, *Taking Trade to the Streets: The Lost History of Public Efforts to Shape Globalization*, Ann Arbor: University of Michigan Press, 2001.

Abbott, Kenneth W., Robert O. Keohane, Andrew Moravcsik, Anne-Marie Slaughter, and Duncan Snidal, "The Concept of Legalization," *International Organization*, 2000, vol. 54, pp. 401–419.

Aggarwal, Vinod K., *Liberal Protectionism: The International Politics of Organized Textile Trade*, Berkeley: University of California Press, 1985.

Agreement Relating Principally to Chemicals, December 19, 1968. Supplementary to the Geneva (1967) Protocol to the General Agreement on Tariffs and Trade, www.wto.org/English/docs_e/legal_e/kennedy_e.pdf.

Alden, Edward, "Companies Seek to Resolve Trade Issues; International Accords Drive to Bridge Political Divide over Provisions to Protect Labour Rights and the Environment," *Financial Times*, January 30, p. 4.

Alden, Edward and Guy de Jonquieres, "Old Friends Struggle to Overcome Rough Start on Trade: Robert Zoellick and Pascal Lamy Have Solved One Bitter US–EU Dispute, but Many Differences Remain," *Financial Times*, April 27, 2001, p. 14.

Alden, Edward and Peter Norman, "'Elephants of World Trade' Set for Talks: EU's Lamy Begins Fact-Finding Mission as US Is Focusing on Americas," *Financial Times*, March 8, 2001, p. 37.

Atlantic Charter, 14 August, 1941, www.yale.edu/lawweb/avalon/wwii/atlantic/at10.htm.

Audley, John and Ann M. Florini, "Overhauling the WTO: Opportunity at Doha and Beyond," Policy Brief, October, Washington, DC: Carnegie Endowment for International Peace, 2001.

Axelrod, Robert M., *The Evolution of Cooperation*, New York: Basic Books, 1984.

Barnett, Michael and Martha Finnemore, "The Power, Politics, and Pathologies of International Organizations," *International Organization*, autumn 1999, vol. 53, no. 4, pp. 699–732.

Bator, Francis, "Memorandum from the President's Deputy Special Assistant for National Security Affairs to President Johnson," LBJ Library: Bator Papers, Box 29, May 15, 1967.

Beane, Donald G., *The United States and GATT: A Relational Study*, Amsterdam: Pergamon Press, 2000.

Becker, W. H. and S. F. Wells, *Economics and World Power: An Assessment of American Diplomacy since 1789*, New York: Columbia University Press, 1984.

Bernal, Richard, "Sleepless in Seattle: The WTO Ministerial of November 1999," www.southcentre.org/info/southbulletin01/bulletin01-05.htm.

Bhagwati, Jagdish N., *Protectionism*, Cambridge, MA: MIT Press, 1988.

Blackhurst, Richard, "The Capacity of the WTO to Fulfill Its Mandate," in Anne O. Krueger, ed., *The WTO as an International Organization*, Chicago: University of Chicago Press, 1998, pp. 31–58.

Blondel, J., *Political Leadership: Towards a General Analysis*, Beverly Hills, CA: Sage, 1987.

Blustein, Paul, "China Agrees on Terms to Join WTO," *Washington Post*, June 10, 2001, p. A19.

Brittan, Leon, "The Outcome of Singapore," Statement given by the Vice President of the EU Commission, IP/96/1172, December 13, 1996.

Burkeman, Oliver, "US Demands Immunity for Its Peacekeepers," *Guardian*, June 20, 2002, www.guardian.co.uk/bush/story/0,7369,740583,00.html.

Burns, James MacGregor, *Leadership*, Hagerstown, NY: Colophon Books, 1978.

Calleo, David P., *The Imperious Economy*, Cambridge, MA: Harvard University Press, 1982.

Chayes, Abram and Antonia Handler Chayes, "On Compliance," *International Organization*, 1993, vol. 47, pp. 175–205.

Checkel, J., "It's the Process Stupid! Process Tracing in the Study of European and International Politics," Arena Working Paper no. 26, University of Oslo, 2005.

Clinton, William J., "A New Covenant for American Security," Speech given at Georgetown University, Washington, DC, December 12, 1991, www.ndol.org/ndol_ci.cfm?kaid=128&subid=174&contentid=250537.

——, Statement given at the WTO Ministerial, Geneva, Switzerland, May 18, 1998, www.presidency.ucsb.edu/ws/index.php?month=05&year=1998.

——, Remarks by the President to the Luncheon in Honor of the Ministers Attending the Meetings of the World Trade Organization, Seattle, WA, December 1, 1999, www.presidency.ucsb.edu/ws/index.php?month.

Clinton, William J. and Albert Gore, "Expanding Trade and Ensuring a Healthy Environment, November 16, 1999," clinton4.nara.gov/WH/New/WTO-Conf-1999/factsheets/fs-005.html.

Cohn, Theodore H., *Global Political Economy: Theory and Practice*, New York: Longman, 2000.

Collier, Robert, "Free-Trade Battles Re-emerge with Bush; Accord with Jordan Likely to Lead Agenda," *San Francisco Chronicle*, January 20, 2001, p. A3.

Components of a Strategy for the Kennedy Round, Confidential White House Report, declassified December 1, 1987, unsanitized, complete, LBJ Library: CD-ROM 19988090102937.

Costigliola, Frank, *France and the United States: The Cold Alliance since World War II*, New York: Columbia University Press, 1987.

Croome, John, *Reshaping the World Trading System: A History of the Uruguay Round*, Geneva: World Trade Organization, 1995.

Curzon, Gerard, *Multilateral Commercial Diplomacy*, London: Michael Joseph, 1965.

Dahl, Robert A., "On the Concept of Power," *Behavioral Science*, 1957, vol. 2, pp. 201–215.

Davis, Christina, "A Conflict of Institutions: The WTO and EU Agricultural Policy," Paper presented at the annual meeting of the New England Political Science Association, Portland, ME, May 3, 2002.

—— "Linkage and Legalism in Institutions: Evidence from Agricultural Trade Negotiations," Paper presented at the International Studies Association Annual Convention, New Orleans, March 24–27, 2002.

——, *Food Fights over Free Trade: How International Institutions Promote Agricultural Trade Liberalization*, Princeton, NJ: Princeton University Press, 2003.

——, "International Institutions and Issue Linkage: Building Support for Agricultural Trade Liberalization," *American Political Science Review*, February 2004, vol. 98, no. 1, pp. 153–169.

Deese, David A., ed., *The New Politics of American Foreign Policy*, New York: St. Martin's Press, 1994.

Deese, David A. and Joseph S. Nye, eds., *Energy and Security*, New York: Harper and Row, 1981.

DePorte, A. W., *Europe between the Superpowers: The Enduring Balance*, New Haven, CT: Yale University Press, 1986.

Derber, Charles, *People before Profit: The New Globalization in an Age of Terror, Big Money, and Economic Crisis*, New York: St. Martin's Press, 2002.

Destler, I. M. "A Government Divided: The Security Complex and the Economic Complex," in David A. Deese, ed., *The New Politics of American Foreign Policy*, New York: St. Martin's Press, 1994, pp. 132–147.

——, *American Trade Politics*, 4th ed., Washington, DC: Institute for International Economics, 2005.

Doig, J. W. and E. C. Hargrove, eds., *Leadership and Innovation: A Biographical Perspective on Entrepreneurs in Government*, Baltimore: Johns Hopkins Press, 1987.

Downs, George W., David M. Rocke, and Peter N. Barsoom, "Is the Good News about Compliance Good News about Cooperation?" *International Organization*, 1996, vol. 50, pp. 379–406.

——, "Designing Multilaterals: The Architecture and Evolution of Environmental Agreements," Unpublished manuscript, 1997.

Druckman, D., *Human Factors in International Negotiations: Social-Psychological Aspects of International Conflict*, Beverly Hills, CA: Sage, 1973.

——, ed., *Negotiations: Social-Psychological Perspectives*, Beverly Hills, CA: Sage, 1977.

——, "Determinants of Compromising Behavior in Negotiation: A Meta-analysis," *Journal of Conflict Resolution*, 1994, vol 38, pp. 504–556.

Dryden, Steve, *Trade Warriors: USTR and the American Crusade for Free Trade*, New York: Oxford University Press, 1995.

Eckes, Alfred E., *Opening America's Market: US Foreign Policy since 1776*, Chapel Hill: University of North Carolina Press, 1995.

Evans, John W., *The Kennedy Round in American Trade Policy: The Twilight of the GATT?* Cambridge, MA: Harvard University Press, 1971.

Fearon, James D., "Counterfactuals and Hypothesis Testing in Political Science," *World Politics*, 1991, vol. 43, pp. 169–95.

——, "Domestic Audiences and the Escalation of International Disputes," *American Political Science Review*, 1994, vol. 88, pp. 577–92.

——, "Bargaining, Enforcement, and International Cooperation," *International Organization*, 1998, vol. 52, pp. 269–305.

Feis, H., "The Geneva Proposals for an International Trade Charter," *International Organization*, February 1948, vol. 2, no. 1, pp. 39–52.

Ferrell, R. H., *Presidential Leadership: From Woodrow Wilson to Harry S. Truman*, Columbia: University of Missouri Press, 2006.

Fisher, Roger and William Ury with Bruce Patton, eds., *Getting to Yes: Negotiating Agreement without Giving In*, London: Hutchinson, 1982.

Garrett, Geoffrey, "The Causes of Globalization," *Comparative Political Studies*, 2000, vol. 33, pp. 941–991.

General Agreement on Tariffs and Trade (GATT), *Basic Instruments and Selected Documents*, 33rd supplement, Geneva: World Trade Organization, 1987.

George, A. and A. Bennett, *Case Studies and Theory Development in the Social Sciences*, Cambridge, MA: MIT Press, 2005.

George, A. and T. McKeown, "Case Studies and Theories of Organizational Decision Making," *Advances in Information Processing in Organizations*, 1985, vol. 2, pp. 21–58.

Gilpin, Robert, *The Political Economy of International Relations*, Princeton, NJ: Princeton University Press, 1987.

Goldstein, Judith, "The Impact of Ideas on Trade Policy: The Origins of US Agricultural and Manufacturing Policies," *International Organization*, 1989, vol. 43, no. 1, pp. 31–72.

——, "Creating the GATT Rules," in John Gerard Ruggie, ed., *Multilateralism Matters*, New York: Columbia University Press, 1993, pp. 201–232.

——, *Ideas, Interests, and American Trade Policy*, Ithaca, NY: Cornell University Press, 1993.

Goldstein, J. and J. Gowa, "US National Power and the Post-War Trading Regime," *World Trade Review*, 2002, vol. 1, pp. 153–170.

Goldstein, J. and R. Keohane, eds., *Ideas and Foreign Policy: Beliefs, Institutions, and Political Change*, Ithaca, NY: Cornell University Press, 1993.

Goldstein, J. and L. L. Martin, "Legalization, Trade Liberalization, and Domestic Politics: A Cautionary Note," *International Organization*, 2000, vol. 54, pp. 603–632.

Grieco, Joseph, Robert Powell, and Duncan Snidal, "The Relative-Gains Problem for International Cooperation," *American Political Science Review*, September 1993, vol. 87, no. 3, pp. 729–743.

Gruber, Lloyd, *Ruling the World: Power Politics and the Rise of Supranational Institutions*, Princeton, NJ: Princeton University Press, 2000.

Haggard, Stephan, "The Institutional Foundations of Hegemony: Explaining the Reciprocal Trade Agreements Act of 1934," *International Organization*, 1988, vol. 42, pp. 91–119.

Hargrove, E. C., *Presidential Leadership: Personality and Political Style*, New York: Macmillan, 1966.

Held, David, Anthony McGrew, David Goldblatt, and Jonathan Perraton, *Global Transformations: Politics, Economics and Culture*, Stanford, CA: Stanford University Press, 1999.

Hufbauer, Gary Clyde and Joanna Shelton Erb, *Subsidies in International Trade*, Washington, DC: Institute for International Economics, 1984.

Identification of Trade Expansion Priorities Pursuant to Executive Order 13116, April 30, 2001, http://www.ustr.gov/enforcement/super301.pdf.

Ikenberry, G. John, "The Myth of Post-Cold War Chaos," *Foreign Affairs*, 1996, vol. 75, pp. 79–91.

——, *After Victory: Institutions, Strategic Restraint, and the Rebuilding of Order after Major Wars*, Princeton, NJ: Princeton University Press, 2001.

Inside US Trade, December 3, 1999, Washington, DC: Inside Washington Publishers.

Jackson, J. H., *The World Trade Organization: Constitution and Jurisprudence*, London: Royal Institute of International Affairs, 1998.

——, *The World Trading System: Law and Policy of International Economic Relations*, 2nd ed., Cambridge, MA: MIT Press, 1997.

Jonquieres, Guy de and Frances Williams, "WTO Optimistic over Agreement on Talks," *Financial Times*, September 28, 2001, p. 2.

Kahler, Miles, "Multilateralism with Small and Large Numbers," in John Gerard Ruggie, ed., *Multilateralism Matters*, New York: Columbia University Press, 1993, pp. 295–326.

——, *Leadership Selection in the Major Multilaterals*, Washington, DC: Institute for International Economics, 2001.

Kahler, Miles and David A. Lake, "Globalization and Governance," Paper presented at the annual meeting of the American Political Science Association, Washington, DC, August 31 – September 3, 2000.

——, eds., *Governance in a Global Economy*, Princeton, NJ: Princeton University Press, 2004.

Kahn, Joseph, "A Trade Agenda Tests Murphy's Law; US Sees Talks as a Test of Leadership, But the Road to Qatar Was Rocky," *New York Times*, November 9, 2001, p. C1.

——, "House Supports Trade Authority Sought by Bush," *New York Times*, December 7, 2001, p. A1.

Kahneman, Daniel and Amos Tversky, "Prospect Theory: An Analysis of Decision under Risk," *Econometrica*, 1979, vol. 47, pp. 263–291.

Kaufman, Burton I., *Trade and Aid: Eisenhower's Foreign Economic Policy 1953–1961*, Baltimore: Johns Hopkins University Press, 1982.

Kennedy, Daniel L. M. and James D. Southwick, eds., *The Political Economy of International Trade Law: Essays in Honor of Robert E. Hudec*, Cambridge: Cambridge University Press, 2002.

Kennedy, John F., Special Message to the Congress on Foreign Trade Policy, January 25, 1965, www.presidency.ucsb.edu/ws/index.php.

——, Annual Message to the Congress on the State of the Union, January 14, 1963, www.presidency.ucsb.edu/ws/index.php.

Kennedy Round, Confidential White House working paper, January 1, 1968, declassified June 7, 1982, unsanitized, complete, LBJ Library: CD-ROM 1984010101475.

Kennedy Round, Confidential White House working paper, January 1, 1969, declassified June 7, 1982, unsanitized, complete, CD-ROM 1984010101475, LBJ Library.

Kennedy Round Crisis, Confidential White House working paper, June 1, 1967, declassified 13 October 1982, unsanitized, complete, CD-ROM 1984010101458, LBJ Library.

Kennedy Round Crisis, Chronology and Annotated Index of Documents, June 1, 1967, Confidential White House report, declassified October 13, 1982, unsanitized, complete, CD-ROM 1984010101457, LBJ Library.

The Kennedy Round of Trade Negotiations, Presented to Parliament by the President of the Board of Trade, London: Her Majesty's Stationery Office, 1967.

Keohane, Robert O., *After Hegemony: Cooperation and Discord in the World Political Economy*, Princeton, NJ: Princeton University Press, 1984.

——, "Governance in a Partially Globalized World," in David Held and Anthony McGrew, eds., *Governing Globalization: Power, Authority, and Global Governance*, Cambridge: Polity Press, 2002, pp. 325–347.

Keohane, R. O. and Joseph S. Nye, Jr., "Redefining Accountability for Global Governance," in M. Kahler and D. Lake, eds., *Governance in a Global Economy*, Princeton, NJ: Princeton University Press, 2004, pp. 386–411.

Kindleberger, Charles, *The World in Depression, 1929–39*, Berkeley: University of California Press, 1973.

——, "Dominance and Leadership in the International Economy: Exploitation, Public Goods, and Free Rides," *International Studies Quarterly*, 1981, vol. 25, no. 2, pp. 242–254.

Koremenos, Barbara, Charles Lipson, and Duncan Snidal, "The Rational Design of International Institutions," *International Organization*, 2001, vol. 55, pp. 761–799.

——, "Rational Design: Looking Back to Move Forward," *International Organization*, 2001, vol. 55, pp. 1051–1082.

Krasner, Stephen D., "State Power and the Structure of International Trade," *World Politics*, 1976, vol. 28, pp. 317–347.

——, "US Commercial and Monetary Policy: Unraveling the Paradox of External Strength and Internal Weakness," *International Organization*, 1977, vol. 31, pp. 635–671.

——, "The Tokyo Round: Particularist Interests and Prospects for Stability in the Global Trading System," *International Studies Quarterly*, 1979, vol. 23, pp. 491–531.

——, "Structural Causes and Regime Consequences: Regimes as Intervening Variables," in Stephen D. Krasner, ed., *International Regimes*, Ithaca, NY: Cornell University Press, 1983, pp. 1–21.

——, *Sovereignty: Organized Hypocrisy*, Princeton, NJ: Princeton University Press, 1999.

Krueger, A., *The WTO as an Organization*, Chicago: University of Chicago Press, 1998.

Lake, D. A., *Power, Protection, and Free Trade: International Sources of US Commercial Strategy, 1887–1939*, Ithaca, NY: Cornell University Press, 1988.

——, "Leadership, Hegemony, and the International Economy: Naked Emperor or Tattered Monarch with Potential?" *International Studies Quarterly*, December 1993, vol. 37, no. 4, pp. 459–489.

Lammers, W. and M. Genovese, *The Presidency and Domestic Policy: Comparing Leadership Styles*, Washington, DC: CQ Press, 2000.

Lax, David A. and James K. Sebenius, *The Manager as Negotiator: Bargaining for Cooperation and Competitive Gain*, New York: Free Press, 1986.

——, "Thinking Coalitionally: Party Arithmetic, Process Opportunism, and Strategic Sequencing," in H. Peyton Young, ed., *Negotiation Analysis*, Ann Arbor: University of Michigan Press, 1991, pp. 153–193.

Lend-Lease Agreement, February 23, 1942, www.yale.edu/lawweb/avalon/wwii/wwii.htm.

Levy, Jack S., "An Introduction to Prospect Theory," *Political Psychology*, 1992, vol. 13, pp. 171–186.

Low, Patrick, *Trading Free: The GATT and US Trade Policy*, New York: Twentieth Century Fund Press, 1993.

McCormick, John, *The European Superpower*, New York: Palgrave, 2007.

Milner, Helen V., *Resisting Protectionism*, Princeton, NJ: Princeton University Press, 1988.

——, *Interests, Institutions, and Information: Domestic Politics and International Relations*, Princeton, NJ: Princeton University Press, 1997.

Naim, Moises, "An Exercise in Futility: International Summits Fail to Provide the Leadership Needed to Solve the World's Problems," *Financial Times*, August 6, 2001, p. 17.

National Security Council, "United States Objectives and Programs for National Security," National Security Council Paper 68, Washington, DC, April 14, 1950, www.mtholyoke.edu/acad/intrel/nsc68.htm.

——, "Basic National Security Policy," National Security Council Paper 162/2, Washington, DC, October 30, 1953, www.mtholyoke.edu/acad/intrel/nsc68.htm.

Nye, Joseph S., "United States Policy toward Regional Organization," *International Organization*, 1969, vol. 23, pp. 719–740.

——, *Bound to Lead: The Changing Nature of American Power*, New York: Basic Books, 1990.

——, "The Changing Nature of World Power," *Political Science Quarterly* 1990, vol. 105, no. 2, pp. 177–192.

Odell, John S., *Negotiating the World Economy*, Ithaca, NY: Cornell University Press, 2000.

——, "Problems in Negotiating Consensus in the World Trade Organization," Paper presented at the annual convention of the American Political Science Association, San Francisco, August 30 – September 2, 2001.

——, *Negotiating Trade: Developing Countries in the WTO and NAFTA*, Cambridge: Cambridge University Press, 2006.

Odell, John S. and Barry Eichengreen, "The United States, the ITO, and the WTO: Exit Options, Agent Slack, and Presidential Leadership," in Anne O. Krueger, ed., *The WTO as an International Organization*, Chicago: University of Chicago Press, 1998, pp. 181–209.

Olson, Elizabeth, "Seattle Failure Weighs on Future of New Trade Talks," *New York Times*, June 26, 2001, p. W1.

One World Trust, "Power without Accountability?" Global Accountability Report 1, January 2003, www.oneworldtrust.org/.

——, 2006 Global Accountability Report, www.oneworldtrust.org/?display=index_2006.

Oxley, Alan, *The Challenge of Free Trade*, London: Harvester Wheatsheaf, 1990.

Oye, Kenneth A., "Explaining Cooperation under Anarchy," in Kenneth A. Oye, ed., *Cooperation under Anarchy*, Princeton, NJ: Princeton University Press, 1986, pp. 1–24.

——, *Economic Discrimination and Political Exchange: World Political Economy in the 1930s and 1980s*, Princeton, NJ: Princeton University Press, 1982.

Paemen, Hugo and Alexandra Bensch, *From the GATT to the WTO: The European Community in the Uruguay Round*, Leuven, Belgium: Leuven University Press, 1995.

Pahre, R., *Leading Questions: How Hegemony Affects the International Political Economy*, Ann Arbor: University of Michigan Press, 1999.

Parker, Andrew and Robert Shrimsley, "Blair Warns Europe on Reform: Prime Minister Says Prosperity Is at Risk unless EU Leaders Deliver Changes," *Financial Times*, July 31, 2001, p. 1.

Paulson, Michael, Transcript of Interview with President Bill Clinton, November 30, 1999, http://seattlepi.nwsource.com/national/trans01.shtml.

——, "Clinton Says He Will Support Trade Sanctions for Worker Abuse," *Seattle Post-Intelligencer*, December 1, 1999, p. A1.

Pollard, R. A. and S. F. Wells, "1945–1960: The Era of American Economic Hegemony," in W. H. Becker and S. F. Wells, eds., *Economics and World Power: An Assessment of American Diplomacy since 1789*, New York: Columbia University Press, 1984.

Preeg, Ernest H., *Traders and Diplomats*, Washington, DC: Brookings Institution.

——, *Traders in a Brave New World: The Uruguay Round and the Future of the International Trading System*, Chicago: University of Chicago Press, 1995.

——, *From Here to Free Trade: Essays in Post-Uruguay Round Trade Strategy*, Chicago: University of Chicago Press, 1998.

Putnam, Robert, "Diplomacy and Domestic Politics: The Logic of Two-Level Games," *International Organization*, 1988, vol. 42, pp. 427–460.

Raghavan, Chakravarthi, "Uruguay Round: At Brussels the Stage Ran Away from Its Managers," *South–North Development Monitor*, December 12, 1990, www.sunsonline.org/trade/process/during/uruguay/tnc/12120090.htm.

Ricupero, Rubens, "Integration of Developing Countries into the Multilateral Trading System," in Jagdish Bhagwati and Mathias Hirsch, eds., *The Uruguay Round and Beyond: Essays in Honor of Arthur Dunkel*, Ann Arbor: University of Michigan Press, 1999, pp. 9–36.

Rode, Reinhard, "Optimism for the WTO Doha Round: The Bickering Atlantic Bigemony and New Pro Free Trade Coalitions," Paper presented at the Central and East European International Studies Association, Budapest, Hungary, June 26–28, 2003.

Rohde, David W., "Partisan Leadership and Congressional Assertiveness in Foreign and Defense Policy," in David A. Deese, ed., *The New Politics of American Foreign Policy*, New York: Harper and Row, 1994, pp. 76–101.

Roosevelt, Franklin D., Annual Message of the President to the Congress, January 6, 1941, http://www.presidency.ucsb.edu/ws/index.

Rosecrance, Richard and Jennifer Taw, "Japan and the Theory of International Leadership," *World Politics*, January 1990, vol. 42, no. 2, pp. 184–209.

Rosendorff, B. Peter and Helen V. Milner, "The Optimal Design of International Trade Institutions: Uncertainty and Escape," *International Organization*, 2001, vol. 55, pp. 829–857.

Roth, J. M., Telegram 3374 to Francis Bator, April 24, 1967, LBJ Library: Roth Papers, Box 3, Tab 84.

Rothgeb, John M., Jr., *U.S. Trade Policy: Balancing Economic Dreams with Political Realities*, Washington, DC: CQ Press, 2001.

Ruggie, John G., "International Regimes, Transactions, and Change: Embedded Liberalism in the Postwar Economic Order," in Stephen D. Krasner, ed., *International Regimes*, Ithaca, NY: Cornell University Press, 1983, pp. 195–231.

Russett, Bruce, "The Mysterious Case of Vanishing Hegemony; or, Is Mark Twain Really Dead?" *International Organization*, 1985, vol. 39, pp. 207–231.

Santer, Jacques, Statement given at the WTO Ministerial, Geneva, Switzerland, May 19, 1998, www.wto.org/english/thewto_e/minist_e/min98_e/mc98_e/default 19_e.htm.

Schelling, Thomas C., *The Strategy of Conflict*, Cambridge, MA: Harvard University Press, 1960.

Schultz, Kenneth A., "Domestic Opposition and Signaling in International Crises," *American Political Science Review*, 1998, vol. 92, pp. 829–844.

——, "Do Democratic Institutions Constrain or Inform? Contrasting Two Institutional Perspectives on Democracy and War," *International Organization*, 1999, vol. 53, pp. 233–266.

Snidal, D., "The Limits of Hegemonic Stability," *International Organization*, 1985, vol. 39, pp. 579–614.

——, "The Game Theory of International Politics," *World Politics*, October 1985, vol. 38, no. 1, pp. 25–57.

——, "International Cooperation among Relative Gains Maximizers," *International Studies Quarterly*, 1991, vol. 35, pp. 387–402.

Steinberg, Richard H., "In the Shadow of Law or Power? Consensus-Based Bargaining and Outcomes in the GATT-WTO," *International Organization*, 2002, vol. 56, no. 2, pp. 339–374.

Stern, Robert M., "The WTO Trade Policy Review of the United States, 1996," Discussion Paper 424, Ann Arbor: University of Michigan, 1998.

Strange, Susan, "The Persistent Myth of Lost Hegemony," *International Organization*, 1987, vol. 41, pp. 551–574.

Submission from the United States of America, October, 2000, World Trade Organization General Council Informal Consultations on External Transparency, www. ustr.gov/wto/wtosub.html.

Sutherland, Peter *et al.*, *The Future of the WTO: Addressing Institutional Challenges in the New Millennium*, Report by the Consultative Board to Director General Supachai Panitchpakdi, Geneva: WTO, 2004, chap. 2, p. 19.

Tallberg, J., *Leadership and Negotiation in the European Union*, New York: Cambridge University Press, 2006.

Tetlock, Philip E. and Aaron Belkin, eds., *Counterfactual Thought Experiments in World Politics: Logical, Methodological, and Psychological Perspectives*, Princeton, NJ: Princeton University Press, 1996.

Thelen, K., "Historical Institutionalism in Comparative Politics," *Annual Review of Political Science*, 1999, vol. 2, pp. 369–404.

Thies, Cameron G., "A Historical Institutionalist Approach to the Uruguay Round Agricultural Negotiations," *Comparative Political Studies*, 2001, vol. 34, pp. 400–428.

Thompson, Leigh, "They Saw a Negotiation: Partisanship and Non-partisan Perspectives," *Journal of Personality and Social Psychology*, 1995, vol. 68, pp. 839–853.

Tocqueville, Alexis de, *Democracy in America*, vol. 2, New York: Knopf, 1946.

Truman, Harry S., Address on Foreign Economic Policy, Speech given at Baylor University, Waco, TX, March 6, 1947, http://www.presidency.ucsb.edu/ws/index.

——, Annual Message to the Congress on the State of the Union, Washington, DC, January 7, 1948, http://www.presidency.ucsb.edu/ws/index.

——, The President's Economic Report to the Congress, Washington, DC, January 14, 1948, http://www.presidency.ucsb.edu/ws/index.

United Nations Development Programme, *Making Global Trade Work for People*, Sterling, VA: Earthscan, 2003, p. 251.

United States Congress, Economic Recovery Act of 1948, Public Law 472, 80th Congress, Washington, DC, 1948.

United States, Department of State, Confidential memorandum, January 15, 1965, declassified 8 March 1993, unsanitized, complete, LBJ Library: CD-ROM 1994090102495.

Vernon, Raymond and D. L. Spar, *Beyond Globalism: Remaking American Foreign Economic Policy*, New York: Free Press, 1989.

A View of US–UK Policy Relations, Confidential State Department airgram, May 23, 1996, no declassification date, CD-ROM 1978070100311, LBJ Library.

Visit of German Chancellor Erhard to Washington, DC, Background Paper: The EEC and the Kennedy Round, September 19, 1966, Confidential State Department document, declassified 9 August 1994, unsanitized, complete, CD-ROM 1995110103183, LBJ Library.

Whalley, John and Colleen Hamilton, *The Trading System after the Uruguay Round*, Washington, DC: Institute for International Economics, 1996.

Whalley, John with Colleen Hamilton and Roderick Hill, *Canadian Trade Policies and the World Economy*, Toronto: University of Toronto Press, 1985.

White, Eric Wyndham, Press Release number 993, GATT, June 30, 1967.

Wiener, Jarrod, *Making Rules in the Uruguay Round: A Study of International Leadership*, Brookfield, VT: Dartmouth, 1995.

Winham, Gilbert R., *International Trade and the Tokyo Round Negotiation*, Princeton, NJ: Princeton University Press, 1986.

——, *The Evolution of International Trade Agreements*, Toronto: University of Toronto Press, 1992.

Yeutter, Clayton, "Bringing Agriculture into the Multilateral Trading System," in Jagdish Bhagwati and Mathias Hirsch, eds., *The Uruguay Round and Beyond: Essays in Honor of Arthur Dunkel*, Ann Arbor: University of Michigan Press, 1999, pp. 61–78.

Young, Oran R., "Political Leadership and Regime Formation: On the Development of Institutions in International Society," *International Organization*, 1991, vol. 45, pp. 281–308.

Zeiler, Thomas W., *American Trade and Power in the 1960s*, New York: Columbia University Press, 1992.

——, "Managing Protectionism: American Trade Policy in the Early Cold War," *Diplomatic History*, 1998, vol. 22, pp. 337–360.

Index

CPSIA information can be obtained
at www.ICGtesting.com
Printed in the USA
BVHW04s1040180818
524897BV00003B/71/P